The Janus Face of the German Avant-Garde

From Expressionism
toward Postmodernism

RAINER RUMOLD

Northwestern

University Press

Evanston

Illinois

Northwestern University Press
Evanston, Illinois 60208-4210

Copyright © 2002 by Northwestern University Press.
Published 2002. All rights reserved.
Printed in the United States of America

10 9 8 7 6 5 4 3 2 1

ISBN 0-8101-1878-5 (cloth)
ISBN 0-8101-1879-3 (paper)

Library of Congress Cataloging-in-Publication Data
Rumold, Rainer.
    The Janus face of the German avant-garde : from expressionism
toward postmodernism / Rainer Rumold.
        p. cm.— (Avant-garde and modernism studies)
    Includes bibliographical references and index.
    ISBN 0-8101-1878-5 (alk. paper) — ISBN 0-8101-1879-3 (pbk. : alk.
paper)
        1. German literature—20th century—History and criticism.
    2. Avant-garde (Aesthetics)—Germany.   I. Title.   II. Series.
        PT405 .R85   2001
        830.9'11—dc21

                                        2001004161

The paper used in this publication meets the minimum requirements
of the American National Standard for Information Sciences—
Permanence of Paper for Printed Library Materials, ANSI z39.48-1984.

Contents

Acknowledgments

This study incorporates in significantly revised, expanded, and updated form the following papers, or parts thereof, delivered at national and international conferences on various aspects of the avant-garde:

"Carl Einstein and Durruti's Spain: The Poesy and the Grammar of Anarchism." In *German and International Perspectives on the Spanish Civil War: The Aesthetics of Partisanship,* edited by Luis Costa, Richard Critchfield, Richard Golsan, and Wulf Koepke, 64–78. Columbia, S.C.: Camden House, 1992.

"Nietzsche, Benn and the Miscarriage of the Avant-Garde." In *International Nietzsche Symposium,* edited by Volker Dürr, Reinhold Grimm, and Kathy Harms, 167–79. Madison: University of Wisconsin Press, 1988.

"Brecht and Grosz in Exile: The Avant-Garde against Itself." In *Exil: Literatur und die Künste nach 1933,* edited by Alexander Stephan, 28–39. Bonn: Bouvier, 1990.

"Crisis as Event: Avant-Garde, Revolution, Catastrophe as Metaphors." In *The Arts and the Event: Aesthetics and Social Transaction,* edited by Stephen C. Foster, 11–28. Ann Arbor and London: UMI Research Press, 1988.

"The Dadaist Text: Politics, Aesthetics and Alternative Culture?" *The Avant-Garde and the Text,* special issue *Visible Language* 21, no. 3–4 (1988): 453–89.

I am grateful to the editors for permission to include them here.

Many thanks go to friends and colleagues who contributed in various ways to the shaping of this project: Volker Duerr, Stephen Foster, Anton Kaes, Klaus Kiefer, Andreas Kramer, Russell Maylone, Estera Milman, Richard Sheppard, Guy Stern, and O. K. Werckmeister. And special acknowledgment is due to the Weinberg College of Arts and Sciences at Northwestern University for the support extended to my research.

Introduction

The current discussion of modernism, the avant-garde, and postmodernism refers to dadaism, surrealism, and Russian and Italian futurism when reviewing the international countercultural movement in literature and the arts that arose shortly after the turn of the twentieth century. With a few notable exceptions,[1] expressionism is significantly absent from this critical context.[2] The reason for such an omission may lie most of all in expressionism's unparalleled aesthetic diversity, its ideological contradictions, and extraordinary tensions between archaic visions and modern views that seem to defy understanding it as a *movement*. The pronounced neoromantic, spiritually heightened utopianism of mainstream expressionists like Franz Werfel clashes with the intensely analytical, self-reflective formalism of writers like Gottfried Benn or Carl Einstein, just as the unique Janus-faced disparity of its aesthetic forms (ranging from the traditional sonnet to linguistic experimentation in the wake of the international avant-garde) appears to resist any such assessment. Yet, for twentieth-century German modernism, expressionism is of singular significance. In fact, the history of the German literary avant-garde is in many ways a story of the legacies (there is not a single legacy) of expressionism.

My study reflects on the developments and trajectories of the German avant-garde in a series of related case studies, critical "constellations," of debates and feuds among writers, artists, and critics, friends and foes of expressionism, a movement that had, for the most part, the aspirations of representing a new, internationally oriented German national culture. In the widest sense of its "legacy," I focus on the countermovement of Zurich and Berlin Dada, on George Grosz, and Bertolt Brecht, writers and artists who originally reacted against expressionism by developing, also on the basis of political differences, a variety of alternative aesthetic forms. On these grounds, I trace the question of the changing significance of literary and artistic production for individual and collective experience from the first decade of the twentieth century through the exile period in Paris, Spain, Moscow, and the United States, up to post-World War II developments in the Federal Republic of Germany, where, for example, Benn and Brecht meet again under most intriguing (and problematic) literary circumstances. In this large-scale historical time frame, literary history becomes a history of competing dispositions toward the significance of aesthetic production in twentieth-century modernity, a history of conflict-ridden, critical constellations. Sublating its critical subject matter into critical under-standing, my study aims to explore a process of the simultaneous erosion of the avant-garde's political identities (its typical association with extremist ideologies), the identity of "art," and the writer's growing sense of skepti-cism toward the medium of literary language. The crisis of literary culture in modernity is a "writing crisis" that also reflects the agon and agonies of writing *about* crisis in the midst of war, revolution, and, above all, political exile.

As case studies, the individual chapters will examine a set of extreme constellations, or critical "moments," between an *apotheosis* and a program-matic *negation* of art. My study focuses on (and is necessarily limited to) developments in *literature* and, for comparative reasons, to some extent in painting as fields in which individual creativity has been the supreme value. As such, literature and painting were most prone to crisis in an age of mass production and mass consumption. By contrast, architecture, of course, the Bauhaus for example, could meet these conditions head-on, and the rela-tively new medium of film was cut out for the times by its very nature as a mass medium, crucially important for Weimar culture. Hence my study is a study of the crisis of the creativity of the individual at the point of ad-dressing a new era by defining herself or himself as "avant-garde" and by attempting to establish alliances in the form of "avant-garde" groups or "movements." As people still make history, artists and writers even more so make literary and art history. Hence my study is also explicitly a study of shifting relations, affinities, and hidden and open hostilities between diverse creative personalities such as Einstein, Benn (in an international context via Eugene Jolas's journal *transition)*, Else Lasker-Schüler, George Grosz, and Brecht, which have their roots in the years of expressionism. Hence also my principle of selection (not only for the sake of a practical pro-portion of this study). Thus, some prominent individual figures or avant-garde circles in the post-World War II period, the "Wiener Gruppe," or the "Fluxus" movement, or politically motivated writers like Peter Weiss receive no or relatively little attention. The latter is discussed only as an antipode to Enzensberger, who responds to the wider legacies which interest me here. Schwitters's Merz version of Dada arises from the relative isolation of the provincial center of Hanover, and it speaks of a highly individualistic artis-tic disposition quite different from the group mentality of Zurich Dada that evolves toward a united stance against expressionism as a movement.[3] Of course, Schwitters's work is among the influences on the postwar experi-mental productions of, for example, Helmut Heißenbüttel. Yet, my study chooses another more pivotal trajectory of constellations which culminate in the latter's "texts." Heißenbüttel here is most representative because of his very specific relation to Carl Einstein's post-avant-garde/postmodern "linguistic turn" and for his problematic affinity to Benn's "absolute poetry." In short, I aim at a surprisingly long-standing context of *intertextual* affinities and polarities that are being revised and rewritten at the various critical stages of the avant-garde.

The concept of "crisis" as referred to in this study thus is not superimposed on literary developments from any systematic position. Neither do I argue in terms of a theory of history in the wake of Karl Marx, from whom Bürger derives his dialectical notion of discontinuity and change, of a "break" with a system, nor, for example, in the epistemological terms of Edmund Husserl, whose concept of a crisis of modern thought is tied to the idea of an underlying unity as telos. For Husserl this unity is exposed—in the struggle of philosophy against skeptical theory—by consciousness turning its *Selbstverständliches* (unquestioned doxa) into *Selbstverständnis* (critical self-understanding).[4] Though such teleological concepts are inherently reflected upon, the notion of "crisis" employed here is arrived at quite basically in historiographical terms. The focus of the "critical constellations" selected is on the *agonistic* polarity of aesthetic "discourses" (not of "styles") through which the Western tradition of aesthetic totality becomes questioned.[5] "Styles" express certain holistic aesthetic perceptions as rooted in the organic "work of art" of a chosen literary genre (poetry or novel), in the work of an individual author, or in a particular epoch (such as classicism). While Dada aggressively exploded that tradition, expressionism most uniquely problematized the concepts of the "work of art" and of "style" as its multiple and divergent forms relativize them, only in its most radical developments consciously so. Thus I read certain typological aesthetic forms, experimentally fragmented, open or "organically" closed, as "discourses" that are related to certain mind-sets, mentalities, and ideological dispositions vis-à-vis tradition and innovation not only in the arts but also in the cultural sphere at large. The notion of the arts being not only tied to developments and changes in the public sphere but actually taking an "avant-garde" role of leadership in a holistic social formation of the present and future is a legacy of the nineteenth century, associated with Saint-Simon's and Fourier's utopianism.[6] In stark contrast to the idea and ideal of the artists' imaginative leadership in consort and agreement with industrialists and engineers, however, the twentieth-century avant-garde has dramatically turned against the rationalist idea of progress and aggressively against economic modernity and its functionaries. The concept of a literary crisis is thus derived from a primary focus on competing discourses, of rivaling dispositions toward the most adequate and consequential aesthetic articulation of the modern experience, and its realization in the life-worlds. Such a concept of crisis is tantamount to a definition of the historical "avant-garde": the avant-garde itself is a crisis phenomenon. By comparison and contrast, literary high modernism constructs an autonomous aesthetic space of subjectivity from which to critique and deconstruct the normative discourses of social modernity. Its adversary stance thus is based on aesthetic innovation that points to the potential of individual transformation through an expansion of consciousness (T. S. Eliot's *Waste Land* being a classical example of high modernism). The understanding of the avant-garde as an unstructured agon of competing discourses for the articulation of renewed experience thus allows for a functional concept of crisis. Such understanding allows its assessment as a subjective as well as objective phenomenon. I am dealing with types of a subjective crisis as much as I am interested in the individual artists' personal experiences and attitudes toward decisive change. As my study traces the trajectory of the avant-garde's agon of discourses in poetological terms, thus gauging its relation to traditional discourses, I can begin to assess the characteristics of an objective crisis. The concept of "crisis" conventionally implies conditions that require speedy evaluation and decision toward a resolution. The agon of the discourses of German expressionism, different from futurism, surrealism, and the other rupture-oriented, relatively undivided international avant-garde movements, appears to consist much more of a series of system-immanent conflicts. These conflicts arise as a contest between innovation and tradition; they continue between postexpressionist avant-garde positions as struggles for the aesthetically and socially most innovative position (cf. Dada versus expressionism, or Grosz versus Brecht in the American exile, etc.). The avant-garde agon contesting the limits of the subjectivity of modernism, but failing to decisively explode them, generates an awareness of a "postmodern" experience as the crisis of modernism. As such, the postmodern is always already latent—its main characteristics being a function of an awareness of the workings of the institution of art. This agon of discourses first of all deserves our historiographical attention before any unified theory of the avant-garde or a theory of (its) crisis.

I thus deal with the most radical and significant instances in the history of modern German literature since von Hofmannsthal's "Chandos Letter"

("Brief des Lord Chandos an Francis Bacon," 1902), which, in the wake of Nietzsche, thematized the crisis of art as a crisis of linguistic subjectivity. Hofmannsthal's language skepsis turned against the validity of signs ("rotten mushrooms") toward the intuitive experience of a "silent language of things." By comparison, the authors most centrally discussed here react to the perceived rupture of the relation of language to the object by turning toward the realm of signs. One explores the sign's capacity to create an autonomous "world of expression" (Benn), or the sheer sensorial materiality of language, of sounds and the visuality of letters ("anti-art" Dada), or one opens up to the emerging forms and images of the unconscious (individual or collective). Carl Einstein's postsurrealist lament about the "blindness" of language and image points to insights into the aporia of metaphorical relations to the "image realm" of experience, which representative poets since the 1950s articulate as a paradigmatic shift toward "postmodern" perceptions.

Part 1 of my study, "The Historical Avant-Garde and the Crisis of Literature," deals with two major antagonistic movements, expressionism and Dada: chapter 1 debates the traditional concept of an "expressionist epoch" (and a corresponding "style") and introduces the construct of an agon of art over art that seeks answers to the crisis of modernity in the aesthetic domain. In these terms I review expressionism as a contradictory movement engaging the antimodernist discourses of the German tradition and, on the other hand, the European promodern avant-garde. My focus on the conflicts between national and international culture, country and city, "primitivism" and cultural modernism, Geist (spirit) and "body," the female writer and the tradition of poetry, illuminates a "cultural schism"[7] with lasting consequences for the literature and politics of the avant-garde in Germany. The expressionist struggle for the complete work of art is ultimately also a problematic question of a metaphysical quest through language. In fact, expressionism can be newly defined as a series of experimental discourses ("styles") to negotiate, more or less consciously, the impact of the physiological and visual, of the ubiquitous, technologically magnified "image realm" of the urban experience, with the symbolic order of the spiritual in art.

Chapter 2 turns to Dada, the first significant reaction to expressionism and, besides surrealism, the chief paradigm for a critical theory of the avant-garde. In debunking the stereotype of two dadaisms (aesthetic versus political revolt), Zurich and Berlin Dada are reconsidered as two *complementary* forms of reactions to the idealistic discourses of expressionism. Both are *aesthetic* anti-art events, anti-art in the sense that they *decisively* break with the concept of "style." My account of the conflicts among Hugo Ball, Richard Huelsenbeck, and Tristan Tzara traces Zurich Dada's metamorphosis from literary cabaret to "Kunstrevolution" (directed against expressionism) and its radical "anti-art" stance. The dadaist event in Zurich and Berlin, as a *performed event* that involved the audience, delivered momentarily—at the point of the dissolution of writing—from the constraints of the traditional production and reception of art. In its published form, however, the dadaist text is—like the expressionist text—accessible only to the individual "aristocratic reader" (Roland Barthes). The most salient achievement of multinational Dada may have been that it was the only avant-garde movement that effectively broke with the idea of a national culture.

Part 2 of my study examines in four chapters the impact that political exile from Nazi Germany has on the avant-garde. It defines its reactions to Nazism and exile as Janus-faced. In the extreme, the avant-garde either radically reverses its course toward traditional forms of *Weltliteratur,* legitimized by NS racist cultural politics as forms of political dissent and of preserving an endangered humanist heritage, or it attempts to debunk the arts altogether. Whereas Dada in the exile of the First World War had been an instance of a shocking, extreme speeding up of avant-garde discourses, the turn to tradition in the exile of the Second World War constitutes a specifically German predicament that amounts to a slowing down, a retardation, if not a taking back of avant-garde developments. The catastrophic, anti-art disposition in exile, on the other hand, accelerates and anticipates certain post-avant-garde concerns, internationally shared in the late 1960s. Chapter 3 thus constitutes an overview of the problems of the avant-garde in exile. It faced the necessity to return to more traditional forms in order to speak to any identifiable audience at all, to stay avant-garde against all odds, or to give up writing altogether in favor of political action. During the period of political exile, a form of "negative aesthetics"[8]—a paradoxical *turn against art in the medium of art* out of disappointed expectations and despair over the political futility of literature—may be the most arresting (though underexposed) reaction by writers, artists, and critics who had their formative experience during the years of expressionism. Self-parody, a dystopian reversal of previous utopian visions, an intense skepticism toward the status of artistic language, or, in the extreme, polemics against the aesthetic amoralism of the avant-garde mark a particularly critical phase in the work of exceptionally reflective authors like Einstein (*Die Fabrikation der Fiktionen* [*The Fabrication of Fictions*]), or Alfred Döblin. Such a crisis of the arts is thematized in Grosz's series of "the Painter of the Hole," also in contemporary modernist novels written in exile, such as Hermann Broch's *Der Tod des Vergil* (*The Death of Virgil*), (hitherto unnoticed) Alfred Döblin's Hamlet-novel, Heinrich Mann's *Empfang bei der Welt* (*Reception with High Society*), and, of course, Thomas Mann's *Doktor Faustus* as an indictment of the amoralism and immoralism of the avant-garde in view of Nazi Germany's political barbarism. I tend to view this phase as of incisive significance. In the specific instance of German literary developments marked by the legacy of idealism, I see this stage as a historical step toward a contemporary global condition in which "art" has become an equivocal phenomenon, where postmodernism may indeed be discussed as "the endgame of the avant-garde."[9]

Chapter 4 focuses on Carl Einstein, his self-exile from Berlin to Paris in the late 1920s, and subsequently his activities as a political speechwriter and member of an anarchist column during the Spanish Civil War. His case illuminates what can be called a *leftist* quasi-mythical vision of political activism. Compared with Benjamin's "messianic," yet epistemologically differentiated critique of surrealism, Einstein's embrace and subsequent rejection of the French movement points to the pitfalls of an exclusively aesthetic critique of modernity. As he "metamorphoses" his surrealist aesthetics (derived from the late work of the painter Georges Braque) into the "pure," elementary action of the anarchists, Einstein returns to a mythical mentality that matches — albeit under opposite political signs — Benn's fascination with the "primitive" collective experience. The tracing of Einstein's developments, from his roots in expressionism to an anti-art stance in the 1930s, illuminates the question: Can the avant-garde really dispose of what it considered an "elitist" cultural legacy?

In chapter 5, I focus on the evolving discussion of expressionism in the early 1930s, and the expressionism debate, occasioned by Benn's embrace of National Socialism, which the Marxist intellectual exiles conducted in *Das Wort* (Moscow 1937–38). At the same time, Einstein was committed to the anarchist cause in Spain and Benn wrote "Weinhaus Wolf" ("Wolf's Tavern"), a highly self-conscious narrative, during a period of extreme isolation after his fallout with the Nazis. Curiously, Walter Benjamin's long-standing antagonism toward expressionism has been overlooked in criticism until now. His critique of its "inwardness" actually predates Georg Lukács's attack and, in spite of his opposition to the latter's all-out condemnation of modernist literature, culminates in also linking expressionism, not just Italian futurism, to a fascist *aestheticization* of politics. Benjamin's critique of expressionism is based on his advocacy of surrealism (his fascination with the "image realm" of intersubjective experience). It is fundamentally a critique of the idealist work of art. Most important to my study is that Benjamin not only continued a long-standing argument against the "disembodying" spirituality of expressionism (and Ludwig Klages) but ultimately raised objections, beyond his attack on futurism, to dadaism and surrealism. It is here that his differences from Brecht's qualified and Bloch's spirited defense of expressionism become most obvious. Arguing that the modern mass medium of film brings about an intersubjective psychophysiological experience, Benjamin ultimately also intends to unmask the historical avant-garde as a *literary* phenomenon that, as such, can be absorbed by traditional culture. His critique of the idealism and *metaphorical* nature of "literature" continues to rank among the most fundamental and still most irritating critiques of "the work of art."

While the expressionism debate in exile revealed the ideological and theoretical conflicts between the critics of the avant-garde, among them Brecht, chapter 6 points to the rising tensions within the avant-garde in exile that would carry over into the postwar period. For the individuo-anarchist George Grosz, the growing political contradictions of the later 1930s and early 1940s erased the ideological differences between communism and fascism as political realities. His American oeuvre, his somber, absurdist allegories of art and politics, oppression and war, compared to his postexpressionist and dadaist productions, constituted a turn to a form of critically reflected aesthetic autonomy that expressed a deep sense of futility of art for social change. His long-standing intimate correspondence with Benn [before and still after (!) the poet's embrace of National Socialism] and his increasingly polemical letters to Brecht reveal the painter's growing opposition to the rigid views of the playwright. In the extreme, "the painter of the hole" (the title of a 1947–48 series of paintings) engages in a negation of any political significance of painting through painting. In other words, Grosz at this moment questions the nature of his own work, while Brecht's rigid insistence on the continued political validity of literary production after his return to East Germany may mark a different form of the crisis of writing. The painter's and playwright's shifting relations here anticipate the postwar conflict in the arts, epitomized by the antagonism between Theodor Adorno's and Brecht's aesthetic theories.

Part 3, "The Avant-garde at a Standstill," opens with a chapter on Gottfried Benn. Chapter 7 renders a contrast to the experience of the political exiles by focusing on the problematic experience of the most eminent representative of expressionism writing in the topography of home. I here deal with the crisis of the poet who had erroneously envisioned (his) expressionism as the official culture of the Third Reich. On the basis of an assessment of Jürgen Habermas's and Paul de Man's views on Nietzsche's prefiguration of aesthetic modernity as opposing critiques of aesthetic autonomy, I critique the unprecedented opening of Benn's pro-Nazi essays toward history and his subsequent reversal. My reading of Benn's philosophical narrative "Wolf's Tavern" (1937–38) reveals that the Nietzschean claim of aesthetic autonomy is at the origin of both, his ideological utopian discourse *and* a skeptical denial of all history that exceeds any previous position by far. Benn's shifting, contradictory readings of Nietzsche come in the wake of his embrace of National Socialism from 1933 to 1934 and his subsequent rejection by the regime. His experience with Nazism proved to be a trauma that needed disguise and made him seek an "inner" refuge (by no means to be confused with the eminently *political* notion of "inner emigration") in his postfascist vision of "bio-negative" absolute art. In these terms the chapter establishes the setting for understanding the spell Benn's poetry cast on a wider, educated postwar German audience that had shared much of the poet's experience.

The last chapter reviews the agon and agonies of the German avant-garde, its turbulent tradition of discontinuities from expressionism through the 1970s. A new generation of poets and writers in the postwar era attempts to restore some of the traditions of twentieth-century German modernism, through symbolist nature poetry or Kafkaesque parables which, symptomatic of a decline of high modernism, bear the marks of a decidedly apocalyptic mentality. By comparison, the experimental texts of Helmut Heißenbüttel and Hans Magnus Enzensberger's poetry of the 1950s and 1960s constitute a significantly changed avant-garde constellation. A self-reflexive focus on the "blindness" of language and image goes beyond the modernist dissociation of sensibility and cancels the utopian/dystopian extremism of the avant-garde as in the instance of Paul Celan's poetry. Helmut Heißenbüttel, who rediscovered Carl Einstein for postwar German criticism, well understanding his importance for defining the boundaries and limits of modernist culture, places his own texts at the other side of the expressionist/surrealist's writer's lament about the epistemological impasse of language. In the German literature from the 1950s through the 1970s, the postmodern experience articulates itself largely within and against the boundaries of modernism. One still has to reconnect with and further develop the international modernist and avant-garde traditions, while the spread of American popular culture and pop art in the visual arts tended toward a break in the terms of global developments. Hence Heißenbüttel affirmatively turns to language experimentation (significantly influenced by Gertrude Stein), exploring the linguistic material in relation to signifying processes and our "language games"(Wittgenstein). His "Lehrgedicht über Geschichte 1954" ("Teaching/Learning Poem about History"), for example, simultaneously engages Benn's formalist and Brecht's "gestic" poetics to explore temporality in language while thematizing history. In fact, the Benn/Brecht polarity very much defines this stage of the German avant-garde. While Hans Magnus Enzensberger declares himself an antipode to strictly experimental writing, his early poetry and criticism is also marked by a paradoxical reception of both Benn's artistic formalism *and* Brecht's poetry for change. In this paradox lies Enzensberger's point of departure for his later self-reflexive critique of leftist ideology and culture, of which the editor of the *Kursbuch* had been a prominent spokesman in 1968. The poetic cycle *Der Untergang der Titanic* (*The Sinking of the Titanic,* 1978) is a central part of such a critique. His literary productions, poetry, and essays of the mid-1970s argue that contemporary writing must continuously negotiate the desire for the wholeness of utopian myth and the insight of reason while staying aware of the blindness of language and image. From such a self-critical point of view, the dialectic of the avant-garde may have become an indeterminate dialectic at a standstill, and there may be no return to utopian visions.

The experience and articulation of a postutopian/postdystopian disposition has become the shared experience of contemporary international Western avant-garde productions. Yet the prolonged, even perpetuated, agon of avant-garde discourses as disparate legacies of German expressionism, in significant traces vital up to and in the aftermath of the student revolt of 1968, amounts to a German cultural *Sonderweg* (exceptional path). Compared with the unified impact of futurism on Italian and of surrealism on French and international literature and the arts, the German avant-garde could never quite agree on a common attack of idealist and elitist traditions (the concern of Walter Benjamin's critique of the expressionist legacy). To sum up: the classical German avant-garde, expressionism, differing from the model of discontinuity which Bürger has deduced from surrealism and Dada, on the whole, is considerably less given to a programmatic break with the institution of art than to a mediation of modernity and tradition. No doubt, this is due to the larger-than-life, monumentalist shadow of German classicism and to the tradition of cultural authority, from Goethe to Stefan George, that continued to loom over the literary and public sphere of Wilhelminian society and, to a degree, still of the Weimar Republic. Hence the avant-garde in Germany continues to assume the function of exploring a number of conflicting discourses for the transition toward and construction of a new cultural identity responsive to national exigencies and the international demands that global modernization processes make on national traditions. German avant-garde developments open up a singularly unstable space of oscillation between a radically new cultural project, the abolition of the special status of art, and the radicalization of a process of aesthetic autonomy (dating back to the emancipation of art from external concerns in the eighteenth century) to that of the apotheosis of art. These tensions will remain informative for an extraordinarily extended time span. The reconstruction of postwar German literary culture in international modernist contexts was a project that, in view of the cold war, had to take place quickly and involved, once more, a clash of multiple traditions that canceled out any "fresh start" at "zero point." In other words, there are different *speeds of crisis,* and there are its corresponding *critically and theoretically* productive aspects. Self-reflexivity is evident already in the postutopian phase of the avant-garde in Germany after the First World War, which begins to consider also its very own institutionalization, a chief characteristic of a postmodern awareness. Criticism, literary agon, and crisis are intertwined, as I will argue more closely in the first chapter and maintain throughout the study. In overall terms, we are dealing with a number of complementary aspects of crisis. We are faced with a progressive legitimacy crisis of the Enlightenment belief in reason and progress turned into a totalization of ratio into instrumental reason. The avant-garde, in its idealistic, messianic camp, responded to this demise of reason with an equally totalizing imaginative critique.[10] Its "naive" utopianism, barring dialogue and mediation, in turn was to be the cause for a subsequent political predicament, often leading into or linking with the totalitarianism of the political Left or Right. More significantly, we are dealing with the question of the "romantic," organic work of art progressively subjected to a demystifying critique of its claim of a unity of appearance (sign) and idea (meaning). This critique in turn is subject to an "intricate play of relapses and momentary recoveries," meaning subject to a crisis of its own,[11] which I trace over an extended time period.

Richard Murphy's recent theoretical study of expressionism as an avant-garde phenomenon arrives at a most important understanding of a "radical" or "cynical" avant-garde discourse (e.g., the early Benn's or Alfred Döblin's) that aims at the "creation of a new kind of 'radicalized' or 'ideologically charged' aesthetic autonomy . . . wary of the affirmative functions which this autonomous status has conventionally entailed."[12] Since such a "cynical" avant-garde critique stays *within* the discourse of aesthetic autonomy, it can be said to desist from any project of alterity and radical change; it is thus assumed to be part of a larger "postmodern condition." Besides going significantly beyond expressionism into its contradictory legacies, my study differs on the basis of its focus on the ideological *contexts* and *substrata* of the expressionist avant-garde's competing discourses. As dispositions against signifying practices of closure and totalization in the construction of the "real," these may be as different as "cynical," on the one hand, and "naive," "idealist," or "utopian," on the other. But a "cynical" avant-garde also reflects a disposition, an emotive response which is not a postmodern characteristic. Moreover, the claims of, for example, a Nietzschean *Lebensphilosophie* (philosophy of life) and the "vitalist" foundations for a Nietzschean "Artistenevangelium" are the grand attitudes underlying the deconstructing practices of the radical expressionist avant-garde (as epitomized through Benn's work). After all, only a much later hindsight reading of Nietzsche's work allows for a clean separation of the ideological from the epistemological. The expressionists themselves read Nietzsche in differing ways, but all of them, whether "naive" or "sophisticated," understood his thought as an expression of an agonistic era, in which an entire Weltanschauung was at stake. Hence I am more interested in theorizing the contradictory legacies and *transitions* of avant-garde developments beyond the expressionist years and somewhat less concerned with establishing firm boundaries between modernism, avant-garde, and the postmodern.

The *rupture* between high modernist/avant-garde culture and popular culture, which pop art exploited in the United States of the 1950s, fully impacted the German public sphere considerably later (though the Fluxus movement and figures like Joseph Beuys took to the stage already in the early 1960s). Pop art's arrival coincided with the revolt of the New Left, which largely appropriated it as a postmodern form of the avant-garde, "as protest and criticism rather than affirmation of an affluent society."[13] Only with the demise of leftist culture in the 1970s, with which *Tendenzwende* (turn of tendency) my study concludes, could the link between pop, the commodity market, and a post-avant-garde postmodern condition in the visual arts and literature come into view. Only then could we begin to discuss the premises of a paradigm change in the arts. These could perhaps be fruitfully assessed in comparison and contrast to change in the terms of a decisive rejection of one cognitive model for another, as theorized by Thomas S. Kuhn (1962) for the structure of scientific revolutions (with occasional minor but interesting comparisons to the arts).[14] Hence, at least for the German context focused on in this study, the postmodern can be defined as a phenomenon not *after* a crisis of modernism but as evolving *within* modernism, with the historical avant-garde as the troublemaker. In these terms, the historical avant-garde functions as the irritant that perceives cultural anomie and produces aesthetic "anomalities." It has the *tendency* to push for a paradigm change—an inherently defining characteristic of the "avant-garde"—and thus it creates a crisis which, as in the sciences, causes "period(s) of pronounced professional insecurity," an " 'essential tension' . . . in a world out of joint."[15] Yet, different from crisis in the objective sciences, a crisis in aesthetic conventions does not necessitate an outright change of paradigm. In the extreme, we encounter writers like Carl Einstein in exile, "the carpenter who blames his tools" (even rarer in the sciences), who rejects the institution of art, as well as the avant-garde, without offering an aesthetic alternative. Otherwise, the resulting crisis in permanence is not stagnation, however. Rather, consciousness of change is reflected in the formal *internal* terms of avant-garde productions, texts, or images, as well as through the recurrence of certain *themes,* of the modern and the primordial, or the utopian and dystopian, and a growing awareness of their intertwinement. While it may be said that the postmodern is the crisis of the modern,[16] expressionism may be perceived as a Janus-faced phenomenon with the double vision of the premodern and the postmodern; hence its problematic yet equally productive and singularly extended legacies for the avant-garde in Germany.

Part One : **The Historical Avant-Garde and Literary Crisis**

The highest reality of art is the isolated, closed work. At times, however, the rounded work is only attainable to the epigone.

—Walter Benjamin, "Baroque and Expressionism," *Origin of the German Tragic Play,* 1925

I. Expressionism

The Janus-Faced Agon

In one of the earliest paintings on his way to abstract art, *Dies Irae (Judgment Day;* 1910), Wassily Kandinsky comments, as it were, on the tools of his craft, at the very moment of the end of all things: In the upper left-hand corner of the canvas, the painter's brushes, the tips of which resemble the cupolas of Russian Orthodox churches, are broken. The spiritual in art has been released from its superficial grounding in the material world. Gottfried Benn's earliest text on the way to his "absolute" prose, "Gehirne" ("Brains"; 1914), the first of his "Rönne novellas" written while he was serving as a medical officer in occupied Brussels, breaks with the mimetic function of language. At the very end of what began as a relatively straightforward narrative, the protagonist Rönne exclaims:

> What is it with those brains? I have always wanted to fly up like a bird from the ravine; now I live outside in the crystal. But now please give way, I am swinging again—I have been so tired—this walk proceeds on wings—with my blue sword of anemones—in the cascading plunge of the light at noon—in Southern ruins—in disintegrating clouds—pulverization of the forehead—the vanishing temples.[1]

At the very moment the protagonist breaks with his craft of medicine, with the tiresome routine of touching and analyzing the human brain, the text breaks the language of representation through a series of verbal "associations" (which constitutes a "novella" as an extraordinary event in terms of

3

his writing). Benn here raises the question of the relation of art (for which "my blue sword of anemones" is his metaphor) to the physical world in the same terms through which Kandinsky raises the question of the religious. In both cases, a totality lost in the material environment is recovered in the realm of art by fracturing the identity of the subject and breaking aesthetic traditions.

In spite of an often radical break with traditional forms, the expressionist embrace of the spiritual in art at the expense of physical experience may be the cause of its marginalization, if not its exclusion from our contemporary debate about the relation of the historical avant-garde to modernist and postmodernist culture, a debate that frequently reflects Peter Bürger's theory of the avant-garde.[2] There are only a few significant exceptions, primarily American studies.[3] The expressionist search for totality and transcendence, illustrated in the foregoing example in its most elevated form, may have led to its image of a more traditional phenomenon (as part of a national German culture, for which neither the case of the Russian Kandinsky nor the momentous formal reception of Italian futurism fit, of course). Yet, a review of the disparate and often contradictory forms of expressionist literature may reveal a physiological aspect that is at the source of the strikingly "visual" quality of the poetry and prose of the best authors who share viewpoints with the international avant-garde. Throughout this chapter we will keep an eye on the oscillating significance of physiological insights that find their expressions in images that, often unconsciously, sometimes consciously, disturb or even subvert the symbolic order of the spiritual in art. In fact, expressionism can be newly defined as a cultural attempt, better as a *series* of different, competing attempts, to negotiate the impact of the ubiquitous, technologically magnified "image realm" of the unconscious in modern experience with traditional forms of interpretation based on the identity of "metaphor" and the stability of "style."

Expressionism as a movement claimed to be future-oriented in the struggle for a better, more humane, "spiritual" modernity elevating art over modern social discourses. The spiritual desire for *Aufbruch* and *Wandlung,* uprising and transformation, the search for aesthetic forms through which to fill the void opened up by the discontinuities and contradictions of modern anomie, may have been anticipated in expressionist art theory, for example, by Wilhelm Worringer. His *Abstraktion und Einfühlung (Abstraction and Empathy;* 1908) was so influential that contemporary art historians were to refer to expressionism as "having characteristics which became familiar to us through Worringer's book."[4] The art critic and theorist Wilhelm

Hausenstein, too, originally identified expressionism with epochal change. Yet, many expressionists were quite conscious of—in fact, took pride in being heirs to—a "romantic" sensibility.[5] Embracing "mystical" visions, they characteristically set themselves apart from French developments focused on an analysis of vision as *seeing*, for example, from the "cubist . . . superficialities,"[6] while owing much to them. The movement's contradictory reactions to social and cultural modernity, the idea of a renewal of art as revival and the idea of the end of traditional art through Franz Marc's "new forms," reveal a Janus-face. The sonnet, for example, in the wake of Stefan George's masterly (envied) employment of its translucent Apollonian properties, remains for some time a challenging form for expressionist poets as diverse as Paul Boldt, Theodor Däubler (with futurist themes!), Georg Heym, Georg Trakl, and Reinhard Goering, before they could break away.[7] Ernst Stadler even wrote the sonnet "Form ist Wollust" ("Form Is Ecstasy") in response to the "master's" condemnation of the expressionist exuberance and lack of formal power and discipline.[8] Nowhere does it become more obvious than in the case of George's influence that while some expressionists were influenced by Marinetti's cult of the rebellion of the young,[9] they never had the futurists' disposition to break as forcefully from the icons of the past. Whether it is the visionary Edschmid[10] or the more reflective Hiller, the gestures toward George always reveal awe beneath rebellion. Hiller himself said, "We are fighting against theories not against masters."[11] Hence the scholarly understanding that expressionism "was not such a radical break with the past as has hitherto been suggested."[12] In this sense, Renato Poggioli's argument for continuity rather than Peter Bürger's thesis of the break of the avant-garde with the romantic tradition and with aesthetic autonomy seems to be more fitting in the case of expressionism.[13]

Yet, there is a significant current within expressionism that was quite open to the anti-idealist techniques of cubism and, most significantly, Italian futurism. Writers like August Stramm, Johannes Becher, or Alfred Döblin felt that new literary techniques, *futurist* techniques, were needed to articulate the physical and material forces in the modern urban world, of sounds and sights that come with its new modes of mass transportation and mass communication (newspapers, film) and new technological means in warfare. Whether or not one had an "experimental" or traditional disposition to the artistic medium, it is abundantly clear, judging from an extraordinary number of self-defining, self-serving, and self-questioning statements,[14] that the majority of the expressionists, before and still during World War I, understood their literary, artistic, and critical activities as *avant-garde* not merely in terms of literary or artistic stylistic innovations. Not just Dada, as theories of the avant-garde have it, but expressionism, too, reacted, in the words of the activist Kurt Hiller, "against the jaded, condescending, heartless, tired and ineffectual aestheticism."[15] Thus Ludwig Rubiner demanded for art and literature a reorientation of "l'homme pour l'homme."[16] "Never before was the aesthetic and the principle of l'art pour l'art so much in contempt," wrote Kurt Pinthus in the 1919 introduction to his anthology of expressionist poetry *Die Menschheitsdämmerung* (*Dawn of Humanity*).[17] For Kasimir Edschmid, expressionism was "not a program of style."[18] These expressionists regarded their creations as representing "a form of lived experience," of a renewal of social life toward a new *Lebensgesinnung* (ethos of life), the "new man." In short, expressionism as a movement perceived itself as the agent of a *Zeitwende* (turning of the age).[19] In this sense, one was against art for art's sake, as Kurt Hiller had implied in 1911, when he said about the members of the "Neue Club" (New Club), among them Georg Heym, Jakob van Hoddis, Ernst Blass, Ferdinand Hardekopf, and Ludwig Rubiner, "We are expressionists."[20] And it was a collective ethical vision of art that inspired Reinhard Sorge, in his early play *Der Bettler* (*The Beggar;* 1912), to make the protagonist plan a "theater of the masses." Ludwig Rubiner's "activist" declaration against art as a separate domain, a purely spiritual call for the immediacy of complete experience, may in these terms be the most characteristic document for the specific *avant-garde* mentality of expressionism:

> We are against music—for the awakening of the community. We are against the poem—for the call for love. We are against the novel—for the guidance toward life. We are against the drama—for the guidance toward action. We are against the image—for the example."[21]

One wanted "to change the world" (Walter Hasenclever) through aesthetic means. More involved than the other historical avant-garde movements (apart from Italian futurism) with the totality of the arts, expressionism's vision of change through aesthetic means was equally pervasive in literature and painting, theater and dance, music and film, sculpture and architecture.[22] This chapter, as that of my study as a whole, is focused on *literature,* with some contiguous consideration of *painting,* as fields in which the creativity of the individual writer or artist has been traditionally valued as the highest criterion. Produced by an individual for individual reception, literature (and easel painting) was most subjected to a crisis of significance in an age of developing mass production and mass consumption. In somewhat overstating the case, one could go as far as understanding the phenomenon of the literary avant-garde, its formation into groups, the proliferating founding of alternative journals, the integration of visual material into their texts, its production of shrill manifestos designed for a mass audience, and its overly pronounced utopianism as attempts to offset what was felt as a growing deficit of literary culture. By comparison, the other arts are inherently devised for imparting aesthetic experience in a communal setting by the nature of their communal reception, the space of the audience ranging from the theater or the dance or orchestra hall to the city as the site of architectural planning. Even when the circumstances of the First World War rather favored the destruction than the construction of buildings, architects such as Bruno Taut and the members of the "Gläserne Kette" (Glass Chain) would communicate their ideas about building in undaunted utopian visions of an organic symbiosis of the human community with nature and cosmos through images, poetry, and prose articulated in the medium of circularies. There was no crisis of the significance of architecture. Altogether new, new in terms of the formal and material exploration of the medium, not at all new in terms of the themes of horror and melodramatic plots of love stories, was the emergence of film on the cultural scene since the turn of the century. The confidence of the upstart in its technological means and visually immediate effects contrasted dramatically with a growing sense of insecurity in the production of literature for modern mass society (to be discussed in some more detail subsequently). Especially after the war, the former advocates of literary expressionism would announce the "death of expressionism" and invariably attribute its demise to the movement's unfettered subjectivity and its ubiquitous commercialization, with Worringer going as far as reviewing expressionism as "great final panic of art loosing faith in itself."[23] Scholarship often approaches expressionism from either extreme, from its rise or its fall.[24] Yet more informative for an understanding of the movement should be a focus on the always already underlying "paradoxes of expressionist culture."[25]

The Expressionist Agon of Art over Art

It is because of the diversity of expressionism that I here propose replacing the still dominant concept of a German modernist *epoch*[26] (and a corresponding *style*) with that of an expressionist avant-garde *agon* of art over art that engages a variety of *discourses* that often clash with each other. Whether one is conscious of it or not, behind the construct of an "expressionist epoch"[27] stands a specifically institutional pressure of "Germanistik" to give the subject of research an importance comparable to the significance of the epoch of Weimar classicism, or that of German romanticism. At any rate, one should be aware of the lingering presence of ideals and values inherited from the norms of a national culture. Historicist constructions of coherence, as implied by the term "epoch," are too sure of what constitutes a break, a beginning, and an end, and largely exclude synchronic discontinuities, which mark the contemporary experience of a metaphysical crisis, and of indeterminate and contradictory relations of art to the social domain. By contrast, neither dadaism nor surrealism are ever understood as "epochs"; they are clearly regarded as movements of the historical avant-garde. Traditionally defined as taking place between 1910 and 1920, expressionism would have been a short epoch, indeed.

Rather, I see expressionism as part of an international modernist *and* avant-gardist response to modernity, a response waging a dynamic battle with tradition for cultural domination. We must recall that Germany's culture, compared to that of France and England, was still under the heavy spell of idealism when the broad impact of European modernism (from the poetry of Rimbaud, in an influential translation by K. L. Ammer in 1908, to the drama of Strindberg) and the avant-garde onslaught (cubism and futurism) largely coincided in *one* critical moment.[28] In the visual arts, the influences of Munch, Ensor, and Cezanne, and in particular of van Gogh, Matisse, and the fauves were most significant. It was such that their "expressionism" was to become the model for the generic international concept "expressionism" applied to comparable artistic and thereafter literary innovations.[29]

There is also no reason to privilege expressionism as a uniquely *German* epoch, spiritually deeper than the other foreign "expressionist trends," as has been claimed, at the beginning of World War I by Paul Fechter and Wilhelm Worringer, later by Ernst Bloch in his *Geist der Utopie (Spirit of Utopia;* 1918), and still by Fritz Martini (1948).[30] Though opposed to such nationalist appropriation, even Hans Mayer would call expressionism "at core a movement of *German* cultural history."[31] Among those addressing "the national side of the question," Wilhelm Worringer may have hit the nail on the head (if a little too hard) when he stated in 1911 that due to a certain "insecurity of instinct," the German artists "always have to receive [their] cue from the outside."[32]

Criticism in the wake of Bürger's theory regards Dada, as well as surrealism, as the dominant avant-garde paradigm. For Bürger, the dadaists "liquidated the possibility of a period style when they raised to a principle the availability of the artistic means of past periods."[33] Their strategies, indeed, engaged the medium of language in order to eradicate the boundaries between art and life. Unlike expressionism, which it opposed, Dada consciously agitated against any vision of an alternative epoch with a definitive style; it aimed to implode *any* telos. Expressionism " 'wanted' something . . . Dada wants nothing," Hülsenbeck wrote.[34] By contrast, expressionism's many "styles" were, in my view, competing (and ultimately futile) attempts "Epoche zu machen" (to define one's time). As Hiller had stated in 1911, "every style is right."[35]

I speak here of expressionist "discourses" rather than "styles" out of necessity; there is simply no other adequate term. We are dealing with *competing* "dispositions"[36] toward cultural problems rather than with "styles" that articulate identity. Such discourses respond on the aesthetic level to contemporaneous ideological conflicts between, for example, international and national culture, city and country, literature and film, "primitivism" and modern rationalism, aesthetic and religious or political values, male and female gender roles, *Geist* (spirit or mind) and body. I will focus on these particular conflicts later; more than others they specifically reveal an expressionist response to the "cues from the outside" (Worringer) given by the international avant-garde.[37] Thus, when dealing in the following examples with the various *discourses* of expressionist poetry, we are dealing, fundamentally, with matters of *language* (rather than "style"). Moreover, one should want to take note of Helmut Heißenbüttel's critique of expressionism (from the point of view of his own experimental "language poetry") that even the most "ecstatic, world-embracing element only indicates that which the changed use of language has laid open: the irrevocable loss of metaphysics."[38] In the following examples, one should keep in mind that the dilemma of the expressionist work of art is rooted in a crisis of literary language, first articulated as such by Hugo von Hofmannsthal that, confronted with an overwhelming experience of modernity's materiality and physicality, attempts to, as it were, once more deliver metaphysical and humanist values. Most significant for an understanding of the problematics of the expressionist work of art, as addressed in my paradigmatic interpretations, is the intrusion of the *image realm* of the urban experience into the space of the poem, often at odds with poetic subjectivity and in conflict with literary metaphor.

The Demon of the Urban Experience

The city-country conflict had a more dramatic and continued impact on the *verspätete* (latecomer) German nation than in any other industrialized society. The conflict was, for example, at the roots of the powerful *Wandervogel* and *Jugendbewegung* (youth movement) in the teens, and it would inform the *Blut und Boden* (blood and soil) dogma of National Socialism.[39] Hence also the marked demonization of the city of Berlin in German expressionist poetry. As it frequently allegorizes the city as an archaic suprahuman force, expressionist urban poetry differs considerably from Ezra Pound's imagist "bottling" of the city of London in his *Mauberley* poems (1920) and Charles Baudelaire's allegories of the poet as a "fencer" in the midst of the aggressive images and sounds of modern Parisian life. On first sight, Georg Heym's employment of the conventional device of personifying allegory seems to be less sophisticated than Baudelaire's. The nineteenth-century French poet focuses on the city from an individual perspective that attempts to parry and absorb the shocks and jolts of the experience of the masses as the bodily unconscious in a formed aesthetic response, as analyzed by Walter Benjamin.[40] Heym's poem "Der Gott der Stadt" ("The God of the City"), by contrast, is often cited for the poet's alleged tendency to avoid a modern confrontation with modernity.[41] What is less known is that Benjamin praised Heym's poetry for its protosurrealist imagery unmasking the lingering ideal of a classical polis and opening the "image realm" of the modern city.[42] Taking the critic's cue, I here would like to attempt a new interpretation of "Der Gott der Stadt" by reassessing its very personification of the modern metropolis (I am quoting the first and last stanza of the poem):

The God of the City

On a row of houses he sits squarely.
The winds camp blackly about his brow.
He gazes full of rage to where in distant loneliness
The last houses stray into the countryside.

. . . .

He thrusts his butcher's fist into the darkness.
He shakes it. A sea of fire races
Through a street. And the fiery smoke roars
And consumes it, till late the morrow dawns.[43]

Heym's poems indeed have an uncanny quasi-visual effect. Stanzas and rhyme (in the German original) here burst with startling images that flood and threaten the poem's formal boundaries, releasing archaic forces (I am quoting the second and third stanza in run-on form):

> Eventide makes Baal's red belly shine, / The big cities kneel around him. / Tremendous numbers of church bells / Well up to him from a sea of black steeples.
>
> Like a dance of Corybantes the music of millions / Thunders noisily through the streets. / The chimneys' smoke, the clouds from factories / Waft up to him like the scent of incense turning blue.

Images of the inferno emerge from the experience of industrial mass society as if in revenge against the constrictions of modern functionalism. Yet, just as the poem is torn between formal conventions and their immanent dissolution, the text seems to be reluctant to look the monster of modernity fully in the eye, to register the powerful forces of technologically produced sights, sounds, and sped-up movements. The influence of Baudelaire and Rimbaud on Heym's poetry can be documented, but it undergoes a metamorphosis. Baudelaire's poetry elected to focus on a seemingly individual type in the crowd (including the poet as "flaneur") or groups of types (for instance, "The Seven Old Men," or "The Little Old Women"). Such selective focus is in the range of the subject's conscious experience that upon visual contact becomes aware of the phantasmagoric "nature" of these types, which modern mass society merely projects as individuals: "For seven times (I counted) was begot / This sinister, self-multiplying fear." As a group, the old men are addressed as "those seven loathsome monsters," an archaic (monstrous) sight that undercuts their "individuality." In Baudelaire's poetry, the masses may be conspicuous through their absence as masses, but they are "accounted" for. Heym's poem, on the other hand, immediately addresses the gigantic aspect of mass society by transforming its *collective* body into a vision of the monstrous. Thus, his vision brings to view an *awareness* that the vast materialism of modernity transcends individual consciousness and understanding. The physicality of the masses is transferred onto the "gaze," "belly," "eyebrows," "head's hair," the "butcher's fist" of the "God of the City." These human features hence are "his"; individual existence has been expropriated by and transformed into the metaphysical, albeit negative, satanic idol of Baal, worshiped by the "millions." In other words, for Heym, modern mass society is *unaccount-*

able and cannot be represented through contemporary *types*. Obviously, the poet in the German metropolis was much more a stranger than the "flaneur" in nineteenth-century Paris, the capital of long-standing democratic, the center of cultural traditions. After all, life in Berlin was marked by a vast population explosion (an increase of over 1.5 million from 1871 to the 1910s) and an enormous surge of modernization, unparalleled in Europe. These developments peaked around 1910, coinciding with the Wilhelminian aspirations for global economic and military influence, if not dominance. Reacting to this environment, Heym's Berlin poem appears to register a rush that floods the subject's capacity to take an individual aesthetic stance; instead, it attempts to uncover, present, and contain the overwhelmingly *visual* experience of modernity as a world of metaphysically uprooted, lost subjects turned into objects in the premodern form of the allegory. As a premodern form, allegory is part of our *collective* language of cultural forms. In the terms of a critical allegory that comes to grips with the phantasmagoric "nature" of modernity, Heym's poem does, after all *consciously* and with a sophistication of its own, articulate the modern experience as that at a threshold. By necessity dissolving the distance of the modern subject, the voice of the poem allows the repressed unconscious its voice.

A reviewer of one of the poetry reading sessions of "Der Neue Club" in *Der Demokrat* (21 December 1910) very well understood the significance of such poetry, as it were, not *seen* in German literature before (after the poetry of the Baroque with its focus on the vanity of appearances from an ultimately stable religious point of view). The review recognizes the very function of its emphasis on the *visual* through which the lyrics attempt to articulate the equivocal "meaning" of metropolitan experience:

> Georg Heym. His poems are a vertigo of seeing. All things roll like orgies before his eyes . . . Every thing "means" something, though its meaning is nowhere talked of.[44]

The achievements of Heym's poem become obvious when compared with Johannes Becher's "Berlin," a poem (I quote only one of its many stanzas) that addresses the city conventionally from the point of view of a stable subject:

> Berlin! You web-monster of a white metropolis!
> Orchestra of the aeons! Field of iron battle!
> Your iridescent serpent-body was chafed as it rattled,
> Roofed over with the refuse and rot of running sores![45]

Poems like these assume an overly self-assured Christian humanist critique of the metropolis, as it were, in competition with Heym's "surrealist" poetics of the city. Straining a rhetoric of condemnation, the poem demonizes the city as a "web-monster" and "serpent-bogy" from a moral point of view. Thus it censors the visceral experience of modernity, suppresses the urban environment's disparate nondiscursive, sensorial stimuli, which Georg Heym's poems gauge in their startling imagery. The conflict between moralizing and physiological perceptions of the metropolis can often be detected in the work of a single expressionist author. Becher's poem "Aus den Höfen" ("From the Yards"), for example, articulates the backyard experience of the poor in the diffuse terms of material images and analogies (such as "balcony dentures") and multiple cacophone stimuli:

> . . . there, suddenly a bang explodes the swollen stone.
> Balcony-dentures flash in grinding.
> And kitchen clang. Carpet beaters batter.
> A human being falls into the circle.[46]

Becher clearly is at his best when he borrows futurist techniques, even though he does so for an indictment of the big city the Italians idolized. The most problematic aspect of a *spiritual* program for the renewal of modernity was the claim that it would specifically "shape the experience of the intellectual urban man." Hiller, for example, asserted that he would endow the experience of Berlin's Potsdamerplatz "with the same strong intensity of feeling as the tiny village in the valley of Mr. Hesse."[47] In spite of its antibourgeois stance, mainstream expressionism's critique of modernity does not altogether transgress the boundaries of a public modernism debate in Germany. To a degree, many expressionist writers even shared in the anti-modern, anti-international mentality of that debate. One of many articles that will (through the 1930s) extol the conservative virtues of the country-side against modernity also turns against the previous "Asphaltliteraten":

> It is today a decisive question for German culture whether the country-side will choose to tolerate the . . . impudence of Berlin intelligentsia. . . . What of the people, whose brains are schooled in Kant, whose sensibilities have stormed the depths with Faust, whose longings for God in the rites of the old church have gained eternal blessing and, in Lutheran faith, an iron resolve? A people of such heritage will not be impressed by Berlin intelligentsia in pan-European style.[48]

A statement like this expresses the pervasive antimodern sentiments of the contemporary public. In terms that are both conventional and stereotyped, it invokes against the expressionist intelligentsia the spirit of classical philosophy, literature, and religion that expressionists like Werfel or Rubiner attempted to keep alive in new or revitalized forms. But it is the modernist formal experiment and the subjective intensity of expressionism that proved most irritating to established tastes of the conservatives and later to Nazi ideology.

Film: The Technology and Aesthetics of the Urban Vision

The conflict between the raw material experience of the modern metropolis and the lingering classical ideal of the polis would manifest itself most poignantly in the conflict between the newly emerging mass medium of film and literary culture between 1909 and 1929.[49] Film, an expression of and development through technological modernity, most incisively articulated the experience of urban mass society. In Germany, film only then became a hotly debated issue when it started to compete with and threaten literary culture, with filmed productions of novels and through enticing famous actors and directors from the stage.[50] The resentment against the "Kinoismus" (Georg Kaiser) of the urban masses was not only that of the representatives of a conservative German tradition (for example, Spengler) but was also voiced by many expressionist artists and writers, contributing to the climate of a cultural schism. In this debate even Franz Pfemfert, editor of *Die Aktion,* indicted film as "the most dangerous educator of the people,"[51] as annihilating the imagination. And even Kurt Pinthus, after all, the editor of *Das Kinobuch* (1913), an anthology of film scripts by expressionists such as Hasenclever, Else Lasker-Schüler, and Yvan Goll, is not quite free of double standards when he polarizes the "merely visual" with the experience "which the word reveals (offenbart)."[52] On the other hand, the playwright Walter Hasenclever intends to defuse such "hostility against film" as a "misunderstanding" by stressing an essential distinction between literary culture and film.[53] Suggesting to look at film from a "physiological" point of view as a reproduction of "God's own . . . world," Hasenclever finds it a "necessary" expression of a fundamentally human "naivité." Most interesting (and far-reaching) here is Hasenclever's "physiological" argument, not exactly standard expressionist. Georg Simmel, whose lectures at the Berlin university the poets of the "Neue Club" attended regularly, had already made a connection between the experience of the city and a changed psychophysiological mode of perception. In his essay "Die Großstadt und das Geistesleben" ("The Metropolis and Mental Life"; 1903), he had written about "the sudden coalescence of changing images, the jagged distance within what is perceived in one glance, the unpredictability of the surging impressions," which the speedy and abrupt sequence of filmed images reproduce and produce most immediately.[54] Heym, van Hoddis, and Alfred Lichtenstein would indeed respond to such changes of perception through the abrupt paratactic arrangement of seemingly unrelated images in their lyrics. When addressing the medium of film itself, however, Jakob van Hoddis's poem "Kinematograph," for example, would resort to an anti-cinematic discourse (while exploiting the parataxis of seemingly unrelated impressions):

> One goes for the revolver. Jealousy erupts,
> Herr Piefke fights a duel without head.
> Then we see the alpine woman with pannier and
> goiter climbing up a mighty steep path.
>
> And into the darkness of the room—right into
> my face—whirs this stuff, terrible! in sequence!
> The arc lamp hisses at the end for light—
> Lecherous and lazy do we shove outdoors.[55]

The poet's criticism obviously focuses on the slapstick banality of the action film and the sentimentality of the mountain film but extends also to the abrupt aggressiveness of the silent medium's delivery of the images buzzing from the dark: "right into my face . . . terrible! in sequence!" As his own poetry, for example, "Weltende" ("End of the World"; 1911) exploits the very same principle of an aggressive montage of unrelated images, the poet obviously privileges the verbal expression of the image in the traditional genre of poetry, no matter how "revolutionary" in terms of composition, over its mechanical production by the "Kinomatograph." On the other hand, the prose writer Alfred Döblin in narratives like "Die Ermordung einer Butterblume" ("The Assassination of a Buttercup"; written 1904–11; published 1913) or the playwright Georg Kaiser in *Von morgens bis mitternachts* (*From Morning to Midnight;* 1916) benefited from a transfer of film techniques into the literary medium. Fast-moving episodes, scenic representations, abrupt constellations of images, montage, and the like were the "physiological" expressions of the urban experience, so that the term

"Kinostil" became a literary term. In Döblin's story, for example, the "sensitive gentleman" from the city ("One becomes nervous in the city"), overwhelmed by an uncontrolled reaction to an unaccustomed encounter with nature, has just beheaded a buttercup (an image of feminine sensuality): "Meanwhile his feet carried on. . . . Even they wanted to dominate him; he was infuriated by their obstinate zeal. . . . It looked as if he was running away from the site of murder. Nobody should believe that." In the fashion of filmed sequences, the author here scenically presents outer motions, motoric, automatic, seemingly independent bodily movements, as the result of inner conflicts.

In 1920, Yvan Goll ventures the most daring prediction about the significance of film for the modern arts: "The basis for all new developments in the arts is film."[56] The expressionist poet and playwright seems to prepare Benjamin's later assessment of the literary avant-garde movements as "precursors" of film (in the 1936 artwork essay) when he addresses the developments of the avant-garde as "premonitions" (*Ahnungen*) of film: "Futurismus, Simultanismus. Picasso in der Malerei. Stramm in der Lyrik. Ahnungen." However, unlike later commentaries by Brecht, who saw "the epic, gestic and montage elements" of film as instrumental for the development of epic theater,[57] and Benjamin's, Goll makes his assertion not on the basis of exemplarily modern *cinematic techniques* proper but in view of a *future* film as a unifying *art* form. His observations on film are made in view of Viking Eggeling's experimental *Kinomalerei* (cinematic painting) rather than of German expressionist film. For Goll, Robert Wiene's immensely successful *Das Kabinett des Dr. Caligari* (1919) or Paul Wegener's *Der Golem* (1920), only formally expressionist, were thematically closer to the tradition of the horror theme, thus symptomatic of a mere "industry."

There is a less conspicuous, but for our concerns most significant, third factor. A focus on film raises for critics and writers like Max Brod or Egon Friedell doubts in literary language, doubts in the "absolute Hegemonie" of the word, resulting in reflections on the word's loss of "credit" in urban modernity.[58] Such reflections on a crisis of literary language as the crisis of language in modernity are not merely learned allusions to the later Nietzsche's language skepticism, Fritz Mauthner's *Beiträge zu einer Kritik der Sprache* (*Contributions to a Critique of Language;* 1901–1902), and Hugo von Hofmannsthal's "Chandos Letter" (1902). Rather, they are the result of a rather sudden, broad confrontation of literary culture with film in the 1910s. Hofmannsthal's remarkably differentiated 1921 essay "Der Ersatz für Träume" ("Substitute for Dreams") is something of a retrospective summary of the positive impact the emergence of film as a powerful mass medium had on the literary imagination. The Austrian poet and playwright now rephrases his early language skepsis that had addressed the distance of turn-of-the century aestheticism from vital experience as the crisis of individual literary creativity. In the former essay, it is the human body that in the moment of crisis and insight (of the eye) rejects the traditional diet of "abstract words," generalized ideas and ideals (such as "spirit" or "soul") as metaphors, and the analytical concepts of language as "rotten mushrooms" (the sensations of mouth and tongue) and opens the clearing for the "silent language of things," in other words, for the image. The early crisis was a crisis of subjectivity within the culture of enlightened individualism (Chandos's fictive addressee is Francis Bacon). The latter crisis, however, is registered in the context of modern mass culture as that of the working masses. Hence Hofmannsthal now points not only to the ontological, epistemological problematics of language but centrally to "language as the tool of society." As a social "tool," language functions as a social divide. The slogans of political parties and the newspaper, the language of the educated and "half-educated" instill the masses with fear, as they feel separated from the elite and from their own selves. Language in the service of others does not speak to their dreams once freely experienced during childhood. It is the medium of film, its "sensual" realm of moving, "silent images," that "in a flash" (*blitzartig*) enables them to reconnect with a "spiritual truth, which cannot be reached by reason," in a moment of flight from "cipher to vision."[59] Of course, Hofmannsthal's sociopsychoanalytic view of film as the medium of the working masses reflects his own point of view as firmly rooted in literary culture. Nevertheless, the steps taken in 1902 and in 1921 amount to a shift from an epistemological to a sociopsychological critique of language, which appears to be also traceable in the various positive comments on film cited earlier that culminate in Béla Balázs's criticism of a modern *Begriffskultur* (conceptual culture) and an idolization of "visible humanity."[60]

By the mid-1930s Walter Benjamin will attempt to most radically privilege film as the proper expression of modernity to the point of debunking the culture of "belles lettres" as a "bourgeois" culture of crisis (see chapter 5). His point of departure will be the "physiological" aspects of experience in modernity and its very own medium cinema (as discussed by Simmel, whose ideas Benjamin would practically summarize in the terms of his reception theory of film). It is the film that registers the "physiological" world of images as already fleetingly noticed by Hasenclever. The technological medium of film focuses immanently (in the terms of its unique visual grammar of montage, close-up, etc.) on the "physiological," the images of which appeared to the early Hofmannsthal in the fluidum of intuitive relations to the "things" from which reemerges the poetic experience, to Heym in a powerful if not overpowering "vertigo of seeing," and to Becher when he borrows from the futurists in order to come to terms with mass experience in the modern metropolis.

At War: Futurist and Expressionist "Language Poetry"

In the wake of the great exhibition of futurist paintings by the Sturm gallery in Berlin (1912), Italian futurism had the most profound impact on the German avant-garde, on expressionism and Dada alike. In view of these movements' essential pacifism and antiwar stance, such influence is almost incomprehensible, unless one considers the expressionists' quasi-religious belief in the formal aspect of artistic creation, a mentality and sensibility that was not even quite dead with Zurich Dada. It was a case of an aesthetically based reception. With the exception of the ideological reception by Moeller van den Bruck, a representative of the "conservative revolution," the identification with the aggressiveness of futurism in some of Johannes Becher's poetry of war, as brought to proper attention by Peter Demetz,[61] and Alfred Döblin's mostly critical response, one simply disregarded the Italians' vitalist ideology of war as "the world's only hygiene," inseparable from their program stated as early as 1909 in the founding Futurist Manifesto and restated in "Futurist Synthesis of the War" (1914):

> We glorify war, which for us is the only hygiene of the world (First Futurist Manifesto), whereas for the Germans it serves as a fat feast for crows and hyenas. The old cathedrals do not interest; but we deny medieval, plagiarist, clumsy Germany, unendowed with creative genius, the Futurist right to destroy works of art. This right belongs solely to the Italian creative Genius, capable of creating a new and greater beauty on the ruins of the old.[62]

Yet, in spite of futurism's militarism and chauvinism, here directed specifically at Germany, the German avant-garde would, on the whole, embrace its formal language in the spirit of a programmatic "radical internationalism."[63] Implying a protest against German nationalism, Franz Pfemfert and Theodor Däubler even dedicated a special issue of *Die Aktion* in 1916 (!)

to futurism. An example for the bluntest futurist fascination with war for war's sake is Marinetti's *Zang Tumb Tumb:* "BOMBARDAMENTO / ogni 5 secondi cannoni da assedio sventrare spazio con un accordo *tam-tuuumb* ammutinamento di 500 echi per azzannarlo sminuzzarlo sparpagliarlo all' infinito. . . ."[64] Nowhere really a *parole in libertà,* if so, then only on a superficial grammatical-syntactical level, quite traditionally favoring the noun in explosive analogies, most of Marinetti's texts invoke a terse, male-centered union of natural-instinctual, primordial energies with the metallic hardness of technology. His vision of "male birth," of the futurist Mafarka, a flying machine with animal and human features, epitomizes futurist dogmatism. The Italian futurists proclaimed a liberation of the body for a radically modern experience. Yet their program of *parole in libertà* was actually far from exploring the realm of the bodily unconscious, as the heroic posturing of their technofascist *artecrazia* superimposed itself on the nondiscursive energies of image and sign.

August Stramm, featured in Herwarth Walden's *Der Sturm* as representative of the circle's *Wortkunst* (language art), employed techniques similar to a futurist *parole in libertà,* but he went much further in experimenting with a dissolution of the distinctions between noun and verb, transitive and intransitive verbs, and the dislocation of prefixes.[65] Though the poet shared the initial war enthusiasm of many expressionist artists and writers, his poem "Wache" ("Guard Duty"), for example, is anything but an ideological reaction to the war, as its language renders a mystical, decentered experience of a self fused with the world of "whispering" things.

Guard Duty

> A star startles the tower cross
> The nag gasps smoke
> Iron clanks drowsily
> Mist brushing past
> Shudders
> Gazing shivering
> Shivering
> Stroking
> Whispering
> You![66]

Stramm's poems on erotic love and war alike diffuse logocentric language, often into the phonemic level (in the German original the intensifying, shrill neologism *schrickt* [startles] instead of *schreckt*). A conscious rejection of the rationality of formal experience (including that of male military order, as implied by the title "Guard Duty") and a passive prelingustic letting go into an intuited preformal totality are blended into one. Entwined with the conscious dissolution of formal literary conventions, such as the poetic line and stanza, is the text's subversion of the subject-object relationship. In a release of aggression and erotic sensations (*streicheln* may better be translated as "caressing" than "stroking,"), the experience of war is articulated as an Eros/Thanatos complex. In that sense, the text transforms the deadly threat to the body into an experience that elides the difference of self/not-self as in "Gazing" (the German *Starren* can mean both a subject's "gazing" and an object "rigidly bristling"). Erased is the difference between the human subject, animal ("the nag") and matter (tower/iron); the animate and inanimate world have become entwined in a "you": "Shudders/Gazing shivering/Shivering/Stroking/Whispering/You!"

Indicative of the mixed reception of Stramm's "language poetry" as a hybrid product of futurist techniques and an expressionist embrace of the "spiritual" self is Edschmid's divided assessment, which represents the sentiments of mainstream expressionism toward the *Sturm* circle's *Wortkunst:* "These poems . . . have more to do with outcry than with art but are nevertheless inspired by the strongest spirituality."[67] Though not as outspoken as Karl Kraus's condemnation of the futurist *Neutönerei* (craze of linguistic innovation) as "spiritual poverty,"[68] judgments such as these typically fail to realize that the "primitive" may be the result of the most refined construction of a highly self- and language-conscious modern poet.

Metamorphoses of the Discourse of "Primitivism"

August Macke's 1912 essay "Die Masken" ("The Masks") in the almanac of the *Blaue Reiter* (*Blue Rider*) contains the earliest revaluation of African masks (among the artifacts from Easter Island to those of Alaska) in the expressionist quest to escape the confines of a "europäische Ästhetik" as Eurocentric experience. Yet such transgression is typically made in the name of the renewal of experience through an emphatic return to the *uralte* (archaic) elements of art, felt to be superior to the formal concerns of "famous cubism."[69] In comparison, Carl Einstein's treatise *Negerplastik* (*Negro Sculpture;* 1915) is the most significant document demonstrating a direct linkage between expressionist "primitivism" and the international avant-garde. This daring analysis significantly displaces the nineteenth-century ethnological discourse in which African masks were viewed negatively as mere artifacts, as fetishes but not as art. Ethnology had defined African masks as products of an inferior or, at best, a still underdeveloped and therefore childlike "primitive" culture. Einstein perceived these artifacts not only as art but as aesthetically superior to the works of the mimetic European tradition. His theoretical breakthrough can be traced concretely to a German-French avant-garde constellation in Paris. Through contacts with the art dealer Daniel-Henry Kahnweiler, Einstein had acquainted himself in Paris not only with the cubist paintings of Georges Braque and Pablo Picasso but also with the African sculptures that had inspired the cubist rupture with the tradition of the logocentric perspective.[70] Such a shift from the dominant scientific ethnological discourse to the aesthetic discourse, such outright aesthetic revolution—and here the much abused term of a "revolution" in the arts is not applied in vain—most likely did not take place in isolation. Rather, it may be tied to a progressing softening of the all-too-rigorous scientific discourse itself. Leo Frobenius, for instance, a leading if controversial German scholar in the study of African cultures, began to admit that the scientific terms of the modern European mind were inadequate to fully experience the significance of African masks: "How often have I charged myself that I am unable to put into words what here before my eyes, under my hands, in front of my pounding heart actively lived and moved. How often, how often! And today I sense in exactly that dilemma the dilettantism of writing, narration and description. . . . Alas, as how thin science here unmasks itself as the pale shadow of art!"[71]

What it took for the cubists and subsequently for Carl Einstein to view African artifacts as art was nothing less than the will to break a barrier. A negative contemporary review of an exhibit of Picasso's cubist works and African sculptures in Paris described that barrier as one which lies "between him [Picasso] and the negroes" as "the whole of art history."[72] The French cubists in praxis and Einstein subsequently in theory did break precisely that barrier. They aimed to excavate, as it were, and *rearticulate* an epoch of "primitivist" European experience. In his 1911 response to Carl Vinnen's "Protest of the German Artists" against the impact of French art in Germany, Worringer had already argued against the dominant "rationalism of seeing," the construct of a "natural seeing,"[73] which had been based since the Renaissance on the logic of the subject-centered perspective—the ordered three-dimensional experience. In *Negerplastik,* Einstein resolutely proposed an alternative definition of the visual function of sculpture:

The task of sculpture is to form an equation, through which the natural-istic sensations of movement and thus its mass are totally absorbed, and its successive differences transformed into a formal order. This equivalent must be total, so that the work of art is no longer intuited as an equation of differently oriented human projections, but as an unconditional, closed independence.[74]

The "new" seeing thus deconstructs the subject-identical relation of the *particular* to conceptual representation, or the dualism between "mass" and "form." *Seeing* thus is said to be freed from binary distinctions; it consists of the experience of a series of *indeterminate* "successive differences" that are coordinated only as far as they present an experiential, intuited totality of vision. The treatise, which still awaits and merits a close reading as a text in itself, has somewhat of a surprise conclusion as it shifts quite abruptly from the discussion of African sculpture to the tattooed body of the African. The effect of this "coda" is the concrete realization that Einstein's rather abstract discussion of the cubist "seeing" is rooted in his understanding of seeing as a fundamentally physiological act, as a function of the body. As such it is literally inscribed in the tattooed body. The tattoo is not the ex-pression of an individual view of the self but a form of collective conscious-ness "metamorphotically" fused with the collective unconscious (the body as a collective body) into an "absolute" ("unconditional") physiognomic structure.

On the other side of the expressionist spectrum of "seeing" are the mes-sianic "visions" of the "soul," or the voluntaristic subjectivity tirelessly advo-cated by Kasimir Edschmid, a virtual promoter of expressionism.[75] The new primitivist energy was to inspire a whole generation of expressionist artists like Max Pechstein or Emil Nolde. The painter Karl Schmidt-Rottluff is re-ported to have carried a copy (not of Hölderlin's poems but) of Einstein's *Negerplastik* in his field pack during World War I. Yet, as Einstein com-plained, the analytic and sensual energy of French cubism would be "deco-ratively" exoticized, sometimes sentimentalized by many German painters. Such judgment is, in cases, not without justification where their extensive travels on location[76] could have raised the question of "authenticity" to the fore. Einstein began to distance himself from the evolving faddish primitiv-ism ("one niggers fashionably"). Thus, in *Die Afrikanische Plastik* (*African Sculpture;* 1921), the second version of his treatise, he attempts to amend his earlier purist aesthetic approach by reintroducing some ethnological con-siderations.

In Germany, African primitivism had its impact mainly on the visual arts. It did not affect literary production[77] except via Marinetti's "bruitist" influence on Dada. For French literature and thought, the long-standing colonial ties to African culture were, of course, of eminent consequence. The significance of primitivism and primitive art for the French avant-garde reaches to Michel Leiris and the surrealist group surrounding Georges Bataille. The self-exiled Einstein here took his part as coeditor of the journal *Documents. Archéologie, Beaux-Arts, Ethnographie, Variétés,* Paris 1929–30,[78] at which point certain "surrealist" qualities that informed his work since its beginning with the "novel" *Bebuquin* (1907–1909) converge with the aesthetic and political project of the French avant-garde (see chapter 4).

The Expressionist Aestheticization of Politics

A fascist *aestheticization of politics,* as critiqued by Benjamin in the case of Italian futurism that bypasses the complexity of modern politics by aesthetically linking it with primordial, primitive energies, is the standard paradigm for a negative legacy of the historical avant-garde.[79] There is also a *leftist* aestheticization of politics, however. Johannes Becher's poetry is a poignant case in point. In "Vorbereitung" ("Preparation"; 1916), Becher writes about the revolutionary task of the poet:

> The poet eschews splendid chords. / He blasts on tubas and shrilly whips his drum. / He stirs the people up with rough-hewn lines, [he] envision[s] a sunny, a carefully organized, a *sculptured* country, / An island of blissful mankind.[80]

The poem may *thematically* proclaim a subversive "shrill" function of art at the expense of aesthetic enjoyment: "The poet eschews splendid chords." Yet it is articulated in aesthetic terms just as conventional as the culture they invoke. The poet envisions something quite familiar: life turned into art ("a *sculptured*" country). Similarly, even before the war, the art theorist and critic Wilhelm Hausenstein had identified the evolving European anti-naturalist style with emerging socialist tendencies of epochal significance. The expressionist style was to anticipate the "public of the future."[81] After the war, Carl Einstein would radicalize Hausenstein's original theoretical vision, conflating the dynamics of what he considered the Russian futurists' "absolute art" with revolutionary (absolute) politics.[82] Proposing such function for art is problematic, to say the least. Einstein here merely radicalizes the notion of aesthetic autonomy: art is to determine social life. In a speech contributing to the *Künstlerdebatte* (artists' debate) of the provisional national council on January 3, 1919, Kurt Eisner similarly proclaimed that "an escape into the realm of the beautiful ought to be no longer necessary . . . but that life itself should be a work of art, and the state the greatest of all works of art."[83] National Socialism would later realize such grand vision of the state as a total work of art in its mass demonstrations from the opposite political spectrum.

Activist texts such as Ludwig Rubiner's "Der Dichter greift in die Politik" ("The Poet Reaches for Politics"; 1908–12) or poetry like Becher's "Hymne auf Rosa Luxemburg" in its fulminating, vitalist, ecstatic "Pathos" reenact a sort of "Storm and Stress" assault on a formal aesthetic sense. Just as Becher's turn to futurist forms, such attack does not represent a real break, however, for he continued to engage traditional contents.[84] Becher's poem virtually disembodies Rosa Luxemburg and elevates her instead, quite conventionally, into a messianic figure, mother and saint redeeming the poor: "Fountain of blood from these fingers it filed through the bars of millions of the poorest."[85] Becher has turned the political revolutionary Rosa Luxemburg into a personified allegory of art ("O most motherly of harps") as a natural, religious, collective force of redemption: "O you spice of paradisiacal meadows/: You one and only! You holy one! O woman!" Some of Becher's truly accomplished "futurist" poems may indeed make him, according to Demetz, "a genius poet, whom (the Germans) have not yet read enough."[86] But—with all due respect for the expressionist Zeitgeist—this sort of poetry lacks in perceptions, thus in perceptiveness (leading to similar, altogether unpalatable later hymns dedicated to Stalin). Contrasting starkly with the poetry of Heym or Benn, Becher's address of a contemporary professional revolutionary in highfalutin hymnic terms is dangerously close to an exhausted recycling of past achievements as rhetorical devices that obtrude as such.

Some of Becher's and others' poetry is, of course, an expression not only of a "metaphysical" forlornness but also of the political isolation of expressionist activism from the Communist Party[87] and the liberal parties alike. Thus, the expressionists were "free-floating intellectuals" (Karl Mannheim) not only on their own volition. By contrast, the Russian and Italian futurists, and later the surrealists in France, were able to establish some connection with the political parties, at least before the inevitable backlash. In Germany, antimodernist views were held even by the reformist USPD (Independent Socialist Party of Germany). Georg Lukács in his later attack on the movement wanted to identify expressionism, falsely as has been thoroughly documented,[88] as the "poetic voice-piece" of the USPD. While the parties, like the expressionists, believed in the universalist nature of art, they were stalwart guardians of the "house of language" averse to the formal exaggerations and transgressions of the expressionists' poetry.[89]

Art and Gender

Among the few women who are generally recognized as significant avant-garde artists in Germany, only Hannah Hoech—the sole female participant in Berlin Dada whose emancipation as an artist is intimately linked to her deeply troubled relationship to Raoul Hausmann[90]—and Lu Märten[91] can convincingly be called "feminist" voices. Of course, the status of women artists or writers was no different in expressionist circles than in the other avant-garde movements. The performer Emmy Hennings and the puppet-eer Sophie Täuber, close companions to Hugo Ball and Hans Arp, respectively, played a relative subordinate role in Zurich Dada. The Italian futur-ists blended Nietzsche's (as well as Weininger's)[92] "scorn for women" with their male-heroic apotheosis of war. In such a climate, Valentine de Saint-Point's "Manifesto of Futurist Woman" was clearly an oddity, a document of female assimilation to rather than emancipation from male domination. The surrealist concept of *amour fou* (crazy love) may, at best, represent a shift from the madonna/whore dichotomy toward an image of woman as a form of *Körpergeistigkeit* (bodily spirituality), as Peter Sloterdijk calls it, that is neither "real" nor "symbolic."[93] Nevertheless, there were no recognized women surrealist artists or writers.

Else Lasker-Schüler was a colorful and irritating presence among the Berlin avant-garde. Her lifestyle as a liberated woman made her the part-ner of many male artists and writers whom she addressed in her poems. Through her letters to these friends and fellow artists, which are not just letters but *letter-poems* that also addressed quite mundane practical matters, she uniquely attempts to overcome the separation of art and life. In her cor-respondence, her self-centered prose and sketches, she may either disclose her psychic complexity or don a mask fitting her competitive male environ-ment by giving herself male attributes as "Prince Jussuf." The protagonist of her novel *Der Malik. Eine Kaisergeschichte* (*The Malik: An Emperor's Story;* 1919) is likewise an androgynous figure. The androgynous there appeals to the overcoming of the gender-based differences of social and political roles and assumes the wider significance of a pacifist stance. The roman à clef reflects the tensions within the expressionist scene, beginning with its early days in the Café des Westens and culminating in the pro- and antiwar divisions brought about by World War I. It is clearly composed around the idea of unmasking cultural differences as conventional constructs. As the story opposes the emperor's oriental culture of the "heart" with German militarism (of which "Giselheer der Nibelunge," Benn, is a chief representative), it should not be read as another exoticist tale, albeit autobiographically. Rather, it is a story that, down to its very details focusing on the significance of clothing (oriental garb versus the "Aryan's" field-grey uniforms), exposes the constructed (masked) nature of identity. Be the "identity" Jewish or German, female or male, it is only a matter of different codes.[94]

Thus her story summons the Malik's powers of poetry as the only means that can dissolve the social and political powers of stereotypes and put an end to the infighting among the artists and writers and to the global conflicts. While the novel invokes a "Reichsunmittelbarkeit"[95] of art, of art partaking in ultimate authority, it does, after all, end with the death of the emperor Malik. This conclusion not only is a resigned reaction to the political realities of the war but may also signify Lasker-Schüler's indecision toward a gender-oriented critique of her cultural environment.[96] Except for continuing to sign her personal letters with "Prinz Jussuf," the poet will no longer pursue the androgynous theme in her subsequent major works.

The issue of gender roles does play a certain role and poses questions in a few of her poems. For example, in "Das Lied des Spielprinzen" ("The Song of the Play Prince"), the "play prince" addresses a male "hard voice" and "deines Kinnes Grube" (the pit of your chin), and in the love poem "Dem Barbaren" ("For the Barbarian"), a male voice (Joseph) addresses himself to his male lover.[97] But the gender issue cannot be isolated as the center of the poet's concerns; it is rather tied to her "experimentation" with the relation of the physical to the aesthetic, and metaphysical realm. Thus, for example, her identification of a male poet with God as in

"Sabaoth" (For Franz Jung)

God, I love you in your rose-robe,
When you step out of your gardens, Sabaoth.
O you God-youth,
You poet,
I drink from your fragrances in solitude.

My first blossom of blood yearned for you,
So do come,

You sweet God,
You playmate God,
Your gateway's gold melts from my yearning.[98]

The poem, dedicated to the anarchist Franz Jung, could be addressed as a quite daring example of a latter-day German "metaphysical poetry" which entwines the disparate realms of the religious and the physically erotic ("You sweet God, / You playmate God / Your gateway's gold melts from my yearning."). Her most accomplished poems exemplify a supreme effort to produce the complete work of art against the odds of her times without isolation from them.

By contrast to Else Lasker-Schüler's refined and stunningly experimental engagement of the metaphysical within the physical, other expressionists often assume a revivalist, fundamentalist concern with religious issues, as Kurt Heynicke's "Psalm" or Paul Zech's "This Is the Hour," from which I cite the opening stanzas:

> You kneel, you pray—: how this God can still
> be persuaded in spite of a thousand lies
> and the mockery of popes grown soft.
>
> Your word assembles in processions,
> the stream forms seven branches in space;
> The virgins carry oil again in vessels.[99]

What purpose would the concept of "style" have where poetry as this expresses, in severely restricted rhetorical terms (indeed, the "word assembles in processions"), mostly an antimodernist disposition? In search of the expressionist "new man" and renewed metaphysical meaning, poets like Rubiner, Heynicke, Werfel, or Zech, even though of different social origins, educational background and political leanings,[100] came together in an attempt to recuperate the moral and/or religious within the aesthetic experience. Helmut Heißenbüttel here, too, speaks of a "mimicry of the lost," finds the "enraptured religiosity" of such texts an expression of a "climax of desperation and disorientation." For the "language poet" and critic of the 1950s and 1960s, they speak "not against the thesis of a definitive departure from the metaphysical realm, but for it." Indeed, the stereotyping symbolism that disembodies the phenomenal world ("seven branches," "virgins," etc.), the subject-centeredness of such poetry as Heynicke's or Zech's speaks of a condition, which the poets were not or did not want to be aware of, a condition in which "the transcendence of the faith in God, has been replaced by language itself."[101] Aesthetic credibility thus depends on how the modern poet, for whom the "lyrical poet with a halo is antiquated,"[102] invokes language, whether as a preformulated figure of speech (*Versatzstück*) reinvoked from past poetic achievements or, as in the case of much of Else Lasker-Schüler's poetry, as an encounter with language as a space of experimentation. Her highly calculated poetry deserves a new critical assessment that indeed puts her work beyond the often invoked stereotype of "neoromantic" and into the center of international avant-garde developments.[103]

On the other hand, some of Lasker-Schüler's poetry—to return to the issue of gender—like that of Claire Goll, after all stresses the traditional "female" characteristics and values of love as compassion and nurturing (with religious traces) as opposed to the "male" qualities of detached reasoning. This is documented in an exchange of poems with an evasively "cool," "glass eyed" Dr. Gottfried Benn (the "Barbarian" or "Nibelunge" of the *Malik* novel). In "Doctor Benn" the poet conforms to the image of the "feminine" in a quasi apotheosis of the male addressee:[104]

> I cry—My dreams fall into the world. / Into my darkness / No shepherd ventures. / My eyes do not show the way / As stars do. / I am a constant beggar in front of your soul; . . . and I do not like the cool day, / It has a glass eye. / Everything is dead, Only you and I are not.[105]

The conflicting attitudes toward gender in poems like "Dem Barbaren" (male to male voice), "Das Lied des Spielprinzen," dedicated to Franz Jung, and "Dr. Benn" may thus be symptomatic for the poet being torn between a liberated and conservative view of the issues. Or, differently stated, Else Lasker-Schüler appears to respond, in one way or another, to Otto Weininger's (today inconceivably) influential *Geschlecht und Charakter* (*Sex and Character;* 1903, with twenty editions by 1920), which set the premises for the male intellectual climate in which she had to compete for recognition as a writer. Weininger's indictment of the female as formless sexual libido lacking spiritual and intellectual creativity, as a danger to the male intellect and his form-giving powers was, after all, shared by some addressees of her poems, be it Benn or Karl Kraus. In poems responding to hers, as in "Kein Trost" ("No Solace"), Benn takes recourse to a rhetoric that echoes Weininger's rejection of a woman's love as too confining to the male creative intellect. At the other extreme, Otto Gross and Franz Jung, the addressee of her poem "Sabaoth" discussed earlier, argued for a sexual-political revolution against the "male-dominated institutions and a return to matriarchy" informed by a "will to love and relationships."[106] "The coming revolution is revolution for the maternal right (Mutterrecht)," Gross had written in 1913.[107] It may be symptomatic for the expressionist mentality in general that Gross's ideas of a sexual-political revolution for communal experience, which transformed Bachofen's nineteenth-century ideas for the modern experience, had an impact mostly only on radicals like Franz Jung[108] and, more problematically, the quintessential dadaist Raoul Hausmann.[109] This is, roughly sketched, the context in which Else Lasker-Schüler writes.

Moreover, the poet's work is to be viewed not only within the Weininger/ Gross (Franz Jung) polarity but also in terms of the underlying sociocultural matrix of an entwinement of a long-standing German discourse of prejudice against women and Jews. Edschmid's quite disingenuous praise of Werfel's and Lasker-Schüler's poetry for a spiritual immediacy that "one would not have credited Jewish poetry with,"[110] stays part of this discourse. Jewish intelligence was stereotyped as "effeminate," merely superficially "smart," thus representative of modernity, but not "creative."[111] Looking at her poetry in the terms of gender, and ethnic/religious divisions, it may be not too far-fetched to assume that she responds as a woman among male writers to the charge that women (and Jews) lack creativity. Weininger, after all, merely philosophically "elevated"—and thus made respectable— a long-standing popular prejudice against women. It informed the higher institutions of philosophy, history, and art when the emancipation movement with the turn of the century became a viable force and threat. In the 1890s, the historian and Reichstags-representative Heinrich von Treitschke had already given voice to an emerging fear by affirming that the "universal" realm of art will remain the citadel of male power: "No woman has the truly creative ability . . . to bring forth a real work of art."[112]

Kunstrevolution: The Work of Art in Crisis

The poetry of Werfel, Rubiner, Zech, and Lasker-Schüler remains, in distinctly varying degrees of success, based on the totality of the work of art. Poets like Jakob von Hoddis and Alfred Lichtenstein, on the other hand, respond to the fragmentation of the modern experience by, as it were, quoting from the disparate world of objects, presenting its *disiecti membra* in montage. Like Heym's, Lichtenstein's poetry is exempted from Benjamin's otherwise relentless critique of expressionism as strained, epigonal idealism. A poem like "Dämmerung" ("Dusk") reflects the dissolution of the subject-centered imagination:

A plump kid is playing with a pond.
The wind has gotten caught in a tree.
The sky looks hung over and pale,
As though it had run out of makeup.

Stooped down crookedly on long crutches
And chattering two cripples creep across the field.
A blond poet may well be going crazy.
A little horse is tripping over a lady.

A fat man is glued to a window.
A youth wants to visit a soft woman.
A gray clown is pulling on his boots.
A baby-carriage screams and dogs curse.[113]

In poems like these, the notion of an expressionist *Kunstrevolution* achieves its most precise meaning. In a first move, Lichtenstein's "Dusk" reproduces the discontinuity of the modern experience, its paratactic lines focus on and, as it were, stumble over the particular. There is, for example, no ready relation between the first and second line, "a plump kid . . . playing with a pond" and "the wind . . . caught in a tree." Yet the situation of arrest (being "caught"), experienced *physically,* constitutes a motif that extends to the "two cripples" *creeping* on "long crutches," the "little horse . . . *tripping* over a lady," to a "fat man *glued* to a window." A counter*motion* articulates itself in terms of the "plump kid's" movement of "playing," of the cripples' "chattering," a youth's desire "to visit a soft woman," and a clown's activity of "pulling on his boots." Nevertheless, arrest and motion meet, as it were, at the moment of standstill: a pond is too large to play with, chattering has no direction, sexual desire may stay desire, one cannot walk while pulling on one's boots. However, the poem is "playing" with the entwinement of stasis and motion, jumping to connections from the "sky . . . hung over and pale . . . run out of makeup" to the "gray clown" (also without makeup). And it is "a blond poet" that may—in this moment of indecision between physical arrest and willful motion—"well be going crazy." Lichtenstein, whose masked alter ego may be the "blond poet," attempts to conclude the textual progression in a culmination of sound and image, in the physical "sound-images" of a screaming baby carriage (toto for pars/object for subject) and cursing dogs. The poem's title "Dämmerung" (unlike its English translation of "dusk," the German word can refer to the twilight of both the morning and the evening) appears to grasp the surreal atmosphere of alienation at a point where experience is inconclusive to interpretation. Lichtenstein himself has commented on his poem as rendering "the reflexes of things in immediacy—without superfluous reflection,"[114] failing to disclose that "immediacy" in poetry is, after all, mediated by a developed aesthetic consciousness of the medium of language.

In these terms, the poem does not "anticipate" the radical dadaist practices of rupture (for instance Arp's, to which these discontinuous lines bear some resemblance). Rather, it may be read as symptomatic of the wider event of an international upheaval in the arts that responds to the material challenge of modernity, and which cannot really be defined in reference to any particular "ism," dadaism or expressionism. Alfred Döblin may be the only contemporary (if distanced) participant in the event of the expressionist *Kunstrevolution* who also understood its workings as its critic. He spoke of a conscious/unconscious "Triebwerk of Erinnerungen und Instinkte" (engine of memories and instincts), where the "artist is only the potential for the opus" and the "opus a tangle of ethical and aesthetical values."[115] In other words, Döblin put his critical finger on the fact that the avant-garde's *Kunstrevolution* is part of a larger cultural system (which he calls "machine," "engine," or "harrow") that, due to the friction between the subjective and objective world, is always in precariously unstable motion and that, contrary to Hiller's activist ideology, no single agency can direct. As an "event," expressionism is not the product "of any interest group"; rather, it may, as Döblin saw its cultural dynamics in 1918, be "a broad fall of tensions and forces flowing from . . . constellations outside of the human being," a "fermentation without a direction." Yet more successful art works may also function in the sense of an "archaeological" uncovering of forgotten, suppressed energies, as Döblin put it.[116] The expressionist movement itself, it seems to me, could be viewed as suspended in a condition of play or motion and arrest between physiological reactions expressed in images and spiritual, albeit mostly fragmentary, responses to the modern experience, well exemplified by Lichtenstein's poem "Dusk."

What, then, is the significance of the tension-ridden relations of the disparate, the "old" and the "new" forms of art for a reassessment of expressionism? How do we understand the coexistence of the closed work of art and the fragment, of neoromantic, neoclassical rhetoric and futurist parole as well as protosurrealist imagery in one literary movement? Does such disparity merely duplicate the conflicts within the modern experience as what Ernst Bloch addressed as the "contemporaneity of the untimely"?[117] Not only was the expressionist revolt formally innovative, but it also recycled, as we have seen, older forms. The purpose was not, as with Dada, to do away with all styles but to try once more to reestablish an authentic relationship of the aesthetic and the moral to the material social domain of experience. Expressionism's contradictory discourses, then, can be attributed to competing attempts to cope with the modern experience.

In his second introduction to the 1922 edition of *Die Menschheitsdäm-merung* (*The Dawn of Humanity*), Pinthus provides us with no small surprise. It is now his opinion that the work of the expressionists may have been "more oppositional than creative."[118] Indeed, a review of the movement may confirm such a revision. There was a great deal of infighting in a group like "Der Neue Club," where Heym's "visual" poetics would clash with Hiller's ethical rationalism, and there were feuds between journals such as *Der Sturm* or *Die Aktion* about the significance of futurism for German art and literature.[119] Infighting among the expressionists could explain, for example, Kurt Hiller's claim of his circle's "energetic fight against 'mysticism in form'. . . the inner hereditary enemy" and his avowed promotion of a "lucid," "latin-like" German.[120] Likewise, Carl Sternheim, typically invoking Flaubert's concern with form, had from the very beginning nothing but mockery for the inflated metaphorical rhetoric of messianic expressionism. In his important, polemical essay "Kampf der Metapher" ("Fight against Metaphor"; 1917), which advocated the cerebral analytic language of the early Benn, he ridiculed expressionists like Werfel, Rubiner, and Heynicke as "foaming at the mouth." He accuses these idealists (in an early version of a "political unconscious") of repressing the fact that they share with the world of stock speculators the same concepts, which are poetically "blown up with both cheeks to the bursting."[121]

One must also not forget, lest the concept of an "expressionist epoch" return through the back door, that even in its heyday expressionism never dominated the cultural scene like the avant-garde did, for example, in Paris. Stefan George, Thomas Mann, Rilke, and Hesse never lost the majority of their readers. While Hesse and Rilke were quite open-minded, if nevertheless concerned about some aspects of an expressionist intolerance for form and tradition, George and Mann fueled with their resentful commentaries the aversion against the cultural rebels.[122] Mann especially criticized the political activism of the mere "Literaten" as "un-German."[123] Seen in this light, expressionism indeed was "Kulturkampf" (a fight over culture) and sometimes even "Literaturpolitik" as a "Hirnkampf" (brain fight), with the "weapon of the will," according to Hiller.[124]

An agonistic view of literary change may significantly replace a preoccupation with a formal history of styles, where each new style is viewed as an evolutionary break with a past form.[125] Reassessed as an "unstructured"[126] agon of competing discourses, expressionism makes visible the crisis of the disembodied "spirit" of German idealism, of the heightened belief in art and the artist. Expressionist works took part in the conflicts of German society, responding in aesthetic terms to the politics of war or pacifism, or revolution, to the conflicts between national and international culture, between the promodern and antimodern voices, the city and the country, between film and literature, the image and the word, of modern rationalism and a new "primitivism," and the conflict between the genders, intensely experiencing the rift between the physical world and a metaphysical realm, in an attempt to find in art a unifying language. As "there was no formed and settled society to which the new kinds of work could be related," writes Raymond Williams,[127] the avant-garde focused on "what could be done in the medium."[128] The expressionists thereby struggled to "solve" (aestheticize or anesthetize) or, in their most successful works, aesthetically mediate the overarching conflict between international and national culture.

Zurich Dada, a grouping of artists and writers of many nationalities in political exile at the height of World War I (the subject of my next chapter), would respond to any attempt to bridge conflicts through art by altogether breaking down the idea of a national culture to the extent that culture as such was questioned. In the era of political exile from Nazi Germany, these questions resurfaced, albeit — except in the case of Carl Einstein and George Grosz (see chapters 3 and 6), erstwhile participants in Berlin dadaism — in less radical form. It can be said that the expressionist agon of art over art *unconsciously* as Dada *consciously* relativized the idea and ideal of aesthetic "styles" (thus also of "art"). As should have become clear in the foregoing discussion of representative poetry and texts, the contesting "discourses" of expressionism represent *conscious* attempts to dominate the cultural domain while *unconsciously* relativizing the idea of a stable identity of art. Moreover, they are also "symbolic" solutions to problems in the social domain (which as such are *unconscious* of the underlying socioeconomic conditions). Differences as to era and genre set aside, Fredric Jameson talks of, for example, Joseph Conrad's impressionistic "aestheticizing strategy" as valorizing an amoral visual approach to the world whose underlying capitalistic dynamics of alienation and reification remain unconscious.[129] He does not, as I do here, place such strategy into the context of contemporary competing strategies of aestheticization, which, of course, also have "economic parallels" (Döblin).[130]

These considerations quite obliquely raise the question what the *Kunst-revolution* in the first decade of our century may have meant for the development of the German avant-garde toward our "postmodern" context where the significance of different "styles" appears to have been set aside with indifference. The question will remain heuristically open throughout this study, which is not per se concerned with a classificatory distinction between modernism, avant-garde, and, particularly, postmodernism, though such a discussion attains a more concrete value for the evaluative, summary parts of the final chapter. The question will be among my concerns in this study of the disparate legacies of expressionism through the period of political exile, and of developments like dadaism or Brecht's epic theater that reacted (at least initially) against expressionism as a movement.

What can be said at this point already about the specific quality of the German avant-garde, if not yet about its *Sonderweg* (exceptional path), is this: The classical German avant-garde, expressionism, is even in its extreme forms considerably much less given to a subversion of tradition in the arts than to a mediation of modernity and tradition. Hence expressionism as a movement objectively assumes the function of exploring a number of conflicting possibilities for the *transition* toward and construction of a new cultural identity responsive to the demands that international modernization processes make on national traditions. The expressionist movement does so in terms that are, in fact, system-immanent to the institution of art, whether or not one wants to break with aesthetic autonomy. Instead, one's faith in art projects and idolizes a suprahistorical *museum* of cultural interiority from which one, as it were, can make aesthetic selections from the past for the present, and to which one can add aesthetic experiences from the present to the future. Different from André Malraux's much later (post-World War II) concept of an "imaginary museum," in which the historical forms of art achieve the timeless status and value of a fundamentally different world, the intent of mainstream expressionism is to activistically fulfill the universal claims inherent in the privileged aesthetic experience for the historical life-worlds. Given the agonistic relations within a movement of a precarious identity, however, one opens an unstable imaginary space oscillating between a radically utopian cultural project and a Nietzschean apotheosis of art.

As already alluded to in the introduction, my concept of an unstructured agon of discourses, reflecting as well as contributing to the tensions between stasis and change in the wider public sphere, serves as a historio-graphically descriptive and evaluative measure of assessing a crisis in the arts and the avant-garde itself as a crisis phenomenon. The concept of an agon of discourses is not a philosophical theorem; rather, it serves as a means for assessing poetological techniques as forms of dispositions in what Paul de Man in his terms addresses as a "successive process of mystifications and partial demystifications" of the idealist notion of the work of art as the "unity of appearance (sign) and idea (meaning)" from romanticism to twentieth-century modernity.[131] My focus on an agon of avant-garde dis-courses allows for insights into an objective, formal aspect of crisis as well as for insights into the individual writers' and artists' subjective experience of crisis, ranging from the political to the moral and aesthetic.

The concept of "crisis" has, of course, become "polysemous,"[132] if not a catchall slogan. In terms of the etymological Greek meaning, from *krinein* as to separate, select, evaluate; to contest, dispute, and *battle*, "crisis" aimed at a final, irreversible decision (as, for example, in battle or in the course of a serious illness). Since the eighteenth century, the term "crisis" has attained a primarily temporal significance, on the level of philosophical-historical (*geschichtsphilosophische*) epochal interpretations which subject the totality of the historical past to the experience of the own present, from which also the future is projected.[133] A critique of avant-garde discourses, of course, cannot duplicate this futurist disposition, shared by all avant-garde move-ments except Dada. Hence throughout this study I first of all go back to the basic etymological meaning of "crisis." As much as an agon of competing discourses means the struggle for resolution and hegemony, the avant-garde strives for an epochal decision (without achieving it). This is the common denominator of even the most conflicting "futuristic" avant-garde visions.

Most typical for German expressionism is an extreme form of a pro-jection of conflicts into a utopian resolution, the "apocalyptical" vision. There is, for example, Jacob van Hoddis's "Weltende" ("Doomsday"; 1911), a much-discussed poem which thematically and aesthetically precipitated a series of doomsday treatments. In the visual arts, there are Kandinsky's abstract compositions on the theme of "dies irae," the Last Judgment, al-ready referred to. The ancient, biblical topos of the apocalypse, implying revelation and redemption, has turned secular with, for example, Ludwig Meidner's paintings intertwining political revolution with the day of reck-oning.[134] The theme articulates the most affirmative (and oldest) under-standing of the notion of "crisis" as designating the "transgression of an epochal threshold," crisis as last decision, producing a definitive resolution in the future; whence "crisis" has turned into a futuristic term.[135] Archaic and modern concepts of crisis are inherently intertwined in the most representative expressionist discourses focused on earlier. They fundamentally bespeak the Janus-faced quality of the expressionist avant-garde. Expressionist utopianism thus may be viewed as the expression of the experience of rationalist modernity as crisis: The experience of the historical, present moment has narrowed in value and richness in regard to the human experience in the past. The tradition of one's culture is richer (as one is looking back on Goethe and Schiller) than the disenchanted modern experience; this deficit of expectations results into aggrandized expectations from the future. In reaction to the anomic experience of modernity, one develops certain *Überzeugungen* (convictions; literally translated, "surplus procreations"), meaning compensatory ideological dispositions, which I here attempt to locate as underlying divergent aesthetical "discourses." Once we have isolated the function of certain forms within an agon of discourses, we can get to terms with the "ideology behind the head" of the artist.[136]

At the same time, as there never is an either-or resolution within or outside of the institution of art, change and stasis are two sides of the same coin, aspects of an open-ended crisis in permanence. The first, the utopian energy appears to drive the international avant-garde in its early stage in the teens of the twentieth century which was poised for an all-out attack on the institution of art. Here we may first of all talk of a concept of crisis that aims at the destruction of a system (as theorized by Marx, for example, or by Peter Bürger for the avant-garde). Such programmatic assault in the arts is, of course, invariably followed by a dystopian awakening, a chief characteristic of developments of the German avant-garde from its very beginnings onward. As much as the avant-garde becomes aware of this bipolar, utopian/dystopian condition, the critical aspect of *krinein* as "discern, evaluate" comes to the fore, so that "crisis" becomes the source for a critique and criticism that reflects, in the second place, on its own aporia within the system, as system-immanent. In other words, there is a critically productive aspect of crisis as most evident in the postutopian phase of expressionism in the wake of the First World War. A postutopian avant-garde, having become aware of the fact that its imaginary museum is a rather stable institution of art, thus in the way of any totalizing vision, reflects also on its very own institutionalization. Instead of rupture, we encounter *transitions* from one phase to another that are not progressive in a linear sense. Yet, as Paul de Man writes, "the fundamental movement of the literary mind espouses a pattern of a demystifying consciousness; literature finally comes into its own, and becomes authentic, when it discovers that the exalted status it claimed for its language was a myth."[137] Hence the postmodern can be defined as a crisis phenomenon not *after* a crisis of the modern but as evolving within the modern as a critique of modern discourses and its myths. The postmodern being the crisis of the modern,[138] expressionism is a Janus-faced phenomenon, its features arising from the extreme tensions between the premodern and the postmodern.

2. The Dadaist Anti-Art Event in Zurich and Berlin, or The Return of the Literary Text

Compared with German expressionism, Italian or Russian futurism, and French surrealism, dadaism was the most cosmopolitan, the least literary, the least given to theoretical statements, the least teleological, the least utopian, and the toughest of the historical avant-garde movements. Looking back on Zurich Dada in 1916, we see that the very radicality of its embrace of the spontaneity and conceptually evasive nature of "life," and its furious, "kynical" rebellion against everything confining and obstructing "life," was the reaction to the death urge of European civilization that had erupted through the surface of reason.[1] Zurich Dada also was the first major contemporary reaction to the expressionist movement, which by 1916 had reached its pinnacle at a point where it became increasingly difficult to tell originality from faddish fake. Moreover, the brutal reality of World War I altogether clashed with the expressionist "spiritual" mission, seriously undermining the utopian claims for a "renewal of mankind" and the "brotherhood of man" as empty rhetorical, if highly marketable, moralizing discourses. The dadaists were the first to fully understand the contingent and transitional character of artworks. This understanding was not derived from any abstract reflections about art but gradually intuited and concretized in the performance of events that threatened to burst and ultimately busted the boundaries of the literary cabaret with which Dada began in the

Spiegelgasse. This understanding became tangible when the dadaists turned the tensions and differences concerning the value of art, as they arose within the group, toward outright aggression against their audience. The shocking of the audience assumed the level of a critique of and attack against the institution of art when Dada turned, most prominently, against mainstream expressionism and its claims for cultural hegemony. Dada engaged in particular expressionism as a literary heir of idealism in a radical agon of discourses: "Instead of continuing to create art, Dada has sought out an enemy. . . . The movement, the struggle was uppermost."[2]

One had found refuge in Zurich in 1915–16 at the height of the war, avoiding censorship and military draft: Hugo Ball and Richard Huelsenbeck from the Kaiserreich; the Alsatian Hans Arp, legally a German citizen, had left Paris as he was unwilling to fight for either side in the conflict. Tristan Tzara and Marcel Janco had come from Romania. Zurich Dada's rebel mentality was to no small degree the consequence of the experience of exile shared by an international group of writers and artists alienated and cut off from their respective national cultures. They were thus strangely "free-floating" intellectuals, yet confined by the circumstances of political exile, thus driven to protest through unconventional means. The multinationals' interest in the most recent developments in the arts turned into rebellion against the concept and value of a "national" culture and, from there, into an all-out revolt against the Western tradition.

Today, the documents of two world wars and the documents of Dada appear to rest in peace in their respective museums and archives, as if in indestructible vaults of rationality and security. Yet, even a "postmodern" reviewer, comfortable with the erasure of meaning, might be somewhat uncomfortable when confronted with Dada's resolute yet ironic negation of meaning: "Death is a thoroughly Dadaist business, in that it signifies nothing at all."[3]

"What is Dada?" This question has been provocatively asked and, as quoted earlier, provocatively "answered" by the dadaists themselves. Scholarly criticism may be at its best when it admits that Dada "escapes definition."[4] Yet Dada, in spite of its protestations to the contrary, is, after all, a *cultural activity* we label as "avant-garde." But what does the label "avant-garde" mean for a movement that refuses history altogether? The contemporaneous Russian futurists, by contrast, had a well-defined cause. They constructively replaced the "illusions" of art in the galleries, journals, libraries, salons, and palaces with a functional art on the walls of houses, fences, rooftops, streets, the back of cars, streetcars, locomotives, people's clothes, or candy wrappings which illustrated the history of the Red Army (by Mayakovsky). The mass media, newspapers, film and radio, the theater, the concert—all were to be put into the service of a "recreation of life." Indeed, Vsevolod Meyerhold would exclaim, "Soon there will be no more spectators, all will have become actors, only then will we have a genuine, truthful art of theater."[5] In other words, before its inevitable repression by RAPP and Stalin's terror, the Russian avant-garde had embarked on a program of abolishing the concept of the everyday and introduced the ideal of the complete man into the world of work.

In comparison with the utopianism of the other avant-garde movements, the accusation that Dada is nihilistic, on first sight, seems to be completely justified. Of the Zurich dadaists, Richard Huelsenbeck felt that only the all-out eradication of all old forms and norms would somehow "usher in" an end (rather than a new beginning) of Western culture. He thus defined dadaism in contrast to expressionism, which was its major target in the aesthetic domain, as a movement that wanted "nothing."[6] Was there, however, really nothing constructive in the dadaist events? Were the dadaists' texts and performances really no more than exercises in "anarchic vandalism," "cynically nihilistic" and against art?[7] And what does "anti-art" really mean? How does the concept of "anti-art" relate to the concept of *Kunstrevolution*? Has Huelsenbeck's rejection of the "the fraud of all art"[8] perhaps been taken too literally? Was Walter Benjamin right when he wrote (in his 1936 essay "Das Kunstwerk im Zeitalter seiner technischen Reproduzierbarkeit" ["The Work of Art in the Age of Mechanical Production"]) that Dada was merely "word salad" and "waste product of language,"[9] content with being merely useless for the consciousness industry as a consumer industry?

As these questions pile up unanswered, one should turn to the dadaist text. Yet where is the dadaist text? Often it was an integral part of the dadaist performance; as such it has vanished. In its published form, it is little more than a skeleton from which the demon of life escaped decades ago, and only the good fairy of art remains. We will here pursue evasive Dada through its specific phases in Zurich and Berlin, phases that have been too easily assessed as altogether different, the former in terms of a *Kunstrevolution,* the latter as political revolution.[10] Both instances, however, involve a displacement of the literary text into an event (without an author) outside the boundaries of the "institution" of art (which, however, proved to be a powerful authority).

From Literary Cabaret to Dadaist Performance; from "Kunstrevolution" to Anti-Art Art

Research on Dada does well to emphasize its character as an *event* and its *performative* aspects. In taking such an approach, one would try to reconstruct the event, an anthropological task that seeks to understand the unknown through empathy, the forgotten image by dramatizing and reenacting the story engraved in the artifacts. Peter Froehlich already made the significant assumption that only the actual reconstruction of the Dada text as a performed event can somewhat recuperate its relations with the audience as an "integral part of the work."[11] His insight leads beyond a stereotyped notion that the dadaists were merely exaggerating the traditional avant-garde impulse of épater le bourgeois. From the point of view of any traditional concept of art, of course, the dadaists do appear to be radical anti-art anarchists. But once it is understood that these texts—in the moment of their performance—are not "literary" in any traditional sense, the criteria for assessing "meaning" lie in the event itself. Obviously, in the moment of actualization, the dadaist event took place in a site outside of Western art traditions. Nevertheless, we do not categorize it, for example, with the folkloric carnival or the violent street riot. Rather, we perceive its carnivalesque energies as part of a complexly performed event that consists of agonistic confrontation and dialogue. The dadaist event can be understood as a multivoiced dialogue that takes place not only between performer and audience but also between performer and performer, audience member and audience member. Where there is no "author," everyone becomes "author" and "audience."

Kurt Schwitters's "Ur-sonate," to take up Froehlich's example of a prominent product of "Merz" or Hanover Dada, has previously been interpreted as a "poetic" text, that is, hermeneutically. But such an approach clearly disregards its performative aspects, the space gained in opposition to traditional individual production and reception. A comprehensive understanding of Dada must depend on historical reconstruction. We need to go back to accounts of its impact on the audience, such as that of Hans Richter, who described the effect of a performance of the "Ur-sonate": It liberated from the constraints of conventional art reception, from the internalizing restraints imposed by the construct of "art." Everyone, whether art connoisseur or layperson, found in the performance a fresh, unmediated form of aesthetic experience.[12]

At the other extreme of the rich dadaist spectrum are Hans Arp's finely tuned texts, which weave in dreamlike fashion patterns of romantic images, onomatopoeia, fragments of everyday language and slang into an intricate texture. Arp's poems are clearly more suitable to be read than performed. Rather than provoke shock, some texts in *Die Wolkenpumpe* (*Cloud Pump;* 1917) stimulate aesthetic meditation instead of breaking with it. "Dem Ausgang zu" ("Toward the Exit"), for example, one of Arp's early poems, reconstitutes "romantic" visions while breaking with the symbolic tradition in a form of "automatic" writing:

Dem Ausgang zu

die nachtvögel tragen brennende laternen im gebälk ihrer augen.
sie lenken zarte gespenster und fahren auf zartadrigen wagen.
der schwarze wagen ist vor den berg gespannt.
die schwarze glocke ist vor den berg gespannt.
das schwarze schaukelpferd ist vor den berg gespannt.
die toten tragen sägen und stämme zur mole herbei.
aus den kröpfen der vögel stürzen die ernten auf die tennen aus eisen.
die engel landen in körben aus luft.
die fische ergreifen den wanderstab und rollen in sternen dem
ausgang zu.

Herbert Read has attempted to render the poem into English:

the night birds carry lighted lanterns in the beams of their eyes
they guide delicate ghosts and drive fine-veined carriages

the black carriage is yoked to the mountain
the black clock is yoked to the mountain
the dead carry saws and timber to the nearby jetty
from viscous goiters crops gush onto the iron threshing-floor
angels land in baskets of air
fish grip their pilgrims' staff and roll through stars to the exit.[13]

Texts like these are produced with the inherent claim to speak from and to a collective unconscious by breaking with symbolic language. Yet the semantic field of "night birds," "ghosts," "the dead" and "angels" evokes a surreal, supernatural realm and, after all, appears to construct a "story": the story of an apocalypse. Qualitatively different from the "event" of the "Ur-sonate" described earlier, the text does point back to an auctorial subject and implies a reading subject. Arp, however, wanted to believe in the naive eventlike reception of the innocent printer, the man of the masses,

whose typesetting errors would generate "chance" creations. In protosurrealist fashion, he invited the typesetter to engage in his own *écriture auto-
matique* (automatic writing), whereas he compared the imaginative capaci-
ties of the "normally organized bourgeois" with that of a "worm."[14] By
breaking with poetic symbol and metaphor, Dada thus wanted to replace
"art" with discourses that erase the barrier between individual author and
individual reader. Nevertheless, Arp was keenly aware of the artistic character of his texts. Turning against all "dead academic" art as well as trendy
avant-gardist posturing, he did claim that "Dada is for nature and against
art." But he qualifies this assertion with the belief in an "original" unity of
nature, man, and the aesthetic experience: "I believe that nature is not in
opposition to art. Art is of natural origin and is . . . spiritualized through
the sublimation of man." Thus I agree with Herbert Read, who writes that
"Arp was always guided by his aesthetic feelings."[15]

At an early stage of the developments in Zurich, the dadaists, in fact,
were much more involved with a "system-immanent critique" of art, to
use Peter Bürger's term, which he applies to modernism as different from
the *avant-garde* strategy to totally subvert the institution of art (for which
Dada, besides surrealism, is his paradigm). Historically speaking, Dada's
creativity was inextricably intertwined with the anarchic bohemian atmosphere—its soirees, its *sabbaths*—of Hugo Ball's Cabaret Voltaire in the
Spiegelgasse in Zurich. From there it spread to Paris and Berlin, Hanover,
Cologne, Leipzig, Prague, and New York. In each of these instances, the
story of Dada is much more irregular than any global theoretical model,
however brilliant, could take into account.

Huelsenbeck's retrospective criticism of Zurich Dada is not disinterested
when he attacks Tristan Tzara as an "expressionist" (!)[16] in order to hold up
Berlin's political dadaism as the "real" dadaism. However, Hugo Ball's account of the Dada years in Zurich, his autobiography *Flucht aus der Zeit* (*Escape from the Times;* 1927), presents a picture quite different from Huelsenbeck's totalization of Zurich Dada as altogether literary, artistic, aesthetic,
as "abstract art," against which the erstwhile Zurich Dada now turned, "gun
in hand."[17] Ball's account is typical of the divided nature of the German
avant-garde, expressionism or Dada: He is torn between regarding his and
his friends' activities as part of the literary and artistic activities "of the last
twenty years" and as a program of radical renewal. He talks of the Cabaret Voltaire as rehearsing "all kinds of styles," of staging an exhibition of
Picasso, Kandinsky, and Arp as a "first synthesis of the most modern trends
in art and literature." He also feels, however, with Huelsenbeck, that the

Cabaret Voltaire as cabaret "should not be sidelined to aesthetics. . . . It is a matter of the human being, not of art." Yet, he hastens to add, "At least not primarily a matter of art." Hence he ponders "the questionable nature of art," as it seems "only an occasion, a method."[18] Hence the program of the Cabaret Voltaire ultimately became, as Hans Richter states it later, "the destruction of art through aesthetic means."[19]

It is at this juncture that minds as different as Hugo Ball and Huelsenbeck meet. Against Tzara's early ambitions to organize the Cabaret Voltaire into a "Voltaire Society" with corresponding publications, both identify Dada with spontaneous creativity instead. Ball agrees with Huelsenbeck's aversion to organize into a school: "One should not make an art trend out of a disposition."[20] Yet, from the very start in Zurich, a traditional cultural mechanism, the need for identity and integration made itself felt, when Ball began more or less distinctly to feel threatened by a momentum of the unknown. Hugo Ball's diary entry of 26 February 1916 reads, for example, "An indefinable intoxication has seized all of us. The small cabaret threatens to burst its seams." At this moment, Huelsenbeck becomes more of a menace than a collaborator: "He pleads to amplify the [Negro] rhythm. He would best drum literature into the ground."[21] With relief, Ball registers the normalizing transition from the Cafe Voltaire to the Galerie Dada: "The barbarisms of the Cabaret have been surpassed."[22]

The more the pace of this new, still undefinable momentum and energy picks up, the greater the need for seeking group solidarity in the common activities, however problematic, and the more aggression is vented against those outside the circle, always "against literature produced at the desk for the spectacles of the collector instead of for the ears of living human beings."[23] Thus one rails in particular against the expressionists, "the rhetorical bombast of the painting gods."[24] Arp's particular notion of formal composition ("Planimetrie") is held up against their ideological zeal and apocalyptic yearning. Arp's commitment to form is emphatically distinguished from mere formalism; it is seen as a formalism to end all formalism of the age, in other words, as ultimate *avant-garde* means (though the term, which my study uses often, but never altogether comfortably, is not used in Ball's diary). In fact, Arp's forms are appreciated as a "triumph of great art over the machine," as *great* art! In the midst of all these affirmative definitions of Dada as a positive cultural activity in times of crisis, the recognition cannot be held back, however: "The normal clock of an abstract epoch has exploded."[25] And now, only now (!), Ball takes recourse to explaining the vehemence of Dada as a reaction against the times, specifically against the war: "The shrillest pamphlets did not suffice to appropriately taunt the reigning hypocrisy."[26]

As a movement of revolt against the art and politics of the times, Zurich Dada was not an escape into the aesthetic realm, as Huelsenbeck, zealously promoting Berlin Dada, was to maintain later on. After all, it was engaged in the "destruction of art through aesthetic means."[27] Huelsenbeck's collectivist mentality would, of course, frown upon the individualist searches of Arp or Ball. Hugo Ball, for example, began to occupy himself with giving the group's language games mystical roots. He went back to an ancient notion of the artistic image that is as close to Walter Benjamin's contemporaneous language mysticism in "Über Sprache überhaupt und über die Sprache des Menschen" ("On Language as such and on the Language of Man"; 1916) as it is removed from the latter's embrace of the intersubjective dynamics of the surrealist image in the late 1920s (as will be discussed further later). In correspondence with Arp's work, Ball defends the nonrepresentational forms of the dadaists as expressions of the "unconditional, typical. . . . The absolute, however, does not need to be abstract." Not so different from expressionism, where one, after all, had come from, Ball is searching for the "world of images and archetypes" (*Welt der Bilder und Urbilder*). No longer is the dadaist effort only an "occasion" or "method" to merely unmask the involvement of "art" with the pernicious discourses of cultural domination: "Perhaps it is not all a matter of art, but of the uncorrupted image."[28] Ball's search for an adamic or divine language transcends aesthetic *as well as* anti-art concerns. His ideas have a tradition, the roots of which are deeply embedded in the mystical and religious.

It is mostly the highly sensitive Hugo Ball—who later became a catholic zealot—who rode such a roller coaster with regard to his view of Dada. By comparison, Tristan Tzara had a fairly stable view of the identity of Dada. He most consistently emphasized the anarchist play of language that serves only one master: life. "Dada has tried not so much to destroy literature and art as the idea that one made of them," Tzara wrote still in "Dada 1957."[29] This retrospective confirms a point of view he had begun to adopt in July 1917. His Zurich chronicle entry of that date reads: "One launches the Dada Movement. Mysterious creation! Magic revolver!"[30]

He will henceforth affirm Dada as an avant-garde movement both in Zurich and later in Paris. Tzara was the theoretical mastermind of Dada. The most learned among the learned dadaists, he insisted that Dada was qualitatively different from the modernist tradition, maintaining that Dada would always be averse to assimilation and would ultimately choose its own end:

> Dada's scorn for "modernism" is based above all on the idea of relativity, all dogmatic codification can only lead to a new academicism. . . . Dada, which wants to be moving and transformable, prefers to disappear rather than to give occasion for the creation of new clichés.[31]

Tzara's "Chronique Zurichoise 1915–1919" also reveals, however, that even he did not accept this radical image of Dada from the start. In the beginning, he seems to have shared Ball's quite conventional scruples. When the Galerie Dada was established, on April 28, 1917, he notes with some satisfaction: "The public accommodates and rarefies the explosions of choice imbecility, each one withdraws his inclinations and plants his hope in the new spirit of the forming of 'Dada.'"[32] On May 12 of the same year, however, he has to realize that the audience's insistence on the ruckus ("bamboula feroce") has to be met and dealt with after all, and the decision for total Dada is not long in coming. But it would take until June 9, 1919, for Tzara to declare the "definitive victory of Dada."[33]

Tzara was to be proven wrong by the actual developments in Dada's *reception*. Its subversive performances degenerated into the tumultuous action of releasing aggression against the dadaist performers. Tristan Tzara's "Le Coeur à gaz" ("The Heart of Gas") staged in the early 1920s in Paris's Salle Gaveau, for example, served as a mere cue for throwing eggs at author and actors. The public's reaction, in other words, did not favor the envisioned eradication of the division between author and audience. The often brutal provocation ("Hoosenlatz"), the "bruitist" primitive rhythm of Huelsenbeck's *Phantastische Gebete (Fantastic Prayers;* 1916) was lost in sheer havoc. The public had degenerated into bad actors, enacting very conventional and predictable roles of violence.

In countering the stereotypical charge of Dada's "nihilism" and "vandalism"—obviously made from the point of view of Dada's *reception* rather than its production—it can be said that the "cultural activity"[34] of the dadaist text consisted in its provocative unmasking of the Western ideology of "L'Art, avec un A majuscule," its subversion of the "oeuvre d'art," of the "rigide édifice de l'art,"[35] in other words, of an idolization of the individual work of art. Politically, it turned against the ideological alliance of the slogans of "individualism" and "patriotism." Inasmuch as World War I triggered the uninhibited release of the dadaists' activities, their "demonstrations" echoed that war's unparalleled violence and destruction in unique forms of artistic violence. In short, the dadaist text operates in the institution of art, based on the traditional "organic" work of art, as a fish bone does in the throat.

But we must not overlook the reconstructive energies of the dadaist discourses, whether we are dealing with texts by Arp or by Huelsenbeck. They are based on language as play turning against its enslavement in the service of instrumental rhetoric. Thus the "Dadaist Manifesto" (1918) closes quite consciously with a retraction of its own assertions: "To be against this manifesto means to be a dadaist."[36] The paradoxical strategies of the dadaist text liberate language from the subject, allow language to play without a player, as it were, and thus break open the realm of inwardness. The dadaists reintegrated extraliterary language into the text, language that formerly had been banned from the aesthetic domain through what they considered the narrowing conventions of the exclusive styles of high culture. In order to decenter subjective aesthetic experience, they montaged into their texts quotations from the public texts of the newspaper, advertising, slang, or simply *language*.

The dadaist text as a written and read text, after all, remains a "work," however it is defined. No matter how heavily it relies on the montage of components quoted from the linguistic realm or pasted in from the visual environment, it will always constitute an aesthetic sign distinguished from the world of objects. Its cognitive potential stems from this distance. Beyond its provocative aspects the dadaist work shares with some works of modernist poetry an intense focus on language. Language, freed from the subjectivity of metaphor and symbol, will be given a chance to manifest itself by *chance* in its *metonymical* relation of letter to letter, sound to sound, sign to sign; letter to sound, sign to image, and so on. This interplay of linguistic elements and the tactile aspects of an anarchic typography reveal the "materiality" of language. The dadaist text becomes what Raoul Hausmann calls a "metalanguage" functioning in an unpredictable relation to "meaning" or the absence thereof.[37] It will demonstrate through multiple, diffuse defamiliarization effects that meaning is generated through signifying conventions. The dadaist montage and collage thus throws a monkey wrench into the subjective metaphorical mechanisms of the "fabrication of fictions," as Carl Einstein called it later.[38] While the dadaist provocation may seem to disillusion to the degree of the absurd, in its deep structure the text will generate energies that can point to as yet unrecognized experiences of the senses, experiences neither labeled nor classified, experiences that resist as the ever heterogeneous the classificatory traps of our rational compulsions. Hausmann, speaking of Arp, interprets the dadaist decentering strategie as follows: "Arp's inspired way of working . . . followed 'without preference' the laws of chance, one would like to say, a creative indifference, in which things are not yet ordered into categories, speaking to us directly without yet being laden with prejudiced meaning."[39]

Stated in broader cultural terms, the dadaist text enriches the realm of communicative forms. It reflects the experience of a group of intellectuals who, as artists, were outsiders to begin with, who moreover had been disenfranchised by censorship and political repression, and who were deeply disturbed by the war. The exiles' reaction is one of anarchism turned against the social realm, which becomes productive in the text's radical disclosure of suppressed forms of communication. While Dada was boisterously antiestablishment, it nevertheless participated, as it struggled to achieve dominance over traditional discourses, in the production of communication (which inheres the most subversive argument). Dada's problem was that, outside of the actual *performance* of the text as an event, its highly differentiated information reached only the ear and the eye of the "aristocratic reader."

Walter Benjamin's point in the late 1930s will be that Dada remained too much of a bohemian reaction, in other words, that it was too "literary" to realize the potential of its antiauratic practices for the modern mass media, such as film. While his view is questionable, not only in view of eminent dadaist film productions such as Richter's, but as far as his faith in film is concerned, it did show a great deal of insight into the conditions of the historical avant-garde.

In short, the cliché of Dada as "anti-art," promoted by its creators, advocates, and critics, must be understood as a historical rather than a cognitive argument. The argument was still being advanced not too long ago by leading theoreticians of "experimental" or "concrete poetry" in an attempt to justify their "experiments" as aesthetically more innovative and advanced than dadaism.[40] By the same token, the retrospective mellowness of the dadaists' later revisions of Dada should not be accepted as evidence for its status as "art," either. For example, in 1920, Huelsenbeck attacked Tzara's texts as ambitious aestheticism and railed against the "fraud" and "humbug," that is, the commercialism of the art world. In the 1950s and 1960s, however, he would insist on Dada's original "faith in the evolution of art" and assert that the movement was "never anti-art."[41] Such reversals are based on the experience of disappointed hindsight: Dada did not succeed in becoming something other than art. Consequently, Dada now must be saved for the history of literature and art. The subtleties of the dadaist texts were realized only in the performative "event" and became conscious only to the "aristocratic" reader. They were thus, in the words of Werner Mahrholz's early assessment of the international avant-garde, "specialty products for specialists": "The circles of the literati and bohemia have generated from within themselves a 'culture' of painting and poetry of their own, which in general becomes known only in the circles of the art specialists and which according to its nature does not want to influence the people as a whole."[42] Zurich Dada, after all, was too learned not to know that its own premises were deeply rooted, if by secession, in a culture of meaning. Thus it seems that the rebellious sons wanted to have their cake (the aesthetic experience) and eat it (its meaning), too.

Berlin Dadaism: Strategies of Politicizing Anti-Art Art

What may at one point in time, in Zurich or Berlin, have been produced to disrupt as "anti-art" was predictably welcomed by the public because of its very eccentricity. The art market averse to stagnation, ready to take "risks," redefined dadaist "anti-art" as artwork. Witness the variety of alternative journals, from *Cabaret Voltaire* (Zurich, 1916) to *Der Bastard* (Leipzig, 1921), part of a flourishing counterculture that operated within the friendly confines of a liberal culture. In a liberal culture, notions about art crystallize and compete within the institution of art that is also an ideological site. This site also takes concrete social forms in the infrastructure of the exhibition hall, the publishing house, methods of distribution, the relations among author, critic, and public. In this ideological and economic space, a dominating concept of art is reinforced, or a contesting notion comes into existence.

Here modern advertising began to beat dadaism at its own game. This happened, typically, in a modern metropolis like Berlin, even though Raoul Hausmann and George Grosz were cognizant of the expropriating power of the consciousness industry. Hence they montaged the sloganeering of advertisement into their artifacts for alternative, decentered statements or, conversely, surreptitiously couched their own statements in advertising's loudly rhetorical terms. An example here is John Heartfield's "Prospekt zur kleinen Grosz-Mappe" in *Die Neue Jugend* (*The New Youth;* 1917), an announcement of the impending publication of Grosz's sketches.[43] In order to avoid the trappings of an *art* movement, Berlin dadaist publicity stunts were delivered with the skill of the advertising industry. The culminating instance of this strategy was the Great Dada Fair in 1920. The Dada Fair was constructed as a "negative total work of art" (*negatives Gesamtkunstwerk*),[44] quoting, exploding, and exposing the sociocultural and political environment as a false totality. This climax of the Berlin movement's visibility and public success was, however, also the beginning of the end of Dada as a dynamic "anti-cultural" group effort.[45] It also brought forth the personal ambitions of the dadaists as individual artists.[46]

In post-World War I Berlin, Huelsenbeck, the painter George Grosz, Carl Einstein, John Heartfield, Wieland Herzfelde, Raoul Hausmann, Franz Mehring, and the "Oberdada" Johannes Baader (through his idiosyncratically self-centered happenings) set out to politicize the dadaist revolt. It is quite instructive to trace Berlin Dada's commitment to concretely revolutionize the institution of art through politically staged events. The pragmatic nature of the dadaists' politics meant, in aesthetic terms, a return to the much simpler, conventional sign systems of the agitprop pamphlet. Art was to become "a weapon" in the struggle for the rights of the proletariat. Captions on Dada posters call for political action. In short, the former complexity of the dadaist text is reduced for the sake of political effectiveness. In Grosz's or Heartfield's splendidly innovative work, this trend need not be one of artistic impoverishment but can be one of genuine "revolutionary beauty," as Louis Aragon put it.

Less convincing was the manifesto "Was ist der Dadaismus und was will er in Deutschland?" ("What Is Dadaism and What Does It Want in Germany?") drawn up by Huelsenbeck and Hausmann in 1918, which anticipates (in letter only, not in terms of creativity) André Breton's political radicalization of the surrealist program by more than a decade. It calls for "the international revolutionary union of all creative and intellectual men and women on the basis of radical Communism." As Huelsenbeck explained, "While Tzara was still writing: 'Dada ne signifie rien' — in Germany, Dada lost its art-for-art's-sake character with its very first move. Instead of continuing to produce art, Dada in direct contrast to abstract art . . . had to say exactly what our Dadaism was after."[47]

Only some of the demands of the "Dadaist revolutionary central council" retain something of the original "creative irrationalism"[48] and anarchism, for example, "Introduction of the simultaneist poem as a Communist state prayer." Other demands are to say "exactly what our Dadaism was after." These demands inherently threaten bureaucratic organization, when the talk is of "a state of freedom" resulting from "the immediate expropriation of property (socialization) and the communal feeding of all."[49] For Huelsenbeck, Berlin Dada was thus to become effective with the "great mass of those who were artistically uninterested," a mass "phenomenon of public morality," as he summarized its objectives in *En avant Dada. Eine Geschichte des Dadaismus* (1920), his precocious story of the "history of Dada."[50]

The 1918 Berlin manifesto clearly bears two different handwritings, Huelsenbeck's and Hausmann's. It is characteristic of Berlin Dada, which was, after all, torn between politics and aesthetics. Hausmann's focus on a material aesthetics and his deeply rooted anarchist sensibility—in which the artistic experience of the material at hand determines and dominates the political drift of the discourse—remains interesting today. Viewed from the perspective of poststructuralist aesthetics, Hausmann's positions are much more advanced than Huelsenbeck's latent political idealism. While Huelsenbeck claimed to reject any commitment to the communist idea or party, promising instead an individuo-anarchist stance, Hausmann saw in the proletarian class struggle the only possible parallel to Dada. But, for him the communist *idea* is, like Dada, a "non-historical,"[51] meaning unprecedented, "revolutionary" vantage point. Most significant is his simultaneous criticism of the *historical* communist struggle: For Hausmann the political movement remains bound to conventional thought, even if "fought by legitimate sons and heirs [of the original idea]."[52] His criticism goes beyond a general anarchist or romantic vitalist rejection of communism as another form of rationalism (as we shall see in the instance of Carl Einstein in chapter 4). In the context of Franz Jung's Berlin journal *Die Freie Strasse* (*Open Road*), which gave rise to the Club Dada, Hausmann's criticism of rationalism was partially based on the antiauthoritarian, anti-Freudian theories of Otto Gross. Gross had set the self (*das Eigene*) up against the estranging pressures of the suppressive authority of sociocultural conventions (*das Fremde*). Only an unconditionally practiced recourse to the self—as a sensorial-intellectual complex open to intersubjective relations—could liberate, as it were, from inner colonization. Thus Hausmann refuses to trace Dada back to the spirit of the romantic lineage (something Ball pursues in Zurich). He wants to radically negate any entwinement of Dada with the Western tradition. The main target of his critique of inwardness is typically the "bloodless" expressionist movement. Thus he defines Dada as beyond an "aesthetic-ethical stance," claiming it as "the first departure from an aesthetic relation to life" ("Der Dadaismus steht zum erstenmal dem Leben nicht mehr aesthetisch gegenüber").[53]

Hausmann's proclamation of a "total break with the past"[54] can be understood only on the specific grounds of his material aesthetics. Only therein can his embrace of Dada's pure "concentrated moment" as a moment of discontinuity potentially avoid the pitfalls of renewed totalization and mythmaking. His anarchic position is consciously undialectical: Dada shall not reconstruct in the space of destruction a new institution of art. Dada is said to be in "conflict with all" because it articulates—as Hausmann puts it typographically—the "PREsente Augenblick" (PREsent moment),[55] a prehistorical moment. The "indifferent" deconstruction of subjectivity's "hallowed categories" is to be the culmination of dadaist experience and creativity.[56] Hausmann's seminal text "Das neue Material in der Malerei" ("The New Material in Painting"; 1918) spelled out the terms for such deconstructive strategies. Where the "visual intellectuality"[57] of the futurists' texts generates new myths of a vitalist unity of man and machine, his material aesthetics are to prevent the reinscription of a new story. For him, the word as material is always a fragment; it forbids both referential meaning and the subjectivity of symbol and metaphor. Language is to be opened up to its contiguous relation to the world, to which it is "complementary" by being "fragmentary." The dadaist poem for Hausmann, therefore, is not a matter of syntax but of the larynx and the vocal cords, of the sound produced through physical friction. The dadaist text thus is *performance* as "DA sein" (existence).[58]

This, of course, is very different from Hugo Ball's idealist language mysticism. It points instead in the direction of Walter Benjamin's view of the "poetic politics" of the surrealist experience as the experience of the collective "image realm" as "body realm." Both Hausmann and Benjamin speak of a psychophysiological experience that explodes the conscious, subjective experience of literary metaphor. Little did Benjamin know, it seems, that Hausmann had already formulated the gist of such an argument in "The New Material in Painting":

Dada: that is perfected benevolent viciousness, besides exact photography the only justifiable visual form of communication and balance in communal experience. Everyone who brings in himself his most unique tendency to salvation is a Dada. In Dada you will recognize your concrete condition: miraculous constellation in concrete material, wire, glass, card board, textile, organically corresponding to your own nearly perfect permeability. . . . Only here no inhibitions, fearful obstinations; we are far removed from symbolic relations.[59]

For Berlin Dada the world (and the word) was at hand as political conflict; and, in spite of Hausmann's efforts to deny the priority of politics,
he refers to the political experience much more concretely than Huelsenbeck does in his reminiscences. Hausmann remembers the realistic details
of political turmoil: police ordinances that declare the right to shoot anyone standing still; at every corner search for weapons; mass demonstrations,
Spartacus-meetings; during the night machine gun fire, and so on. How
could Dada, then, have been "indifferent," wanted nothing, and yet claim,
as Hausmann did, that not the proletariat but his Berlin Dada reacted ade-
quately against the assassination of Karl Liebknecht and Rosa Luxemburg?
It reacted by introducing Dada texts into the public realm as a "weapon,"
simultaneously undermining the political and artistic culture of the status
quo: "The Oberdada and I carry literature and poetry into the streets, in
the true sense of the word. The word is a signal in the streets. The word does
not belong to the future; it is present, it is not black on white, on any kind
of paper."[60]

    Is this not what Walter Benjamin had in mind, when, a decade later,
he eulogized the revolutionary "poetic politics" of surrealism, which, in
his view, made short shrift of all metaphorical idealism in literature as
in politics? For Benjamin this space of discontinuity would, for the first
time, bring into view the "one hundred percent image realm" of an experience (*Erfahrung*) that sublates individual experience (*Erlebnis*) into the collective, ultimately the "metaphysical" into the physical realm ("the body
sphere"). Had Benjamin known of (or acknowledged) Hausmann's text on
the new material in painting, which according to its author caused an up-
roar when delivered at the first Berlin Dada soiree on April 12, 1918, he might
not have been able to talk quite as disparagingly of the "linguistic garbage"
of Dada later on.

    In contrast to Huelsenbeck's growing ideological zeal and Hausmann's
cognitive fervor, Grosz's and Herzfelde's contributions to Hausmann's *Der
Dada* (1919) are still characterized by the comparatively harmless discourses
of "play" as revolt, familiar from Zurich Dada. Journals such as *Der Blutige
Ernst* (*In Bloody Earnest;* 1919), edited by Einstein and Grosz, are indicative
of a transition toward revolutionary pragmatics. "Ludendorff's Tagebuch"
(in No.3) fuses the original dadaist practice of play with relatively straightforward political satire in the vein of Heinrich Mann. In No. 6, Einstein's
text "Abhängigkeit" ("Dependency"), which should have been of interest
to Hausmann, analyzes the repressive ideological function of "bourgeois"
slogans such as the "nebulously religious term *necessary.*" Journals such as

Die Pleite (*Bankruptcy*), edited by Grosz and Heartfield, give further evidence of a trend inseparable from the activities of the Spartacus League and the communists. The journal's 1923 issues are devoted to topical events such as the Stinnes affair and von Ludendorff's endorsement of the memorial for Schlageter, the Nazi hero idolized for sacrificing his life in the uprising against the French occupation of the Ruhr (ten years later the protagonist of Hanns Johst's first National Socialist play *Schlageter*).

During the First World War, George Grosz had already transferred the subversive dadaist play into politically staged events. At parties of the rich he postured, for example, as the "merchant from Holland," offering for sale engraved bullets from the front. In the early years of the republic, similar antics mark the politically constructed dadaist *happenings* at the numerous trials against Grosz for his notorious sketch "Maul halten und weiterdienen" ("Jesus with Gas-Mask; Shut Up and Keep Serving"), and against Einstein (a major figure in my next chapters) for his drama *Die Schlimme Botschaft* (*Calamitous Tidings*), in which Jesus Christ returned to the temples of the money-mongering Weimar Republic. "Happenings" such as these attempt to define the art of revolution as a practical political form of staging events within the social institutions. The very negative *reception* by the authorities of the Berlin dadaists' event-related performances, texts, and sketches provided them with a great deal of visibility. Bertolt Brecht's killer instinct for publicity drew him to these events, too. At one point he planned to exploit them for his *Lehrstück*-stage (learning plays). Similarly, the Malik Press's hit-and-run distribution of Grosz-illustrated pamphlets on Berlin street corners constituted, momentarily, a form of convergence of politicized art and political life. Minutes later, of course, the police would intervene.

In this dynamic process, constituted by the text and the political context, art did become a "weapon." Over the long term, however, the story did not change: While literary history, constituted by the insatiable institution of art, proved extremely receptive to the dadaist "revolutionary" discourse, political history, of course, was less inclined to tolerate its political contextualization. Dadaism, like other avant-garde "anti-art" movements, instead of debunking "art" ultimately became part of the art world simply because it was the only domain (besides, of course, advertising) to which it could contribute tangible, lasting change. This change consisted in making visible that "art" is a historical construct, its "identity" subject to a continuously changing consensus, open-ended in its relations to popular and political culture. Dadaism demonstrated that "styles" and their holistic, universalist assumptions about an "epoch" have lost their significance to "techniques" which define the relations and tensions of aesthetic perceptions in regard to the utilitarian experience and ideological prejudices. While dadaism derived its "anti-art" disposition to a major degree from its historical stance against the experience of World War I, it developed its own antisymbolic and antimetaphorical discourses, aesthetic techniques and images, in opposition to the idealist discourses of mainstream expressionism. After all, expressionism spoke out against the war in the very inflated terms that Dada held responsible for or at least complicit with the misled mentality of heroic patriotism and militaristic nationalism. At the same time it can be said, and I did so at the end of the last chapter, that the dadaists consciously pushed the crisis of art to the edge, to the very rupture and gap between language as symbol and language as material, which some expressionists had sensed and attempted to express in their conflictual and contradictory quest to once more establish a comprehensive identity of art.

Part Two : **The Crisis of the Avant-Garde in Political Exile**

3. From Weimar Culture to Political Exile

Two Phases/Faces of the Crisis
of the Avant-Garde

The history of the twentieth-century avant-garde is a history of the crisis of literary culture. It is a history of an agon of discourses that articulate differing political, moral, and aesthetic experiences as well as conflicting experiences of language as art. By no means is the history of such literary crisis one of decline in creativity. On the contrary, it is the richer from the very contradictions that brought about an unparalleled variety of aesthetic forms, which as such prevented resolution and closure. The previous two chapters focused on the movements of expressionism and dadaism as a constellation of antagonistic, yet productive relations. Expressionism articulated a certain crisis of literature in the disparity between traditional and, on the other hand, mostly iconoclastic, albeit highly cultivated poetics, which amounted to a measure of relativizing (unconsciously) the idea of "style," and the complete work of art. Dada meant to liquidate the work of art, at least by program, through its "anti-art" productions and did away with the notion of "style"—all this amounted to an exceptionally accelerated speed of a short but consequential literary crisis. The activities of multinational Dada in the exile of Zurich specifically forced the crisis of *national* culture. Richard Huelsenbeck and Hugo Ball, for example, reacted predominantly against German expressionism, which they perceived as the continuation of a culture of *Geist* (spirit), as a movement that had the makings of renewing

German national culture. Obviously, the dadaists made the most of their exile conditions. Their performances, experiments in bruitist sounds and visually tactile typography, borrowed from the French and Italian avant-garde, generated a provocative new international language that spread from Zurich to Paris, Berlin, and finally New York.

Dada in Zurich had aimed to explode the boundaries of literature, if not literary culture per se, staging in its place the *performance* of manifold texts that simultaneously engaged audiovisual techniques such as chanting, sheer noise, masks, puppets, and weird makeshift costumes. Weimar culture in its technologically most advanced manifestations attempted to expand the significance and scope of literature in modernity by fusing it with filmed projections on the stage, or channeling it into radio productions for mass consumption and influence. While the reception of literary culture thereby moved from the privacy of the *gute Stube* (best room) to a public space, it lost in this process some of its once singular status and aura.

During its political exile from Nazi Germany, the avant-garde did by no means fall silent from despair and disillusionment. The avant-garde that had to leave behind its following often sought a restoration of literature in the order and values of previously shunned traditional forms. Some of its most stubborn representatives, among them quite remarkably Else Lasker-Schüler, did, however, continue its iconoclasm in the international context of the antifascist struggle. And when writers like Hermann Broch or Carl Einstein did relinquish their faith not only in literary innovations but in literary culture per se, they often did so in voluminous literary or theoretical statements, which here deserve our special attention. The discontinuity and continuities between Weimar culture and the literature of political exile are the subject of this chapter. The chapter not only will continue to pursue the precarious trajectory of the avant-garde but also will set the premises and elucidate the contexts for the three ensuing case studies of a writer, a critic, and a painter in exile.

Weimar Culture: The Outsider as Insider

What we refer to as "Weimar culture" was mostly the product of the outsider turned insider, as Peter Gay observed. The critical culture of the first German republic arose from the crystallization of formerly opposing trends: expressionism, dadaism, and Brecht's experiments with the stage. It was brought about by the mutual experience of war and revolution as a turning point for the politicization of previously developed innovative forms. During the first years of the republic, a radically politicized Berlin dadaism, which Huelsenbeck noted "made literature gun in hand," competed with the expressionist theater of Kaiser (*Gas II*, 1920) or Toller (*Masse Mensch* [*Man and the Masses*], 1921), plays that most poignantly projected the spiritual claims of the movement onto the political issues of war and revolution in the age of the masses. While postwar expressionist theater may have peaked in terms of the sheer number of performances, it is wishful thinking to understand its increased visibility on the stage as a "coming to its own" or even "triumph," as described by Jost Hermand. After all, these plays not only attacked the political status quo but also quite manifestly admitted to the impasse, if not defeat, of a spiritual tradition they represented. As we recall, by 1920 expressionism had already been exposed by its former theorist Wilhelm Worringer or the author Yvan Goll as a utopian "as-if" projection, as a movement of exaggerated expectations. Of course, no one could really foresee the manifold ways in which the expressionist legacy was to live on through 1933, in an extreme, with Hanns Johst and Gottfried Benn prostituting it in the service of Nazi ideology. Altogether convincing, however, is Hermand's wider argument that the mass culture of the Weimar period put the literary culture of inwardness, the culture of a traditional "elite," to a severe stress test.[1] At stake was its viability to interest and influence the masses, which film (as pointed out in chapter 1), radio, and show business catered to with more effective means than did the book and the canvas. The focus on literature I choose here (over film, music, and the visual arts) is most revealing, because the problematics of artistic changes can best be "read" in the written medium, as Jost Hermand and Frank Trommler have shown in their large-scale study *Die Kultur der Weimarer Republik*.[2] In fact, from the beginning to the end of the Weimar Republic, the exuberant if not hectic spirit of experimentation within traditional genres and the interest in the new media were accompanied by a shadow that cast itself over traditional literary culture (a shadow that will come to the very fore during the exile period).

In 1920, at the beginning of the contested republic, for example, the impact of a bullet, fired during the rightist Kapp Putsch, on a painting by Rubens in the Dresden Zwinger, sparked the so-called *Kunstlump* (art rogue) debate between the expressionist painter Oskar Kokoschka and the collaborators George Grosz and John Heartfield. At stake was the question whether bourgeois culture should be valued higher then the life and interests of the working class. Kokoschka had pleaded that armed confrontations ought not to take place at locations where cultural treasures are endangered, to which the dadaists responded with a ferociously derisive attack on the bourgeois "art market, public opinion about art . . . art stupidity and art impudence and arrogance," in short, "the whole insolent art and culture swindle of our times."[3] Toward the end of the decade, the communist writers Johannes Becher and Egon Kisch, the latter a proponent of documentary working-class literature, leveled a similarly indignant attack on Gottfried Benn's elitist aestheticism. The 1930 radio debate "Können Dichter die Welt ändern?" ("Can Poets Change the World?") between Becher and Benn once more pitched the argument for politically committed writing to meet the challenges of the day against the poet's Nietzschean insistence on the suprahistorical autonomy of aesthetics as metaphysics. The call for *Gebrauchskunst* (art for social use) dominated the Left's agenda, ranging from Brecht's notion of poetry for and even by the common man (like "He! He! The Iron Man!"—a bike racer's poem) to Kisch's documentary reporting.

The 1920s are "golden" only to those who mistake the sheer exuberant productivity of these years, epitomized (and overly glorified) with Brecht's *Dreigroschenoper* (*Threepenny Opera;* 1928) and Fritz Lang's (very) late-, or better, retro-expressionist film *Metropolis* (1926), as a new "flowering" of the arts. As years of political crisis, they rather prepared the way for the rise of Nazism. As such they finally brought to awareness that the Berlin avant-garde had failed in the attempt to displace the mythical-irrational strain of German culture and politics. And one had tried everything to expand the significance of literary culture for the age of the masses: from the writing of political literature as "a weapon" by Friedrich Wolf to the leftist appropriation of the popular medium of opera by Brecht and Weill, the integration of film onto the stage by Piscator, the political refunctioning of communal music (*Laienmusik*) in Baden-Baden by Brecht and Weill, or the utilization of radio, in Germany a public medium since 1923, for addressing the masses.

I will here have to limit myself to a few exemplary, albeit relatively little discussed, instances. With *Der Lindberghflug* (*The Flight of Lindbergh;* 1929), for example, Brecht attempted to move from the stage into the wider public space of the annual festival of lay musicians in Baden-Baden, where it was demonstrated as a model performance, and—the radio. Kurt Weill composed the American part of the score, Paul Hindemith the European part of the "radio play." The musician listeners (beyond the setting of the festival) were to fill in their musical part in front of the radio at home. In other words, the radio, "an epochal event," was to be turned, as Brecht theorized in his observations on this mass medium, from a mere "Distribu-tionsapparat" (distribution device) into a collective participatory medium.[4] A falling-out between Brecht and Hindemith over the playwright's attempt to radically politicize the *Laienmusik* (lay music) festival at Baden-Baden — *Die Maßnahme* (*The Measure Taken;* music by Hanns Eisler) had been com-missioned but then rejected by the organizers for a performance — fully bore out the *Kulturpolitik* behind these moves toward the larger public space. Hindemith now sought the collaboration with Gottfried Benn. The composer wrote the score for the poet's "Oratorium. Das Unaufhörliche" ("Oratory: The Unending"; 1931) a sort of poetic *Lehrstück* (learning play) without a lesson, namely a cycle about the senselessness of history and its transcendence by art as an absolute cipher. It is evident from the correspon-dence of Benn with Hindemith, in which the poet does not shy away from Brechtian terms like "demonstrieren" ("in the sense of *The Measure Taken*"), the "Oratorium" was to implicitly function as an antidote to Brecht's highly successful turn to music.[5] For further collaboration, Benn even projected, among several other suggestions likewise aborted, an opera, in fact — in his own words — a "Lehrstück" demonstrating the unchangeable irrational-ism of capitalism and the dubious nature of technological progress. The "Weizenstück" (wheat play) was to have its setting in America (the site of the Brecht and Weill *Mahagonny* opera). Its story is fully accounted for in an essay Benn wrote later in 1932: Carleton, a petty employee with the United States Bureau of Agriculture, had introduced, on his own venture, a durable Russian winter wheat that was resistant to the extremes of the climate and could be stored and sold throughout the year. While Carleton's initiative brought immense profits to the middleman and large corporations, it led to the dependence, impoverishment, if not demise of the small farmer (as well as the ruin of the pioneer who was unable to pay off his debts).[6]

Benn's correspondence with Hindemith clearly reveals that he was quite eager to compete, on conservative aesthetic and ideological grounds, with Brecht in the wider public space of musical performances. At this time he also ventured into what he somewhat disingenuously calls the "lowly busi-ness of radio lectures."[7] In fact, his 1930 broadcast debate with Becher, the ideas of which are at the core of his letters to and his production with the composer, had caught Hindemith's attention and caused him to contact the poet to begin with. These episodes may suffice for understand-ing Weimar culture as a result of productive, politically motivated confron-tations over the relation of *literature* to popular institutions like music fes-tivals, opera, and modern technological means of production.

The culture of the Weimar Republic has been much discussed and extensively illustrated—with a meanwhile somewhat dulled focus on the critical Left versus the irrational Right as represented by Benn or Ernst Jünger. Interesting, however, remains Ernst Bloch's claim and regret made in *Erbschaft dieser Zeit* (*Legacy of Our Times;* 1935) that the leftist intelligentsia disregarded the power of myth in their attempt to compete with the Right for influence over the masses. Much more adept in recognizing the dangers that lie in the lure of myth but also aware of its potential had been representatives of liberalism such as Thomas Mann (from *Der Zauberberg* [*The Magic Mountain;* 1924] to the *Joseph* novel, first volume, 1933), Hermann Hesse (*Steppenwolf,* 1927), and Hermann Broch (*Die Schlafwandler* [*The Sleepwalkers;* 1928–31]). As to the place of the avant-garde in this constellation, it is quite telling that the dominant expressionist legacy never allowed the surrealist project of merging modernity and myth to take root in German culture, even though "surrealist" elements can be detected early on in the poetry of Heym and Lichtenstein (see chapter 1), in Benn's Rönne novellas, in Robert Walser's prose, and, of course, in Franz Kafka's works. Here the battle was waged between the *Geistige* of all shades and colors and anti-idealist movements such as Berlin dadaism, which explored the means of a "material aesthetics," or Berlin avant-garde theater such as Erwin Piscator's that was influenced by Soviet constructivism and agitprop, and Brecht's epic theater. Thus still relatively little, and only quite recently, has been said about singular attempts to transplant from France into conflict-ridden German culture and politics the surrealist experiment with the "marvelous" and the collective unconscious as an aesthetic factor with political potential. Some writers of the Left and, much less exposed, of the Right considered surrealist forms of writing to be more potent than the German expressionist legacy of *Geist* (spirit). Not only Walter Benjamin with *Einbahnstrasse* (*One-Way Street;* 1928), his fascinating essay of 1929 on surrealism, or his attempt to read Brecht's epic play *Mann ist Mann* (*Man Is Man*) in quasi-surrealist terms, but also Ernst Bloch with his *Spuren* (*Traces;* 1930) tried to gain a new dimension for German literature from the experiments and experience of the French avant-garde. On the other side, there is Ernst Jünger, whose *Das abenteuerliche Herz* (*The Adventurous Heart;* 1929) has to be placed into this context. His views on cities, war, the writings of the Marquis de Sade, sexuality, insects, coral fish in an aquarium, and dreams are "stereoscoped," in a moment's flash, with dream images and visions that ominously amalgamate the primitive with technological modernity. The interest of the "conservative revolution" in surrealist visions, images, and myths could not be understood properly without a new look at Gottfried Benn's poetic practice of the "hallucinatory-constructive" deconstruction of rational subjectivity. Benn's "hallucinatory-constructive" poetic method is, quite simply stated, the common denominator of his "absolute" poetry, prose such as the "Urgesicht" ("Primal Vision"; 1929) — "I saw the I, the gaze from its eyes, I dilated the pupil, saw deep into it, saw deep from inside out" — and his pro-Nazi essays. These projected his "Urbilder" (primordial images) inside out, from the solipsistic self onto the body politic of the state as an organism. Hitler's rejection of modern art as "entartete Kunst" (degenerate art), of course, meant the end of the avant-garde in Germany. The infamous exhibit of 1937 could conceivably be discussed as a perverted variant of the "end of art" thesis that has haunted Western culture since Hegel. Hitler's address at the simultaneously staged exhibit of "German art" at the "Haus der deutschen Kunst" (House of German Art) and the catalog to the "Degenerate Art" exhibit posit the *end* of ever changing "so-called modern" developments: the "art" of the avant-garde (always referred to in quotation marks as *nonart*) would in the era of a conclusive and comprehensive cultural revolution be displaced by German racial art as "eternal" art.[8] In 1933 and 1934, Benn had participated in the dissemination of Nazi ideology with a series of scandalous essays, among them "Confessing Expressionism," and predictably failed to reassure Hitler and Goebbels of the "Aryan" nature of expressionist literature and modernist art as an aesthetic expression of the transhistorical "mutation" of the times. His inconceivably crude (let alone immoral) political manipulation of the expressionist heritage — after all, half of the expressionist writers and artists were Jewish — was not to achieve what, in his view, the futurist Marinetti appeared to have accomplished in Mussolini's Italy.

The exuberance of the German avant-garde's experimenting extensively, extensively also in the sense of reaching out to the media and beyond national traditions, with literary and artistic culture during the Weimar Republic contrasts starkly with the introspective self-questioning and self-doubting in its political exile from Nazism. Yet, these years of exile were by no means less productive, though characterized, on the whole, by a restorative withdrawal into traditional forms of art — such as the historical novel or even the sonnet. On the other hand, there developed, in the extreme, a most profound cultural pessimism and skepticism that cast into doubt the function of art, if not the very language of art.

The late start of the study of German exile literature[9] reflected a mentality of forgetting also outside of the academy. In the Western zones of occupied Germany during the immediate postwar period, a quasi-religious search for existentialist experience surfaced, the yearning and need for pure, or "absolute" art in the vein of Gottfried Benn, on the other side of which was a pervasive aversion to dealing with the past and engaging in historical analysis (in spite of the efforts of the "Gruppe 47"). In the midst of the ensuing cold war, Marxist writers (such as Brecht) were outright silenced, and one continued the prejudice against liberal leftist traditions, the very traditions which the student revolt in the late 1960s were to muster in an effort to alter the mentality, if not the course, of German society. Since the early 1960s, "Exilforschung," the study of literary and artistic production in political exile, most eminently in the United States, France, Spain, and South America, has proliferated into a vast international discipline with subjects that go beyond the traditional focus on literary culture. Given these circumstances, surprisingly little research has been conducted that would specifically thematize the German *avant-garde* in exile. By that I do, of course, not mean that research on the exile experience and production of writers such as Bertolt Brecht, Alfred Döblin, Carl Einstein, Yvan Goll, Georg Kaiser, Else Lasker-Schüler, Ernst Toller, or Fritz von Unruh, or minor poets such as Erich Arendt, Albert Ehrenstein, or Alfred Wolfenstein, or artists such as Hans (Jean) Arp, Max Beckmann, or George Grosz would be missing. In fact, the volume of research on German literature and art in exile has become, it appears, near exhaustive. Moreover, its activities have been critically incisive. The findings of exile research have been incisive to an extent that no discussion of twentieth-century German literature and art should any longer bypass this period as being somehow separate—as a matter of exceptionally unique "politics"—from its main currents. After four decades of intensive research, the period of literary exile should also not be outside the concerns of scholars who investigate the cultural traditions of modernism and the avant-garde in their relation to modernity, as last still maintained by Silvio Vietta in his ambitious, large-scale 1992 study *Die Literarische Moderne*.[10]

On the contrary, due to the very fact that exile research has established the period as one of significant continuities and discontinuities, a consistent focus on avant-garde literary and artistic production in exile as a crisis phase of the project of the historical avant-garde may bring some new insights into the role it plays within modernist culture as a whole. This would mean a specific concern for what happened to the writers' and artists' utopianism, in its various spiritual and political forms, and what happened to their techniques of linguistic innovation and experimentation as forms designed to subvert literary and cultural traditions. In short, the issue of the crisis of the avant-garde in exile as the *crisis of avant-garde writing* warrants further investigation. A probe like this chapter may contribute to differentiating the typology that research has developed for the overall literary production in exile as marked by a restorative turn toward traditional themes and forms. It will implicitly also serve as a kind of miniature *Forschungsbericht* (research report) that explicitly cites findings by American and German scholars that are essential for my reassessment. Such a discussion will have to take its point of departure from what Paul Michael Lützeler has addressed in the case of Hermann Broch as "negative aesthetics,"[11] as a relatively extreme case of exile writing turning, for mostly moral and epistemological reasons, against art (to be fully discussed subsequently). My own study chooses, besides the poet and critic Carl Einstein, the critic Walter Benjamin and the painter George Grosz as representative of the most radical avant-garde. In these cases, the identity of not only "art"—that had already been the experience of Dada in exile during the World War I—but, this is a further step, the identity of *avant-garde productions* is eroded in the course of the exiles' experience. Hence the question arises: What would come after such extreme response, if not utter silence? During their exile, writers as different as Broch and Einstein, for example, sought their answers in political activism as a temporary response to a perceived futility of literary culture. As literary creativity survived the harshest conditions in exile, as even its self-questioning or self-negation came in a form of creativity, the question—here limited to the German avant-garde—poses a different problem for us today. In what ways is the exile period, which apparently shook the belief of even the most dyed-in-the-wool avant-gardist in avant-garde art, not just an "exceptional" period of politically motivated discontinuity but one that throws into relief the contours of the before and the after? For example, can it perhaps be viewed as an intensely self-reflective phase that, in addition to the long-standing crisis of literary culture, first and most incisively articulated by Hugo von Hofmannsthal in his "Chandos Letter" (1902), contributed to an experience which we today address as the "postmodern," for which art may have become a highly diffuse, if not questionable, phenomenon? Of course, such a question cannot be solved ad hoc, perhaps not at all, even when posed, most appropriately, in the context of postwar developments (my final chapter).

A complementary, less ponderous, but, aside from individual accounts, still surprisingly underexposed question would be, for example: Did the German avant-garde in exile, beyond the participation in various writers' congresses in the 1930s, significantly converge with the creative efforts of the French avant-garde in Paris, or with the international avant-garde in New York, with fellow exiles and American artists and writers, so that one could speak of an evolving paradigm shift in the arts that was internationally anticipated? The eminent exile scholar Guy Stern already in 1986 asked for a "comparatistic history of influence,"[12] so far in vain. I, too, can here no more than allude to, for instance, the question of what may have been the impact of the exiles from the various European countries on the formation, self-image, and public reception of a "transatlantic" international avant-garde. At any rate, no matter how "subversive" once, in the postwar cold war era the international avant-garde would be raised and promoted, by institutions and critics on both sides of the Atlantic, to the status of an international "modernist" culture, representative of an individualist, democratic Western culture. Such change of status from revolt to representation constitutes, as it were, an *affirmative* paradigm shift, quite different from the crisis of the avant-garde my study pursues, as the following brief illustrations may illuminate by way of contrast.

There were some significant contributions of German writers and artists to this other context of "positive" creativity that would warrant a further, separate investigation. Typically, writers and artists like Yvan Goll or Max Ernst had been in the vanguard of "surrealist" developments, sometimes even before surrealism fully evolved into the French movement. By contrast, expressionist writers and artists (like initially even Max Beckmann in Paris and the Netherlands) were perceived and beheld themselves much more as "German" than was good for ready assimilation, let alone impact abroad, not even in the United States where expressionist theater had earlier influenced playwrights such as Eugene O'Neill (*The Hairy Ape;* 1921) and Elmer Rice (*The Adding Machine;* 1923). Even the painter George Grosz, received as *the* political satirist of German society between the wars and unable to relinquish that perception in spite of his attempts to become an *American* artist, had little chance to compete with the growing influence of European surrealist and, subsequently, American abstract expressionist painting. For the latter, represented by Jackson Pollock or Mark Rothko, critics like Clement Greenberg most successfully made the claim that the new American art was the vanguard for a global postwar renewal in the name of individualism and democracy.[13] By contrast, Grosz was a case of a German artist in exile who had begun to fundamentally and persistently question the validity of art in times of political disaster (which deserves discussion in a separate chapter). The painter had shunned contacts with his German fellow exiles in New York as well as any involvement with American artists' political organizations. His experience with the German Communist Party in the 1920s and early 1930s before his emigration to the United States had made him incurably allergic to any group alliance, artistic or political. Grosz's growing skepticism also reflects to some degree his failure to reach the American art market. Before America's entry into the war, there was little understanding from the public at large, nor from the American Left, for his grotesque satires which equated Hitler's with Stalin's totalitarianism. They were reproduced in a very expensive, limited edition *Interregnum* (1936; 300 copies at $50), with a rather general introduction by John Dos Passos, who failed to point out its political exigencies. Even less understanding could be found for the painter's proliferating existentialist-absurdist allegories and self-portraits which questioned the purpose of the political artist and of art. By contrast, there was an immense interest in the "surrealist" developments of Paul Klee, who had no success in the exile of conservative Switzerland, while his works became best-sellers in New York. James Johnson Sweeney, an American critic and staff member of the Museum of Modern Art whose interest in expressionism also extended to Carl Einstein's theoretical writings, gave Klee's work as early as 1940 the significance that modernist culture was to achieve in the West for the postwar period as a whole:

> Today . . . we see a world torn between the two great forces, democracy and totalitarianism. . . . Yesterday, in a blind, self-satisfied world, Klee was forced to withdraw into himself to protect the sensibility his art cultivated. Tomorrow will find Klee's work a delicate distillation of those qualities most needed to give life to a renewed art in a renewed world.[14]

In other words, the creative individual's inwardness (rather than despair or doubt) that comes with the experience of exile was the source from which to "distill" a postwar democratic modernist culture with universal significance.

For a poet like Yvan Goll, of Jewish origin, accustomed to the instability of identity as he grew up and began to write in the bilingual, bicultural, conflict-ridden borderland of Alsace-Lorraine, exile caused no real break from previous internationally oriented activities. His self-understanding as a "born exile" always transcended his identity as a "German expressionist" (as documented by his presence in Kurt Pinthus's anthology *Menschheits-dämmerung/Dawn of Humanity*). On the contrary, his exile in New York was a chance to vigorously reconnect with surrealism that would triumph with the overly spectacular success of the painter Salvador Dali in the 1940s. While Goll's more romantic (i.e., "German") concept of surrealism had differed with Breton's in the Paris of the mid-1920s,[15] the editor of the journal *Hémisphères* now not only collaborated with Breton but also connected with American poets and writers such as William Carlos Williams, Kenneth Patchen, and Henry Miller. In other words, Goll continued his surrealist production in exile, even though his momentous poetic cycle *Jean sans Terre* (*John without Land;* 1944) was written in the conservative form of the sonnet. And the painter Max Ernst, since the early 1920s in Paris, was among the fifty Parisian members of the *Freie Künstlerbund* (Free Artists' Union) in exile. Identifying with surrealism as a political and aesthetic movement, his efforts were to further a collaboration between French and German anti-fascist artists. Most notably his was one of the rarer avant-garde attempts to cooperate with aesthetically more conservative minds.[16] When his flight from Nazism brought him in 1941 to New York, the surrealist artist found an enthusiastic audience.

Similar in circumstance, yet quite different as to his reaction to efforts to ally the avant-garde with antifascist organizations of intellectuals, writers, and artists, is the case of Carl Einstein. Einstein had left Berlin for Paris in 1928; like Ernst's, his was initially a case of "cultural emigration" that would fully turn into political exile. The former expressionist writer, one of the most advanced theoreticians of the movement in Germany, turned into a leading critic and spokesman of French cubist and surrealist developments. In the late 1920s and early 1930s, he was fully active in international avant-garde circles, as advisory editor for Eugene Jolas *transition,* "An International Quarterly for Creative Experiment," where, as far as one can see, the term "experiment" was for the first time connected with avant-garde writing. Here appeared the first translations into English of some of Kafka's most important short narratives, a sample of Gottfried Benn's Rönne prose, and an excerpt of Alfred Döblin's Berlin novel. In 1929–1930 Einstein was, with Georges Bataille, coeditor of *documents,* a journal for "Archéologie, Beaux-Arts, Ethnographie, Variétés." It is quite significant that with Hitler's rise to power, the self-exile, now truly a political exile, began to withdraw from these connections. Communications with German culture restricted as his friends left the country, avenues of publication in Germany closed, a lingering sense of isolation, now strongly felt, left its mark on the vitality of his production. It resulted in an abrupt doubt in the mission and nature of the avant-garde, which is the focus of my preliminary concerns here and in the following chapters. Unlike Max Ernst, Einstein was no great believer in the political organization of creative intellectuals, as he never took much stock in "rational forms of revolt" (such as the Communist Party, or any party, let alone the Popular Front); he simply had no stomach for the compromises involved. This attitude appears to be a common denominator for a certain type of hard-core avant-garde that had exaggeratedly pure expectations from the revolutionary function of aesthetic production in itself (that, in cases, reproduced the traditional belief in aesthetic autonomy, albeit in radically iconoclastic forms). Rather than looking for political and thus aesthetic compromise in the humanist, liberal leftist terms of antifascist alliances like the Popular Front, Einstein and the critic Walter Benjamin in Parisian exile (chapter 5) or, at a certain point, George Grosz in the American exile felt compelled to question all aesthetic production in times of extreme political crisis. Their questions were to lead to a fundamental review and analysis of a change in the function of art in terms that, paradoxically, doubt the language of art in the medium of art. Or one altogether questions "literary culture" in the way of Benjamin's film essay of the mid-1930s, which, as has been overlooked, also turns against the literary avant-garde.

Einstein and Benjamin had become true refugees; thus their experience is not quite comparable to the alienation many modernist writers — such as the expatriates James Joyce, Samuel Beckett, or Ernest Hemingway, the members of the "lost generation" — felt in self-exile. While these classical expatriates of the 1910s and 1920s had developed the international language and aura of the avant-garde, the political refugees of the early 1930s were now radically questioning both traditional and avant-garde culture. This was something somehow more "German," a matter of systematic thought, not quite Parisian. Pablo Picasso, for instance — his powerful *Guernica* mural alone speaks against it — cannot be at all imagined as having been plagued with politically inflicted anti-art thoughts. Einstein's and Benjamin's hypercritical, intensely cerebral mentality must have contributed to their outsider position in the Parisian exile (where they, according to existing documentation such as diaries, address books, etc., never met). I will return to the issues involved with these extreme cases after an overview of some mainstream developments in exile.

That the issue of the German avant-garde in exile as a specific question of the *crisis of avant-garde writing* has not yet been sufficiently addressed is the more surprising as it is intimately linked to the larger issue of what happens to the writing of any writer in exile, traditional or avant-garde. One is, of course, quite aware of the implicit effects exile has on literary language in general, as addressed by Manfred Durzak in 1973 in his introduction to a major collaborative project of exile research. As language for the writer is the primary means of expression, his or her work is now produced outside the context of national relations and reception, in an unfamiliar linguistic environment. The writer's intense preoccupation with literary language thus becomes a major obstacle to assimilation. Second, the focus on artistic forms may engender, with lack of immediate critical feedback from one's accustomed audience of readers and critics, features of artificiality.[17] While such developments, as pointed out by Durzak, are critical for any writer, they become a matter of creative life or death for the avant-garde artist.

By definition of his or her iconoclastic identity, the avant-gardist would, so one expects, be excluded from the refuge many writers found in the traditional forms of their national literature as part of world literature. On the whole, it appears, exile research will agree with the nutshell assessment that Ernst Schürer makes for the dramatic production in exile as characteristic for writing in exile as such:

> Most exiled writers were opposed to the prevailing social conditions and the reigning political philosophy and party and had often expressed this opposition in their previous writings, but they were not rebelling against any prevailing literary trend or in the process of developing a new one. Or, if they had been members of the literary avant-garde and had been experimenting with modern forms, this had nothing to do with their exile. On the contrary, these authors were forced by the exigencies of exile and by political and economic considerations to turn away from experimentation, to reject modern forms and use traditional, usually realistic styles and structures to make their plays acceptable to as many stages as possible and their message understandable to the whole audience instead of just a few insiders.[18]

I here will turn to the genre of poetry, and subsequently to a certain type of novel that inherently deals with the issue of the avant-garde.

Poetry has been considered the "stepchild of exile research," as if to say, critically, with Bertolt Brecht that exile was a "Schlechte Zeit für Lyrik" (bad time for poetry), though there is a sheer abundance of poetry from the period. For our purposes here, the genre of poetry, a prime question of *language*, is most important, of course. And language is the prime concern of the historical avant-garde, as it had attacked the "bourgeois" confinement of language into literary "genres" and corresponding "styles" from its very beginning around 1910. Critics point to the restorative tendencies of exile poetry, its "premodern styles . . . classicist norms of style," poems apparently written "far from the movements of the aesthetic and political avant-garde in the teens and twenties . . . almost as if this avant-garde never existed."[19] The consensus is: "The service performed by exile lyric had more to do with preservation than experimentation." Most provocative is an overall understanding that "there could be no avant-garde in exile,"[20] to which issue we shall, of course, want to return.

Theodore Ziolkowski identifies such restorative tendencies, culminating in a renaissance of the sonnet, with many exiles' programmatic, emphatic belief in the mission of literature as political enlightenment and heightened faith in the power of form. The critic goes as far as contrasting such belief in the "power of form" held by those deeply endangered in the jails of the Gestapo, in concentration camps, or at the front with the "often faddish doubt in the usefulness of art of writers who were not immediately exposed to the threats of the Third Reich." Which doubt he sees as a prominent topos of exile literature: "the denial of all aesthetics which so often resulted from the ethical desperation of the emigrants."[21]

In political terms, the sonnet, rich in tradition, came to represent for many exile writers a medium that is as international as it was considered by the cultural politics of National Socialism *entartet* (degenerate). The sonnet thus constituted a form of "protest against the Aryan cultural politics of the Third Reich" as well as a form-conscious antidote to chaos, here of exile. As the form also enjoyed a long political tradition in German letters (e.g., Rückert's "Geharnischte Sonette" ["Armored Sonnets"]), the exiled Rudolf Hagelstange understood the recourse to the sonnet, at first somewhat ambiguously, as a "fashionable form of resistance." While he had employed the form before exile out of a traditional aesthetic disposition, finding it for some time in exile "senseless, to write poems,"[22] he began to use it himself as a form of aesthetic resistance. In this environment, the sonnets of Johannes Becher and Erich Arendt represent the case of the avant-garde in exile. The former expressionist poet Becher, whose early poetry was at its best when employing futurist techniques, had written almost no sonnets during his *Aufklärungszeit* (period of enlightenment) from 1917 to 1933. From 1933 to the end of war, however, he writes 350 of them,[23] some abusing and perverting the genre's ideal of form for the affirmation of Josef Stalin's totalitarian regime.

The aesthetics of resistance in exile in only a few cases involves the employment and further development of avant-garde forms. The case of Erich Arendt is such an instance. Much of his poetry in exile displays an energy that manifests itself in the context of political action. Arendt's "(late)-expressionist poems,"[24] published from 1924 to 1928 in *Der Sturm* (*The Storm*), are here much less interesting than those written in the Spanish exile. The member of the 27.(catalonian) division "Carlos Marx" writes stories and reports from the front, also "surrealist" poems like "Die Hände" ("The Hands"), from which I quote:

> Tot lag im Acker er. Und weit von ihm die Hände.
> Sie schlossen sich zur Nacht. Im Dorfe hörten sie
> die Fäuste kommen und an alle Scheiben blutig klopfen.[25]

(He lay dead in the field. And far from him the hands. / They closed themselves for the night. In the village they heard / the fists coming and bloodily beat on all window panes.)

Arendt also writes sonnets, sonnets not smooth but of "raw sound, . . . in rhythmic syncopes."[26] As the author himself offers, "During the Spanish Civil War I read Rimbaud, and I . . . have come to the conviction that one can master in the sonnet also a lived experience."[27] The form of the sonnet here is employed as a "means of contrast," in other words, as a medium in which to explore and exploit—in avant-garde fashion—aesthetic contradictions. Obviously, here an exiled author "did not lose but found his language in exile."[28] Arendt's is a case of a continued genuine avant-garde disposition toward literary culture that has much to do with the utopian optimism that brought many German intellectuals into the "good fight" for Spain. Somewhat comparable is Ernst Toller's (albeit more liberal) fund-raising, speech-making activism for the Spanish cause. The dramatist, too, kept, if not strengthened his belief in the political power of the word, as literature, speech or pamphlet, so that his suicide in 1939 in New York came as surprise and shock.[29] In contrast to Arendt and Toller, Carl Einstein had, as we shall see subsequently, given up on avant-garde writing already in the relative isolation of the later years of his Parisian exile and thereafter sought salvation in anarchist "pure" action in Spain.

Otherwise, the resistance against the betrayal of tradition in the Third Reich favored communicative forms over continued formal experimentation. Thus there was, on the whole, a "return to tradition" that had been disrupted in Germany.[30] And many writers widened the scope toward the Western tradition with a marked emphasis on biblical themes or the Ulysses topos.[31] The spectrum of avant-garde reactions to political exile is much more diffuse and unpredictable than that of other writers. Readers who have a special interest in the plight of also minor poets of the German avant-garde will most readily agree with this assessment.

Poets like Karl Otten and Paul Zech, for example, turned to the writing of altogether realist novels, taking up their expressionist legacy only after the war.[32] Albert Ehrenstein, the author of the experimental narrative *Tubutsch* (1911) and some of the early better expressionist poetry, upon his exile in New York resigned from all literary activity, as it were, waiting for his death in the isolation of his small apartment. The dadaist Richard Huelsenbeck, apart from writing some poetry to be published in France and dwelling on his Dada memoirs, was mostly preoccupied with practicing psychiatry. The talented expressionist poet Alfred Wolfenstein, too, who managed only a few literary essays in French exile, was unable to complete his novel *Frank*, which dealt with the experience of his son, and committed suicide only a few months after the end of the war.[33] The expressionist playwright Fritz von Unruh turned from drama to the novel; however, he was unwilling or unable to relinquish his hyperbolic expressionist language and idealism, which made for poor sales and accounted for his failure as a writer in exile.[34] The major expressionist dramatist Georg Kaiser kept on writing in Swiss exile. While his earlier plays were given to a pathos of exalting the great, lone individual in history (e.g., Napoleon over Hitler), his later ones turned from direct attacks on National Socialism to the tragedy of the genius artist in an age devoid of meaning.[35]

An altogether unique case of continued creativity is Else Lasker-Schüler, the oldest representative of expressionism. Together with the continued creative activities of Arp, Goll, and Ernst in New York and Toller and Arendt (albeit inspired by direct involvement in political action) in the context of the Spanish Civil War, her work disproves the assumption that "there can be no avant-garde in exile." While Karl Kraus, with whom Lasker-Schüler had a closer relation during the expressionist years, folded his *Fackel* (*Torch*) already in 1933 in view of the insight that Hitler had made satire impossible, this remarkable woman found enough cause, energy, and satirical imagination in Jerusalem to write with *Ichundich* (*IandI;* 1940–41), a powerful dramatic satire of Nazism that awaits renewed attention. The daring parody of the Faust theme is critique and continuation of the German tradition in one. Characteristic for German exile writers was the sense that tradition was theirs inasmuch as it was betrayed at home. Werner Vortriede's still remarkable and often quoted early reflections on a typology of exile literature (1968) thus pertain as much to Lasker-Schüler's as to Thomas Mann's later treatment of the Faust theme, namely, that parody in exile is dialectically related to a faithfulness to tradition as well as being a form which disallows "restorative" acquiescence.[36] Indeed, Else Lasker-Schüler's parable, employs Brechtian techniques of outright defamiliarization.[37] By contrast, the poetry of *Mein blaues Klavier* (*My Blue Piano;* 1943) occasionally shares some of the language skepticism of other poets in exile, expressing a prolonged and increasing feeling of isolation from her home, the German language. The Jewish German poet may have—like Einstein or Goll—already felt a "stranger" in Germany as the land of her birth.[38] At any rate, the separation from the German language as a *lived* language is crucial to the poet in exile, as expressed in her poem "My Blue Piano," from which I quote a few central lines:

> Ich habe zu Hause ein blaues Klavier
> Und kenne doch keine Note.
>
> Es steht im Dunkel der Kellertür,
> Seitdem die Welt verrohte.
>
> . . . .
> Zerbrochen ist die Klaviatür. . . .
> Ich beweine die blaue Tote.[39]

(At home I have a blue piano / Yet I do not know any note. / It stands in the darkness of the basement's door, / Since the world has become barbarous / . . . Broken is the keyboard / I cry over the blue dead one)

The poet's "piano" had to be left "at home" (now Nazi Germany), the notes, the German language of the lived moment, are inaccessible to her, the keyboard broken by the Nazis (the "rats," the poem's next stanza refers to as "dancing in the clanking"). The piano becomes the subject of the exile poem. The poem as *Klage* (lament) becomes the "blue" piano, as such situated nowhere but in nostalgia (a stimulus for creativity in exile). Sigrid Bauschinger accurately assesses the significance of such poetry as exile poetry: "The magnificent paradox of such poetry from exile is that in poetry its impossibility is expressed and overcome."[40] By contrast, Einstein's last poem, "Entwurf einer Landschaft" ("Design of a Landscape"; 1930), written in Paris, differs significantly from Lasker-Schüler's poem as much as there is no overcoming, neither in content nor in form. Nor is there any "restorative" dimension that comes with nostalgia. "Design of a Landscape" constitutes, as we shall see (also chapters 4 and 8), an extreme case of "negative aesthetics," of a negation of poetic language in the form of poetry, that shares with other exile writing only the tenor of *Klage*.

Our review so far of the various writers and their forms of writing in exile already allows the conclusion that there is no separate typology of the German avant-garde in exile. As for the surviving representatives of the once powerful expressionist movement, we can say that the variety of contradictory forms they employ in exile reinscribes, in a pronounced political context, the crisis of expressionism in the 1910s to the early 1920s (see chapter 1). Some predictably negate and take back expressionism's original utopianism, reverting to parody or other traditional forms. While there is a common restorative element shared with mainstream exile writing, that does not mean, however, that there is no avant-garde. Else Lasker-Schüler's *IandI* is not only a Faust parody but also an aggressive satire on Nazism. Arendt transforms the sonnet into an activist avant-garde expression. Toller develops a politically motivated, if rigid, belief in the continued power of the word for speech making and political satire (e.g., *Nie Wieder Friede* [*No More Peace*; 1937]), whereas Becher holds on to the formal tradition and magic of the sonnet. Others like Goll and Ernst continue to practice surrealism in New York, as if to say that their surrealist critique of modernity found its justification in developments that led to their exile.

"Negative Aesthetics"

There is, however, a singularly avant-garde subtext determined by a far-reaching concern for the continued viability of aesthetic production in exile, shared with more traditionally minded writers but expressed in ultraradical terms. These terms are *avant-garde* inasmuch as they risk to explore, paradoxically in continued creativity, a danger zone in which art may cease to exist, in which the creative individual has to face up either to complete silence or to the action of total politics. In polar opposition to a restorative mentality in which many writers of the avant-garde shared, there is a tendency toward altogether questioning the significance and value of art and literature. Different from the silence of Ehrenstein and Wolfenstein as a personal reaction of submission to exile, writers like Broch and Einstein, for example, develop such fundamental skepticism at the threshold of sublating art into politics, if not relinquishing art for politics. Yet they come as such from two different directions: While Broch's critique of art is predominantly *morally* rooted, in that sense more traditional, Einstein's is predominantly *aesthetically* rooted, in that sense more avant-garde.

Here I would like to focus more closely on these two obversely related dispositions that seem to be tied mostly to the genre of the novel. On the one hand, there is a critique of art in moral terms, a reversal of the avant-garde's original delinking of the aesthetic from the moral in the wake of Nietzsche. The moral now becomes significant again for the modernist writer of novels, a genre traditionally given to the exploration of social mores and individual ethics. As far as I can see, such a self-critique of the "immoral" nature of a continued preoccupation with aesthetic production in the era of singular political immorality and barbarism informs besides Thomas Mann mainly three novelists in exile, the later American exile, namely, Heinrich Mann, Alfred Döblin, and Hermann Broch. On the other hand, Carl Einstein's *BEB II*, written in the Parisian exile, represents an avant-garde novel that continues to reflect on its relation to politics in predominantly aesthetic terms, even as these become questionable epistemologically but *not* morally. Einstein's text is avant-garde inasmuch as it continues its tradition to put into question the genre concept "novel"; it will thus serve as a kind of control.

Thomas Mann's claim that "not all literature but mainly the novel has gone into exile (while) poetry grows and looms, serene and undisturbed in sweet oblivion of the world"[41] documents that the novelist had little insight into the nature of lyrical production in exile, mistaking its surface "conservatism" as the expression of a "timeless" disposition of the poet. His statement is, of course, self-reflexive of his own work in exile. His major exile novel, the *Doktor Faustus* (written 1943–1946, published 1947), for example, exemplifies the productive influence exile had on some writers. *Doktor Faustus* is a document of a uniquely paradoxical nature. The novel thematizes the creative spirit of the avant-garde at an extreme: the composer Adrian Leverkühn is a fictive, as it were, montaged alter ego for Nietzsche, the "expressionist" twelve-tone composer Arnold Schönberg, and Theodor Wiesengrund (Adorno). Mann pursues the avant-garde experiment from a moral point of view, however, as he links a Nietzschean amoral, aestheticist disposition toward the world to the political barbarism and immoralism of Nazi Germany, a strategy that can be criticized as a demonization of German history. The novel is a profound indictment of the avant-garde, albeit delivered from the perspective of the "bourgeois" Zeitblom, whose narration is based on the traditional realist device of the *Rahmenerzählung* (narrative frame). In these terms, representation is, in spite of an extended tension exemplified by the split, *ironic* overall perspective of the novel, privileged over avant-garde experimentation — *morally* (less decisively formally). Thomas Mann hereby not only deals with, if not exorcises, his own Nietzschean aestheticist heritage but also points at the moral implications of the avant-garde's "devil's pact." In the wake of Nietzsche, the avant-garde had unleashed aesthetic creativity from its classical ethical roots, once more enabled a boundless creativity — at great cost, the loss of "the soul" of art as an aesthetic and *moral* phenomenon. "Isn't it amusing," proclaims Adrian Leverkühn in the vein of the historical avant-garde's project to sublate art into collective life,

> that music for a long time considered herself a means of a release, whereas she herself, like all the arts, needed to be redeemed from a pompous isolation, which was the fruit of the culture-emancipation, the elevation of culture as a substitute for religion — from being alone with an elite of culture, called the public, which soon will no longer be, which even now no longer is, so that soon art will be entirely alone to die, unless she were to find her way to the folk, that is to say it unromantically, to human beings.[42]

One should add, "unromantically," these were to be human beings or an entire nation released from the ethos of the Judeo-Christian culture of sublimation and compassion.

In view of the supreme significance of Thomas Mann's *Doktor Faustus* as a most comprehensive moral and aesthetic critique of the German avant-garde, it sticks out that exile research has not yet substantially pursued the theme of the self-critique, the confrontation of the exiled writer with his or her Nietzschean heritage of amoralism and aestheticism which had prominently informed the older generation, some of whom were once close to or part of the expressionist movement. This is the more remarkable in view of Theodore Ziolkowski's insight that the indictment of literature as "useless or even immoral, almost belongs to the characteristic topoi of German literature in exile."[43]

The case of Hermann Broch here stands out as a major example of the exiled avant-garde's tensions between ethics and cognitive interests. In terms of his cognitive disposition, Broch belongs to the avant-garde; concerning its ethical tendencies, his work is traditional. It is on these grounds that Broch takes part in the critical debates of the 1930s, which see him shift from an advocacy of James Joyce's new cognitive efforts in the literary medium (*Ulysses*) versus Lukács and Bloch to the critique of Joyce's *Finnegans Wake* in 1934, of the Irish recluse's radically esoteric, "antisocial" stance. The year 1934 is Broch's year of crisis, as Paul Michael Lützeler in a seminal yet little noticed 1988 essay, "The Avant-Garde in Crisis: Hermann Broch's Negative Aesthetics in Exile," concludes, of most incisive significance:

> [H]e now makes a total reversal and becomes a writer who despises and gives up his trade, an opponent of the task of writing, a plaintiff against the world of aesthetics, a judge who condemns the poet's occupation, an iconoclast in the picture gallery of literature. However, the basics of his positive aesthetics—ethics and cognition—are also the basics of his negative aesthetics. He is convinced: the appropriate medium in the antifascist struggle is not literary writing but political publication.[44]

Consequently Broch dedicates himself for one year to his "League of Nations Resolution." As we shall see, Carl Einstein also turns against literature before turning, albeit on extremely radical anarchist grounds, to the cause of the Spanish Civil War. The difference between the two writers is that Broch's disclaimers of the significance of literature are always phrased in ethical terms: "The present world in its ethical decline has no room for artistic feats . . . and it is almost unethical to force something upon it that it doesn't need," or: "The simple telling of made-up fables is absolutely no longer worth it; it becomes utterly immoral in view of the age and its horror." Broch's statement "Artistic writers, be it Joyce or Th. Mann (are) simple atavisms . . . , velvet couches,"[45] could have been made—it is the same polemical language—by Einstein as the author of the polemical auto-da-fé *Die Fabrikation der Fiktionen,* contemporary to his novel *BEBII,* albeit in cognitive terms. Einstein here addressed the avant-garde's failure to integrate the subjective with collective experience. He addressed this failure in view of the tendency of the institution of art to assimilate, aestheticize, and, as it were, anesthetize the impact of the most subversive discourses. Broch never wrote anything as radical as Einstein's *Die Fabrikation der Fiktionen,* but he wrote *Der Tod des Virgil* (*The Death of Virgil;* 1939–1945). Lützeler, whose insights deserve closer attention in a review of the status of exile research pertaining to the avant-garde, accordingly states that "what Broch undertakes now is something paradoxical and probably unique in the history of literature; namely, to write a modern novel from the perspectives of a negative aesthetics, a literary work against literary writing. . . . In this unpolitical plea for the acceptance of political responsibility, the whole self-contradiction of the avant-garde is formulated, here is crisis most clearly expressed."[46] Lützeler points to the novel's reflection (and self-reflection) of the failure of the avant-garde project to sublate art into life (in the sense of Bürger's theory of the avant-garde); and, indeed, there is ample evidence of such a self-critique in the work. It proclaims as vain the "hope for a life away from art, free of literature;" it focuses on Virgil's self-critique as a "man without cognition as the bringer of cognition to those unwilling to accept it, the wordsmith as language revivalist for those unable to speak, the irresponsible as obligator of those ignorant of their duty, the cripple a teacher of the lame." And the novel zeroes in on the shortcoming of literary writing: "It is not literary writing which can proclaim such purest truth of reality . . . literary writing lacks the power to discern."[47] All this is altogether comparable to Einstein's indictment of the writer and of literature—except for the fact that *The Death of Virgil* indeed is an "aesthetically beautiful condemnation of the aesthetically beautiful." In my view, Broch's maintaining a *nostalgic* position of writing *within the beautiful* implicitly also allows the potential of a return of the beautiful at the end of the novel, just like Virgil at his death bed decides against burning the *Aeneid,* admitting his work into the safekeeping hands of the emperor as patron of the arts. And at its end, the novel allows the images of the unconscious to articulate a space in which the borders between the subject and world are elided, where, for the dying subject, the realm of collective, universalist images discloses itself within the horizon of the beautiful (the novel's language).

Alfred Döblin, in *Hamlet oder die lange Nacht nimmt ein Ende (Hamlet or the Long Night Comes to an End;* written 1945–1946; published 1957) pursues the unmasking of the emptiness and moral turpitude of a once rich aesthetic experience of "autonomous" art that valorizes and absolutizes pure form. It has been said that the historical avant-garde once exposed aestheticism as the most extreme, as it were, final form of the belief in aesthetic autonomy and thereby made visible art as an institution separate from life.[48] By contrast, these exile novels critique aesthetic autonomy through moral perspectives. The "restorative" aspect of *Hamlet or the Long Night Comes to an End* consists in a turn to a traditional form of narration within the structure of the novel: storytelling. As a form of premodern personal and communal communication, the telling of stories apparently is inherently intended to subvert the "impersonal" modern structure of the novel. In other words, here we encounter a critique of literature's distance from life with literary means, an undertaking that appears to be unique to the exile literature of this period. The story of the story in exile has been incisively addressed by the question of whether literature (the story) "can enter the political arena directly without revealing all too vividly its inherent weakness as a house of words."[49] Döblin's novel appears to answer this question affirmatively in favor of the magic of the immediacy of oral *storytelling*— thus, to a degree, against itself as a novel.

While once the expressionist writers and artists confronted their Wilhelminian fathers with their utopian aesthetic and moral demands, in this novel, it is the artist—the father is a most successful and established writer —who needs to answer to his son, just returned from another world war. Physically and psychologically wounded from that experience, and in search of explanations, the son requests from his father information about the parental generation's past. In a foil to circumvent his son's request, the writer suggests that one should start communication by telling stories. The telling of stories (or novellas) in Boccaccio's *Decameron* was a design to find respite from the threatening danger of the present (the plague that has befallen the city) through the exchange of oral communications. In Döblin's work, the artist-father begins with telling "his" story—in the entertaining, albeit calculated, cerebral form of narration for which he had become famous. He thus appears to lead his family audience away from the "lost generation's" communal ethical concerns into a realm of mere imagination. His story, an oriental tale of courtship, love, and amorous relations as a series of deceptions and self-deceptions, seems to perform perfectly that diversionary function. Yet, as the other participants respond with their stories, which more or less consciously represent their very own stories, the therapeutic and moral effect of narration in a communal setting gains the upper, the moral hand. The father's "lying" has, after all, led to the truth, as impalpable as the growing insight into the underlying conditions of personal corruption, lack of compassion for others may be for all involved. The deceptive story of personal deceptions has led to a cleansing experience, from which the son can look forward into a new day. In a certain way, then, Döblin's work may be read as a subtle self-critique of its very own genre, the novel as a form of solitary production for solitary consumption that, in the extreme, may valorize form as mere formal perfection by allowing into its inner textum, as it were, the Trojan horse of storytelling. Döblin's employment of the healing power of storytelling in this exile novel is not new but markedly exceeds its use in *Berlin Alexanderplatz*, where the story told by the red-bearded Jew has a certain tonic effect on the disoriented Franz Biberkopf.

Altogether underexposed by exile research remains Heinrich Mann's *Empfang bei der Welt* (*Reception with High Society;* 1941–1945). While Heinrich Mann felt reinvigorated by the manifold contacts he enjoyed with French writers and the international exiles in Paris, he greatly suffered from his isolation in the intellectual climate of his California exile. The novel, perhaps on purpose less than engaging reading, may reflect that predicament, as it exposes the "schöne Schein" (beautiful appearance) of aesthetic production as commercialized aestheticism. The author focuses on the (lacking) significance of the construction of an opera house by an uprooted, alienated elite. The members of high society live out their desires and neurotic quirks in a grotesquely opaque space of interiority that seems to have no identity and memory as to locale or historical time. It is in art— the opera house is constructed at the expense and exclusion of the common man—that one feels "at home." As Mann illuminates through a series of fragmented bizarre episodes, this feeling "at home" in a space of aesthetic seclusion is merely the flip side of one's intrigues against and exploitation of others, a continuation of estrangement with aestheticist, meaning empty, decorative means. If Thomas Mann referred to his brother's work as a curious form of "Greisenavantgardismus" (senile avant-gardism), he may not only have pointed to Heinrich Mann's advanced years or his work as a late "expressionist" critique of the age's lack of "Geist und Tat" (spirit and deed). "Senile avant-gardism," may this coinage by Thomas Mann, for lack of a proper concept, then, not perhaps point to what we today perceive as the late ahistorical mentality of a postmodern critique of conditions in which the aesthetic experience is always already entwined with, falsely sublated into a global (space- and timeless) commercialism? At any rate, the novels discussed here share in a refusal or inability to engage the concrete "local color" of the American exile, as the exiles found in their work a "refuge, in which they allowed the new world and language only to a degree."[50] Yet, as today's global experience has increasingly erased the uniqueness of "local color," their experience may also have adumbrated a world with diminishing identities, which is ours.

Nevertheless, distinctions within international postmodern developments still ought to be made on the basis of national cultures. As far as I know, literary and cultural criticism has not looked into this issue yet, at least not beyond the circumstance that the American brand of postmodernism was in direct reaction to popular culture cultivated in the terms of pop art. In the case at hand, one should at least take note of some basic distinguishing characteristics. Typically Heinrich Mann, the German exile in the 1940s, responded to the Californian experience by critiquing modernity from a still traceable point of view of a universalist idealism. Samuel

Beckett, the Irish exile on the war-torn European continent, shares some of this perspective, notwithstanding differences in the intensity of sarcasm, of absurdist phrasing and imaging. In both instances, notwithstanding differences in radicality, we witness a disposition of high modernist culture that has turned against itself, in a "postmodern" turn. While for the German émigrés, mandarins of European culture, American popular culture was all "Mickey Mouse," thus to be disregarded, an American author like Thomas Pynchon would later head-on and on the spot, of California as in *The Crying of Lot 49* (1966), engage the experience of a sprawling, anonymous multimedia popular culture that disseminates images by the millions, makes the image of "personalities," uproots identities, and effaces origins and originality. Pynchon would do all this—in a response to the anonymity of mass-produced popular culture—without supplying the reader a clue (much less so than Beckett) as to how to gauge affirmative reproduction or quotation from critical distancing, parody from pastiche.

Carl Einstein's novel *BEB II*, his long poem "Entwurf einer Landschaft" ("Design or Sketch of a Landscape"), and his treatise *Die Fabrikation der Fiktionen* written in the Parisian exile of the early 1930s represent the case of avant-garde writing that does not turn or return to a, as it were, "restorative" *moral* questioning of itself. By contrast to the novels discussed previously, Einstein's *BEB II* is a text that attempts to radically continue the *aesthetic* project of the avant-garde at the stage of its being severely put to question by extreme political developments that culminate in exile. It is a consciously experimental novel, a fragment of fragments, begun some time after the author's cultural *emigration* to Paris in 1928. Much of it was written before his departure to Spain in 1935, meaning at a stage where his emigration had turned into genuine political *exile*. Klaus Kiefer is the only critic so far who has attempted not only to "construct" a reading of this immensely heterogeneous text (at this point still unpublished) but also to establish its relations—fictive, not fictional, in terms of an "autobiographical pact"— to the exile period. His reading of the text ascertains as its most fundamental structure the "ambivalence of utopianism and thanatography."[51] Such a structure appears to correspond to the trajectory of the German avant-garde's visions from its heyday within the context of its national culture to the experience of exile. The protagonist's search to reconnect with the archaic mythical, premodern language and life-world of childhood as an original *home,* for example, reverts to the awareness that language is "totemistic," in other words, tribal.[52] Here it is quite significant that the text omits any identifiable reference to Einstein's early years in Berlin as it constructs the space of a premodern experience. In fact, it is most revealing that Einstein's BEB wakes up from the isolation of his utopian-archaic childhood dreams only when confronted with an event that takes place outside the realm of such interiority. A fragment of the text, dated January 31, 1934 (that is, two weeks after Hermann Göring's emigration edict), relates this awakening:

> BEB now understands that he had belonged for his entire life merely to a separate clique, that had fought itself in aesthetic vanity and desire for success; thus BEB had been, as he now sees, an emigrant for his whole life. his whole effort had been to be an emigrant, i.e. to be isolated and an exception. he always had been in flight of a binding milieu. he now understands to where one has ousted him.[53]

In other words, Einstein-BEB here self-critically exposes the avant-garde, and his participation in it, from its beginnings at the turn of the century, via expressionism to surrealism as a form of regressive "childhood dream." The reality of political exile reveals his "emigration" into the culture of the avant-garde as an escape into fictions ("[H]e had always been in flight of a binding milieu"). Thus his polemical treatise *Die Fabrikation der Fiktionen* will aim at a delivery from the realm of aesthetic "fictions," "narcissistic" and infantile," into the experience of political experience as action. In *BEB II,* such turning point is still addressed in the terms of a discourse that is shared by German expressionism, Italian futurism, and surrealism: that of the *apocalypse.* In its utopian-thanathographic structure, this exile text articulates the protagonist's awakening from a narcissistic preoccupation with the self toward the reflection of an epochal experience, the "demise of a generation" of isolated intellectuals. As a "roman von der wirkungslosigkeit des " 'geistes' " ([*sic*]; novel of the ineffectiveness of the spirit), it articulates the end of utopianism, a "collapse of a society" that had raised the aesthetic experience to the status of transcendental autonomy.

There is also something of an exile's "moral of the story" here that is tied to but goes beyond mere cognitive issues. Namely, Einstein criticizes the German avant-garde's "infantile regression" into poetic metaphors (Mss. 37) from the point of view of his writing in the radically "metamorphotic" terms of the surrealist experiment. The French avant-garde's "revolutionary" experiment with the unconscious/conscious relations of the human experience ("the immediate human being") is closer to life than German "literature":

[T]his is my danger: my writing does hardly stand in any relation to today's German literature; my figures are much sharper and more aggressive than that of the Germans. my thought and speaking wants to be revolutionary as far as the immediate human being is concerned. writing as metamorphosis and not conservation of types, forms of experience and conditions.[54]

Einstein criticizes "German literature" that as "literature" it conserves "types" (in the sense of expressionist drama, for instance) rather than constituting experience (*Erfahrung*). Thus this exile's adoption of the surrealist writing techniques of the host culture is altogether different from the majority exiles' attempts to save German traditions from corruption at home. Such "treason" does not, however, come without split feelings, as the Jewish German intellectual spotlights himself as a loner, gone astray, as it were, and he painfully accuses himself of a "willed" and "artificial" separation from his home (tribal) culture:

[T]he lamps shine over the one without connections; I avoided every relation and closeness. Now, however, everything is different. every willed separation was vain voluntarism and artificial; now, however, *I have been separated*. that is different.[55]

In these terms, the significance of the Parisian avant-garde for Walter Benjamin as a critic in "cultural emigration" and his ensuing separation from Berlin as political exile in Paris was quite comparable. Notwithstanding Einstein's and Benjamin's substantial epistemological differences, their production in Paris may have been, consciously or unconsciously, for a fictive "ideal reader"[56] who was neither "at home" nor really in exile. Benjamin's experience of writing in Paris, the city of his previous attempts to gain a productive distance from German culture, was a case of severest difficulties to continue the publication of his criticism, written in German, in German exile journals. There were the well-known difficulties with Klaus Mann (*Die Sammlung*), most importantly with the demands and ideological restrictions Adorno and Horkheimer made on his work for its publication by the Institute for Social Research from the safe exile in New York. There was little significant contact with French journals, instead the rejection of his essay on Bachofen by the *Nouvelle Revue* and the *Mercure de France,* and the critic had only spurious contacts to the Collège de Sociologie. And there was Benjamin's provocative attempt to place his essay "The Work of Art in the Age of Mechanical Reproduction" into the center of the cultural politics of the Popular Front, to have it published in *Das Wort,* well knowing that the exile journal in Moscow was dedicated to "leftist belles lettres."

Occasions like the 1935 International Writers' Congress in Paris, which for Heinrich Mann were events that stimulated a new sense of significance and identity in an international context, for minds like Einstein's and Benjamin's were further proof for the questionability of organized culture politics. Conference topics such as "Creative Questions and the Dignity of the Spirit," the theme for June 24, 1935, were anathema for Benjamin as for Einstein. For the critic, the total agreement with Brecht in the rejection of a humanist enterprise concerned with "creative questions" and the "dignity of the spirit" was "the most enjoyable—almost the only enjoyable—element of the event."[57] As he was writing on his *Passagenwerk* (*Arcades Project*) at the time, the liberal exiles' affirmation of the "spiritual" provoked the theorist to reflect on an extended project that would address, by contrast, the "fatal hour of art" in its "present form," a fathoming of the issue "from inside" the space of aesthetic production, "in avoidance of unmediated relation to politics."[58] In chapter 5, I will show that the question of the "fatal hour of art," the gist of his artwork essay, constituted a turn to the visual image against literary metaphorical language, including that of the avant-garde. Benjamin's and Einstein's developing doubts about the literary avant-garde's language as an aesthetics of resistance, let alone utopian anticipation, was certainly also a result of their exile experience. At the same time, these doubts about literary language connect with those that run like a critical current from Hofmannsthal's "Lord Chandos" letter to the impact of crisis film had on literary culture (as discussed in chapter 1).

The three case studies on Einstein, Benjamin, and Grosz and Brecht I offer later are little-discussed cases of a most pronounced *reversal* of long-standing, highly advanced avant-garde positions that culminate in a profound questioning, if not denial, of literary and, respectively, artistic culture. Grosz's political allegories also focused on the futility of aesthetic resistance and, in a series of paintings and sketches, the role of the artist and his "'outmoded' profession"[59] even before events like the Hitler-Stalin pact of 1939 that shook Benjamin to the core. For his part, Grosz, the visual artist, began to doubt the artistic image as a politically effective sign. His "Painter of the Hole" (1948) questioned the paradigm of art as a political weapon from an existential point of view, pointing to the absurdity of political experience and aesthetic reactions to it. His growing skepticism ultimately clashed with Brecht's dialectical attempts to refunction and reconstruct meaning from the experience of political crisis and exile. Though the exile Brecht was no less isolated and ineffectual within the American scene, his personality, his internationalist Marxist project, and his plans of a return to Germany at the earliest possible moment made him immune to the doubts of other exiles.

In sum, I agree with Wulf Koepke's and Michael Winkler's assessment that exile writers did not seek "in the beautiful semblance of art a refuge free from politics,"[60] even if they turned to conservative forms such as the sonnet or novella. Writing in exile was, indeed, more often than not, a question of a "consolidation or taking back the two previous decades." But there obviously are, beyond continued stalwart avant-garde writing in case of Arendt or Lasker-Schüler, some radical exceptions to such typology; these stay avant-garde while they question the avant-garde. More than most of the other cases here discussed, they most drastically underscore the significance of exile literature for the study of the complex modernism, avant-garde, and postmodernism.

In the conclusion of his essay on Broch's "negative aesthetics" as a paradigm for the exiled "avant-garde in crisis," Paul Michael Lützeler wrote that "the history of German speaking literature of the avant-garde in our century with its discontinuities and crises when literature and politics intersected in Dadaism, the literature of exile and that of the student movement requires a consideration of the negative-aesthetics aspects in a—yet to be written—comprehensive work on aesthetics."[61] My own study as a history of "constellations," and "moments" of the avant-garde in crisis, from expressionism, Dada, via Einstein's, Grosz's, and Benjamin's literary, artistic, and critical activities in exile to Helmut Heißenbüttel, and Hans Magnus Enzensberger before, during, and after the student revolt in the late 1960s and early 1970s, appears to go a ways in that direction. At the same time, it seems to me, a "comprehensive work on aesthetics" in an extreme sense of a "negative aesthetics" cannot be written. This is so as even the most radical "anti-art" stance, be it that of Dada, of Broch, George Grosz, "the painter of the hole's" painting the beautiful "grey in grey," with the possible, yet qualified exception of the development of Carl Einstein's writings in exile, cannot be "negative," if understood as tending conclusively toward an "end of art." My findings seem to indicate that we will not see the displacement of art by politics, as Einstein envisioned and Enzensberger held decades later at the height of the student rebellion; by philosophy, in Hegel's terms; or by theory, in Fredric Jameson's view. Instead, we will witness mutations and further developments of what Adorno addressed as the avant-garde's continuous dialectical negation of any consensus about art in its productions as "fragments." In this sense, a review of German avant-garde writing in exile, of a crisis of the avant-garde torn, if not split, between relinquishing its project in favor of traditional literary forms as politically timely moral discourses of dissent and a radicalization of its antiaesthetic strategies, may result in an understanding of the *concretely historical* premises for *specific* developments in *German* literature and art which we today address as *postmodern* developments. After all, these are conditions in which the notion of "art" has become destabilized, the subject of continuous renegotiations, discussions about its "affirmative" or continued critical character. Specifically German developments are, of course, *not unique* developments as their significance extends beyond the exile period, before and after, where they meet and blend with the wider developments of twentieth-century European modernism and the avant-garde (see the evaluative summary of chapter 8). Even before political exile, the Berlin dadaists' political radicalism and the technological aspects of Weimar culture pointed to the erosion of the singular, privileged status of literary culture, as we have seen at the beginning of this chapter. And in the wider terms of the history of Western culture, the modernist writer has increasingly become aware of the precarious nature of poetic production as an always already late, epigonal creativity for which the experience of "originality" has vanished with a growing sense that what is left is a form of "copying and interpretation of that which may once have been original," a continued creativity against increasing odds.[62] Nevertheless, a review of the German avant-garde from the 1910s to the late 1970s, with a special focus on its period in exile, would assure that a concept such as the *postmodern,* which is often treated from philosophical and theoretical vantage points that have generated among valid concepts also quite nebulous assumptions, could—at least in the arena of German avant-garde developments—be quite poignantly reassessed on the level of historical research.

Certain historical constellations can be selected, constructed, and understood as critical constellations, critical in a twofold manner. The critical constellations chosen here reveal the agon of discourses reaching pivotal points, crisis moments tending toward a resolution in the alternative paradigm of a "negative aesthetics." Second, by way of their extreme positioning, they permit a critical hermeneutical review of the function of traditional as well as avant-garde literary and artistic texts. They appear to rupture the privileged literary discourse toward collective political action (Carl Einstein), to break with metaphorical subjectivity (*Erlebnis*) toward the tactile intersubjective metonymy of the mechanically reproduced visual image (Walter Benjamin), or to abandon a belief in the political/moral value of art in the medium of art (George Grosz). In all instances, however, we are dealing with subjective projections of a crisis demanding a radical "resolution" rather than with objective conditions of closure. As such they retain their significance beyond the experience of exile.

4. The Self-Effacement of the Avant-Garde Author, or The Metamorphosis of Surrealist Myth into Action

Carl Einstein and the Anarchist Movement
during the Spanish Civil War, 1936–1937

The last decade has seen a spectacular surge in literary and art historical criticism concerning the once nearly forgotten poet and critic Carl Einstein.[1] He was rediscovered in the early 1960s by the "experimental" writer Helmut Heißenbüttel, who saw in his late work a "turning point" from the modernist embrace of the vision of a complete aesthetic world to a painful awareness of the emptying out of its fulfillment into mere signs[2] (which I will further discuss in my last chapter). I will here focus on this *turning point* in the context of Einstein's political experience in the 1930s that reveals the contradictory, agonistic and agonizing, nature of changes in literary and critical insights, which we scholars usually tend to address as an abstract process. His work still poses a challenge, not only because of its difficult theoretical underpinnings (and, as we shall see, often irritating, idiosyncratic critical terminology) but also due to its extraordinary reach. His oeuvre extends from the very beginning of the German expressionist *Kunstrevolution* (art revolution) to the very end of a politicized European avant-garde before World War II. Participating in the expressionist movement, Berlin Dada, as we recall from the previous chapters, thereafter in

Paris associated with surrealism, Einstein contributed to all major phases of the avant-garde. As a critic and theoretician of the *avant-garde* in literature and the visual arts, his range surpasses that of Benjamin and Adorno, whose major criticism primarily deals with high modernism.

Among the numerous topics that still need to be examined more closely is Einstein's active commitment to the anarchist cause in the Spanish Civil War. It calls for further scrutiny for a fuller understanding of the relation of the avant-garde to political activism in exile, which had an enormous impact on the writers' and artists' assumptions and on their aesthetic production.[3] Einstein's written contribution to the cause of Spain was modest, as he himself had previously (in the early 1930s) downgraded the artist's role in the course of a revolution. He wrote an obituary speech, broadcast by Radio Barcelona in November 1936 (published in German in *Die Neue Weltbühne*, December 10, 1936), in commemoration of the anarchist leader Buenaventura Durruti, who had been shot on the twenty-first of the month in the fight for the Casa de Campo at the University of Madrid. There is also an activist report on "Die Front von Aragon" (*Die Soziale Revolution*, 1937), in which he calls for the support of the anarchist revolutionaries at Zaragoza, who by that time were forsaken even by their own major organizations. On the surface, these documents read like mere political propaganda; as such they will not speak to today's reader. Yet they retain the traces of a grand surrealist vision. Once these features are recognized, the texts point to the dilemma that the intellectual faces when attempting efface himself in collective action.

To understand this issue better, we must determine whether there was indeed a stable continuity between the "quasi-anarchistic moments in Einstein's thought [as] the result of his epistemological insights" and the activities of the anarcho-syndicalist in Spain. I agree with Jochen Schulte-Sasse's assessment that Einstein's anarchist position "cannot be simply dismissed with an exclusively political critique of anarchism,"[4] but for quite different reasons. To my understanding, the anarchist activist is no longer informed by the "deconstructive rhetorical strategy" that characterizes the main body of his poetic and theoretical work. As a militia man and political journalist committed to a highly isolated and militarily precarious anarchist cause, he is led, in my view, to a *nostalgic* vision of "primitive" communal experience.

In my view, Einstein's commitment to political anarchism in Spain breaks with his previous critique of cultural and social modernity that can indeed be understood as symptomatic of "an early transformation of modernism into postmodernism."[5] His *Die Fabrikation der Fiktionen*, written around 1933, did provide insight into the cultural assimilation of even the most subversive avant-garde discourses. Such insight does characterize a postmodernist reaction to modernity; Einstein's ardent demand for a *sacrifice* of art for the sake of communal priorities does not fit such assessment, however. His call for a *social* "production of the real" in *Die Fabrikation der Fiktionen* can be understood neither as a postmodern premise nor as a tenet of the historical avant-garde whose aim was, after all, a reintegration of the aesthetic experience, if not an *Aufhebung* (sublation) of art into communal experience.

Moreover, the angry rhetoric of Einstein's monumental, manifesto-like polemic against modernism *and* the avant-garde always undermines its own analytical argument through contradictions. Nowhere in this treatise does he critique the "real," the principles of the capitalist system or, on the other hand, those of organized communism from a socioeconomic point of view, as one would have to assume. It would be an exaggeration to say that the failure of the avant-garde, which Einstein addresses in *Die Fabrikation der Fiktionen,* necessarily results in a "materialist turn,"[6] since he did not develop a consistent position. It would also require taking Einstein's polemic *Die Fabrikation der Fiktionen* as his last word on the subject. One would have to regard Einstein's treatise *Georges Braque* (written 1931–1932, published 1935, in a French translation) on surrealist myth as the "real" as completely overruled by the text that he must have begun to write within a year. But Einstein's texts never *end* that way; they have a way of returning in different forms, openly or in disguise, and they are never free of contradictions, as we shall see. For example, in 1933 Einstein was still staging an exhibit on Georges Braque in Basel. In the exhibition catalog he wrote: "These paintings are based on nothing that would lie outside of painting" (*W* 3:178).[7] In other words, he there still maintained a position of aesthetic autonomy.

As I will show in detail in this chapter, Einstein's treatise *Georges Braque* embraced surrealism as the production of the "real" in mythical form: Myth *is* "the real." In the sense that "the real" is myth, he began to advocate action as a primordial event requiring no justification beyond itself. His embrace of "pure" action will mark his subsequent activities in Spain and the activist texts he wrote as a member of the anarchist brigade.[8] These activist writings, I maintain, constitute a shift of his "surrealist" discourse into lived communal experience. As never before, Einstein here absolutizes action for action's sake. In terms of Einstein's life, *this* was his last stance (in 1940 he committed suicide at the Spanish border under the same circumstance as Walter Benjamin).

The attempt to consider Einstein's previous critique of modernism and social modernity together with those of Brecht and Benjamin as "one of the most consistent models of a leftist-radical, grass-roots democratic theory of art to date"[9] is tempting, but it also remains open to discussion. Instead, Einstein's criticism is, indeed, more significant for an understanding of the arts in a process of an "early transformation," thus not equivocal, shifting of modernist to postmodernist conditions. As there was no contact between Einstein and Brecht, there is no documentation of any communication between Einstein and Benjamin during the exile in Paris, although they could have at least met through the circle surrounding Georges Bataille, to which both maintained relations.[10] But that is not the point here. More interesting are the differences between Einstein's and Benjamin's positions, which I will address subsequently as much as pertinent. A comparison with Benjamin's positions on the avant-garde[11] will make clear that Einstein's writings after 1930 were very much part of a crisis of the arts, as he was a poet and not only a critic, who reacted much more spontaneously to the whirlwind of fast-moving political developments. Benjamin's critical theory of the avant-garde in the late 1920s and 1930s, by contrast, was an integral part of a long-standing epistemological project to critique the organic work of art (fully discussed in chapter 5).

My account of the transition of the anarcho-individualist, expressionist poet and essayist to the anarcho-syndicalist stance he adopted in Spain focuses on his outsider status that led to exile. The former Spartacus affiliate and leader of the revolutionary councils in occupied, wartime Brussels had left Berlin for Paris already in 1928. His study of European modern art, *Die Kunst des 20. Jahrhunderts,* published by the prestigious Propyläen Verlag (Berlin, 1926), was a culminating achievement of the art critic and theorist, granting him immediate international recognition. The German Left regarded Einstein as the rightful successor to the prominent art historian and theorist Wilhelm Hausenstein, who, in the course of the war, had abandoned his previous political sympathies. Nevertheless, Einstein chose voluntary exile in reaction to censorship and public attacks on himself and his friends and collaborators, John Heartfield and George Grosz. A major scandal was his trial and conviction for blasphemy stemming from his play *Die Schlimme Botschaft (Calamitous Tidings),* a devastating satire of what he perceived to be the reactionary mentality of Weimar Germany.[12]

Einstein's years in Paris were outwardly very productive and successful. It was here that he was to consolidate an international reputation with his essays in art criticism, the subjects of which ranged from French cubism and sculpture to the art of the nomads in Central Asia. Until 1933, Einstein maintained close contact with his intellectual friends in the German capital through correspondence and travel. Hitler's rise to power, however, closed the doors to the German Jew and leftist activist. At this point, the poet Carl Einstein realized that he had been shut out from his real home—the German language. He bemoans his loss in a self-revealing entry in his diary on January 18, 1933:

> I realize I will always be alone. A German-speaking Jew in France, a Jew without God and without knowledge of our past; German-speaking, yet not like my countrymen willing to let the German language go to rot, lazily and tired. In France that means without readers. From now on, I will briefly converse with myself every day; for a long time I have been totally cut off from people and books in my language, never will I be at home in French literature, because I dream and ponder in German. Thus I have been condemned by Hitler to a total loss of home and to estrangement.[13]

The outsider and exile, barred from his native country for his political views and his Jewishness, apparently had not found a home in France, either. An exception was his relation to Eugene Jolas, editor of *transition. An International Quarterly for Creative Experiment,* the journal that published James Joyce's *Finnegans Wake* in serial form and for which the "advisory editor" Einstein recommended seminal texts by Benn, Sternheim, and Kafka for translation into English. In *Man from Babel,* his autobiography (which has finally been published, nearly half a century after its fragmentary conclusion), Jolas wrote about Einstein's assessment of the German conditions around the mid-1920s:

> He felt that a new and dangerous jingoism was coming up in Germany and that the "Prussian spirit was not dead." "Expressionism was the last form of the human equation in German," he said. . . . He did not believe, however, that the racist infantilism of the nascent Nazi movement would ever triumph. "The German is organically ambivalent," he would say. "Sentimentalism and power lust are in him in equal portions; but there are still a few humanists left who will prevent the Teuton berserk spirit from getting the upper hand. Even Thomas Mann, whom I do not like, as you know, will have enough influence over the young writers to stop the evolution towards military nationalism."
>
> Einstein, Hans Arp and myself spent hours in Einstein's book-

cluttered studio near the Boulevard de Grenelle, talking about poetry in the German language. Einstein was determined to launch a cry of revolt against what he called the "Fichte spirit" among the German poets then writing on the other side of the Rhine.[14]

Apart from such contacts with like-minded writers of a split national identity—both Jolas and Arp grew up in the "borderlands" of Lorraine and Alsace, respectively, and experienced the conflict between two cultures and languages creatively before embarking on their international "educational travels" and delivering their "regional" experiences and energies to the metropolis—Einstein stayed relatively isolated even after 1933. He seemed to have sought no significant relationship with the international antifascist front and the exile organizations.[15] This is striking indeed, since even the highly eccentric Georges Bataille, with whom he had edited the unique journal *Documents. Archéologie, Beaux-Arts, Ethnographie, Variétés* (Paris 1929–1930), had involved himself, however briefly and inconsistently, as the founder of the antifascist organization Contre-Attaque (Counterattack).

In Berlin, Einstein had had a closer intellectual relationship with Gottfried Benn. Throughout his life, Benn would virtually revere Einstein as the foremost critical genius of expressionism—in spite of the growing divergence in their ethics and politics.[16] In turn Einstein's theoretical study *Georges Braque* still displayed a great deal of affinity to the aesthetics of Benn's *Ausdruckswelt* (world of expression). In spite of attempts to distinguish his views from the poet's view of "absolute" art (*W* 3:189), Einstein's advocacy of surrealism's "hallucinatory" dimension marked a certain convergence of his and Benn's aesthetics, as affirmed by the significance which Jolas attributed to the latter's work for *transition*'s "Revolution of the Word."[17]

We here witness a basic ambiguity inherent in the avant-garde's aesthetic discourses in relation to the political domain. Both writers share a pronounced extremism that leads them to a growing sense of isolation and subsequently to a desire for reintegration; the differences are ultimately ideological. In 1933, Benn embraces the National Socialist myth of the "Volk" in a veritable salto mortale. For him, the rise of National Socialism was the epoch's inevitable "mutation" toward a "new biological type."[18] Nevertheless, he claims for art and the artist a suprahistorical autonomy that would give his essays of the period from 1933 to 1934 an "inner" authority for an *aestheticization* of fascist politics. Einstein, on the other hand, intends to turn Braque's surrealist myths against the solipsism of Benn's "späte Ich" (the self as a late development; $W$3:224). He views Braque's surrealist myths as the *final* expression of subjective creativity at the breaking point. At that point, art is said to "metamorphose" into a "primitive" collective experience. Hence Einstein's concept of "metamorphosis" and Benn's notion of "mutation" are equally problematic; both return to a biological model of change. Both writers thus displace the analytical episteme of modernity with visions of a discontinuous epochal turn toward "primitive" social organisms. "Urbilder,"[19] "archaic images" are the source for imagining and imaging the "new man" at the stage of a fundamental historical change.

Georges Braque: Myth as Reality

With the treatise *Georges Braque,* Einstein begins to abandon his early understanding of the avant-garde as deconstructing the subject-object dualism of modern rationalism *within* aesthetic discourse. His position had been that the avant-garde would uncover the "mythical in the present" without relapsing into "an atavism."[20] *Georges Braque* is a very late espousal of surrealism. The theoretical treatise disqualifies the movement's Marxist position as based on a "narrow" concept of reality as "economic reality"(W 3:198). Contrary to Breton's and subsequently Benjamin's concept of surrealism developed in his 1929 essay on the movement, Einstein proposes a surrealism without political alliance.[21] Instead he attempts to privilege the "work of art as a living force and practical tool" ($W$3:187). The essay discards traditional art as an "aesthetically isolated phenomenon" that in the liberalist era is said to have degenerated into a pluralism of multiple styles without collective significance. The essay also disqualifies, in implicit reference to Aragon, who had defected from surrealism, "proletarian art" because of its "antiquated rational methods" ($W$3:209). Italian futurism is criticized as a movement that idolizes technology and worships the modern state. For Einstein, Braque's surrealism thus is the most advanced aesthetic position. In going beyond the formal experimentation of French cubism, it uncovers tangible "visual myths" ($W$3:204) that arise from the dissolution of the subject. The painter's surrealist images, in Einstein's view, are mythical "images" that virtually embody "practically effective energies and facts" ($W$3:206), as they explode the subjective "fictions" and "metaphors" of autonomous art. For the critic, they are the result of a dialectic that begins with the "psychogram" of the artist's "private myth." From there the painter proceeds to externalize the depths of a "primal chaos" as "dictation" by the collective unconscious. In Einstein's idiosyncratic terminology, the surrealist image thus is defined as a "dialectical organism" ($W$3:236). In other words, it is seen as the result of a spontaneous fusion of a subjective *vision* with images surging from the unconscious, thus "dictating" the content, if not the form, of the experience. As an *organic* complex, it *disallows* individual conscious-ness's function to parry, absorb, and suppress the "shocks" that arise from the surfacing of the collective unconscious ($W$3:204, 339). As a "*dialectical* organism," the surrealist image jars a historicist absorption of its "archaic" energies by projecting these energies toward a collective experience of the future ($W$3:212). Braque's surrealist "production of reality" ($W$3:206), in Einstein's view, thus *bypasses* the rationalist structures of modernity. From its beginning in the quasi-seismographic registration of a solipsistic, "pri-vate" vision ("psychogram") that provokes, evokes, and merges with the "primal chaos" within, the surrealist "production of reality" thus takes place in a space of rift and *rupture* from the reality constructed by consciousness and rationality as the *outer*. Critically assessed, Einstein here endorses the total displacement of outer experience, rejected as an overwhelming false construct, with a virtually overwhelming inner experience. Hence Einstein's organic vision of the surrealist image is, in spite of some similarities in terms of the rejection of subjective *metaphorical* language, after all, fundamentally different from Benjamin's view of surrealism. Benjamin carefully analyzed collective experience as a matter of the relation of language, *image* (versus abstract *metaphor*) and physis, the bodily, to the experience of the subject, of the masses in the midst of modernity, in the city of Paris, within its his-torical structures and political movements (see chapter 5). His construct of the surrealist "dialectical image" takes great pains to reflect on the relation of conscious versus involuntary memory in terms that insist on a *media-tion* of subjective experience (*Erlebnis*) with intersubjective experience (*Er-fahrung*). Benjamin attempts to link his critique of consciousness with a critique of political modernity, surrealist writing to communist activities, not to speak of his messianic concept of time, so different from Einstein's socially unmediated vision of fulfillment. In terms of the political implica-tions—after all, these are the early 1930s—Einstein's avant-garde project is as blunt as all visions of spontaneous change. He welcomes in surrealism outright "the beginning of an epoch of primitivism, even barbarism" (*W* 3:209). Such an assessment brings him closer to Gottfried Benn's visions of a "new order" than to anyone else's. Clearly, Einstein was much more fascinated by the surrealist vision as the "primitive" per se than Benjamin, who was concerned with its aesthetic as political potential within modernity (however problematic and questionable at that).

Given the precarious relation of Einstein's epistemology to social experience, it is by no means incomprehensible that the critic who had just finished *Georges Braque* would respond to the Nazis' rise to power by turning around in order to liquidate the significance of art altogether. His *Die Fabrikation der Fiktionen* was tantamount to an auto-dafé of modern art as such. The polemic was a complete reversal of his long-standing enthusiastic support for the avant-garde, of his advocacy of cubism, of the Russian futurists, *and* of surrealism. Einstein now perceives at the core of the modernist *and* avant-garde projects merely the legitimization of "bourgeois" culture. The avant-garde, in fact, is in the way of the "production of the real." It, too, is nothing but fiction. It falsely claims "anonymous forces of individual hallucinations" without establishing a "link between the work of art and communal experience" in "action" (*FF* 316).[22] After all, "hallucination, dream, or the unconscious can *only* be articulated in the medium of signs" (*FF* 303; my emphasis), he writes. Such dismissal of aesthetic productions as "only . . . signs" obviously must pertain also to his own previous Braque exegesis. The polemic treatise thus is a total critique of modernist culture: "Modernism contains within itself romantic chiliasm. One believes in the better, more imaginative human being who can oppose reality and disprove it." Modernism is now rejected as a "rejection of the real" (*FF* 24). The "hallucinatory" energies of its discourses, which Einstein still valued in the final instance of Braque, now are nothing but "atavistic romanticism . . . counterfeit modernism" (*FF* 227).

Einstein's polemic thus constitutes a spontaneous *reversal* in interpretation; it is not a dialectical reassessment of the avant-garde in the sense of Benjamin's reappraisal of Dada and surrealism in favor of Brecht's epic theater or of film. In fact, Einstein's moves are also emotional, hence also paradoxical, reactions to political crisis. As *Die Fabrikation der Fiktionen* alludes to the surge of National Socialism since 1930, a significant portion must have been written in disillusioned response to Hitler's triumph in 1933. Nevertheless, Einstein does not further analyze the relation of specific avant-garde movements such as Italian futurism or German expressionism to fascism, as Benjamin does at the time. Instead, his reaction to the failure of the avant-garde is totalizing. It also reflects personal experience.

Not by chance, the bitter polemic coincided with his despair over the demise of his own creativity as a poet. Einstein had been obsessed with attempts to reproduce the cubist and surrealist experiments in the visual arts in the medium of literary language. However, *BEB II,* an epistemo-logical experiment to go beyond the transcendental problematics of his early "novel" *Bebuquin* (1907–1909), intended to explore the openness of decentered, hence intersubjective, experience within the medium of lan-guage (signs), had failed. This meant the end of his own literary produc-tion and the beginning of his turning against the avant-garde as such. His last poem is "Entwurf einer Landschaft" ("Design of a Landscape"; 1930); I will return to a full discussion of the poem's significance for Helmut Heißenbüttel's "experimental" writing in the 1960s in my last chapter. "Entwurf einer Landschaft" articulated a deep-seated despair about the total "blindness" of the language of art, disallowing an articulation of the self (as in these lines translated by his friend Eugene Jolas, the editor of *transition*): "You fade away into icy cloud / Of narrow grammar / Stum-bling hunted / in swindling / Word stealing from you / Rope over bottom-less sea / Of sentiment."[23] A 1931 diary entry concerning his poetic work reads: "Finis—a poem."[24] A corresponding statement in the contemporary polemic itself condemns the avant-garde's attempts to deconstruct indi-vidual toward intersubjective experience. They are nothing but the fabrica-tion of "dream-collectives for the elite"(*FF* 272).

The polemic *Die Fabrikation der Fiktionen* in its rhetoric of repetition, its sarcastic tenor, and moody digressions therefore is also the document of dis-appointment. Anger (an affect far from any postmodern indifference) tinges its critical argument, which comes in two moves. The first is a critique of the always already assimilated status of avant-garde discourse. As such, the argument represents, indeed, a "postmodernist" point of view. However, the second strategy, dominant toward the end of the treatise, constitutes a distinct break from the first; it shifts to privileging a social construct of reality as "action." Apart from allusions, however, neither "action" nor social "reality" are defined anywhere in the book. In these parts, *Die Fabrikation der Fiktionen* can thus appropriately be considered a radical expression of a *post-avant-garde* crisis that responds to rupture with rupture.

Einstein writes that once having surrendered its subjective, "magic" sig-nificance ("aura" in Benjamin's terminology), art will retain merely a "mod-est" socializing function in a postrevolutionary era:

> A new *spiritual style* is possible only after a revolution which creates changed social facts and has brought forth other human types. The intel-lectuals must regain a sense for useful cooperation and surrender the utopia of an aesthetically perfect yet non-purposive activity. . . . The

foremost goal is to destroy the dictatorship of individualistic fictions and to bring about the *primacy of action* and factual processes . . . Within this project, art can regain its place when it modestly participates in the production of a new reality. (*FF* 326f.; my emphasis)

Emphasizing "the primacy of action and factual processes," Einstein thus turns—more abruptly than Benjamin does in any of his writings—against the tradition of artistic culture that the Braque treatise had stretched to its limits. His definitive answer to Benn, who had defined poetry as an absolute "monologue," an essential voice of an autonomous historical process, now is: "Monological poetry is finished" (*FF* 327).

On occasion, *Die Fabrikation der Fiktionen* addresses practical issues, such as the "Gebrauchswert" (use value) of art in a revolutionary society. But contrary to Brecht, whose term he uses, he does not see much "use value" left for aesthetic expressions. The communal newspaper, for example, will replace individual creativity as the so-called literati become "writers" in the collective interest—an argument he will restate verbatim in his speech "Die Kolonne Durruti" a few years later. At points like these, Einstein does engage in a "demystification of art," which Benjamin focused on, beginning with his essay on "The Political Grouping of Soviet Writers" (1927). It is Benjamin, however, who in the wake of his interest in the work of Brecht (with whom Einstein never had any relation) articulated a developed critique of production and reception processes. Only after a carefully argued turn to the mass media of newspaper and film did Benjamin critique Dada and surrealism as surpassed. Einstein, on the other hand, here rejects the modernist and avant-garde tradition wholesale and without much ado. In Einstein's revolutionary society, the newspaper is to have a direct "factual" function, which Benjamin formulates much more specifically as a *dialectic* between writing and reading, where the reader may become a writer at any time (*GS* 2:688). Mass media like radio or film typically do not play any role at all in Einstein's writings. His critique of the "bourgeoisie" thus always remains a critique of its aesthetic culture. His rhetoric is of a Marxist provenance, yet, typically, it recalls more of Rimbaud's turning his back on art. In fact, what he writes in *Die Fabrikation der Fiktionen* about Rimbaud turning away from art toward a life of action can be understood as a commentary on his own position: "Poem and adventure for him meant one and the same—namely a means for social freedom. The contemplative revolt failed, because it was isolated. Rimbaud understood the senselessness of artistic revolt, thus he was through with art" (*FF* 114). In Spain, Einstein will scoff at "les littérateurs . . . avec leur Rimbaud" (the literary writers . . . with their Rimbaud),[25] because he now felt himself an active part of a community in action.

At the Front in Aragon

In 1936 Einstein joined the cause for Spain and became a member of Durruti's column and the general's staff. "Die Kolonne Durruti" (1937), Einstein's penultimate published testimony, advances the anarchist's exemplary conduct of self-effacing leadership as a timely model for the leadership of the writer: "Durruti, this exceptionally objective man, never talked about himself, his own person. He had banned the prehistorical word 'I' from grammar. The column Durruti only knows a collective syntax. The comrades will teach the literati to renew grammar in a collective sense" (*W* 3:459). Einstein here redefines "bourgeois" history as prehistory; the new era is the result of the self's surrender to the collective. The leader Durruti was "self-less," as it were: he "never talked about himself, his own person." Thus the military leader is said to set an example for the intellectual as well. As the anarchist leader "banned the prehistorical word 'I' from grammar," language is realized as a "collective syntax." The subjectivity of the "bourgeois" literati *erased* (not mediated), the intellectual thus becomes an integral part of collective action. In *Die Fabrikation der Fiktionen*, too, Einstein had addressed the relation of thinking, writing, and action in terms that canceled the difference and distance of reflection. Thus, for example, he had idiosyncratically interpreted Lenin's writings as generating a spontaneous activism: "This man had understood that it was not a matter of an intellectual problem which would have to be theoretically jacked up. He worked out the Communist formula so stringently and unequivocally that it guaranteed at the right moment instant action" (*FF* 43). Einstein's antirationalist impulse here and elsewhere in the treatise saw in "reflection . . . merely a *transition* between a situation and an action through which alternative conditions are enforced" (*FF* 217; my emphasis). As a *transition*, Lenin's communist formula thus is a formulaic sketch which is instantaneously absorbed in *action*, apparently without residue.

In terms of the relationship of Einstein's treatise on Georges Braque to his auto-dafé of modern art, the writer at the crossroads of art in its final stage and the beginning of total politics appears to have taken an unequivocal turn toward the latter. Yet the anarchist artist in the anarchist militiaman, submerged in "action and factual processes," cannot be as easily displaced in reality as in theory. Einstein's obituary speech for Durruti draws, after all, albeit in traces, on the notion of a "production of the real" as advanced in the treatise on Braque's surrealism. The treatise had envisioned a "meta-morphotic" coalescence of art and the social life-forms: "Myth has been reintegrated into reality, and poetry becomes an original element of the real" (*W* 3:341), Einstein had written. Hence we can assess also Durruti's (alias Braque's) "self [as] expanded toward a metamorphotic person." As the rational self has been dissolved in the experience of a "comprehensive reality" (*W* 3:327ff.), the "prehistorical I" has vanished and given expression to a "new collective syntax." In other words, Durruti's new syntax has replaced the "weak metaphors" (*W* 3:338) of the "literati." The anarchist experience articulates "a totally changed selection of history" (*W* 3:341).

Only when the political situation reveals its precarious, unstable utopian/dystopian character with the death of the charismatic Durruti on November 21, 1936, does Einstein emerge from action, become a *writer* again, a speechwriter. His obituary address rejects the attempts by the government of the socialist Caballero (since September 1936) to reintegrate the anarchist militias into the discipline of the Republican army. And it repudiates the subsequent turn against the revolutionary collectivization of industry and agriculture. Einstein reiterates the fundamental anarchist dogma of the Confederación National del Trabajo and the Federación Anarquista Ibérica (National Work Confederation and Iberian Anarchist Federation), CNT-FAI: "War and revolution for us are a single, inseparable act." His speech thus identifies the meaning of the new "collective syntax," the new "grammar in a collective sense," as *performance* in action: "Others may discuss in select and abstract terms. The column Durruti only knows *action,* and *in action* we learn. We are simple empiricists and believe that *action* fosters clearer insights than a scaled program that evaporates in the force of *deeds* "(*W* 3:459; my emphasis).

The question, of course, is what Einstein means by a "simple empiricism" of "action." In the context of Durruti's anarchist column, "primacy of action" means, very concretely, expropriation of private property: "Wherever the column penetrates, collectivization occurs" (*W* 3:461). Yet, Einstein's speech goes beyond the pragmatics of the CNT's political statement:

> The earth is given to the community, the country proletarians are being changed from bondsmen of the kazikes to free human beings. One *metamorphoses* from country feudalism to free Communism. (*W* 3:461; my emphasis)

This statement clearly transcends any empiricist understanding of "factual processes" (*FF* 327). Rather, Einstein interprets the column Durruti as an "organic" unity (*W* 3:460) — as a "dialectical organism" in the terms of the Braque essay, as it were. The key for understanding Einstein's speech obviously lies in the (surrealist) code word "metamorphose." The statement is tinged with traces of the Braque essay, as it implies a "metamorphic" identity of "action," "the earth" (rather than concretely "land"), "community," and "free human beings." In other words, while seemingly speaking about facts in the manner of *Die Fabrikation der Fiktionen,* the text engages in a reconstruction of a mythical dimension. It identifies myth with the "real" in terms of the *Georges Braque* essay.

Underlying such vision of a "metamorphic" unity is Einstein's understanding of action as an unmediated form of a life process (*Vorgang*) endowed with a unique aura. For the critic of Braque, the "aura of an event" (*W* 3:339) had found its immediate expression in the subject's "psychogram" (*W* 3:340). For the militiaman, authenticity reveals itself in Durruti's direct action. All other forms of experience are merely derivative temporal forms (*W* 3:191). He thus envisions the new era as a nonmetaphorical, in that sense nonliterary, nontemporal "original" event. The experience of that *moment* is defined as the lived experience of "human freedom." Einstein thus addresses in existentialist terms what Benjamin had objected to as the "humanistic concept of freedom" in the epistemological, albeit ultimately messianic terms of his 1929 essay on surrealism. The essay had envisioned the surrealist experience of the "image/body realm" coalescing with communist action at a moment of complete liberation.

Einstein's long-standing abhorrence "of rationalist Communism [as] only a continuation of rational capitalism,"[26] of the communist proletariat as "rationalist primitives" (*W* 3:198), is unequivocally based on a nostalgic counterstance against social modernity. It is his principally "expressionist" mentality that refuses to view poverty as an economic issue. Already his essay "Der Arme" ("The Poor,"1912) had elevated social disadvantage — in pronounced opposition to the reformist program of the Social Democrats — to the status of an existential experience. As human beings, the have-nots, undetermined by social possessions, are beyond the concepts of "rich" and "poor," thus open to the *Wunder* (miracle) of life as such (*W* 1:131). Such visions of immediate experience extend to the militiaman's utopianism. Indeed, Einstein's belief in the liberating force of pure action resembles a faith in religious salvation.[27]

The rejection of abstract concepts for the sake of "primitive" experience

(W 3:341) has a long history in Einstein's work. It goes back to his treatise *Negerplastik* (*Negro Sculpture;* 1914–1915). This theoretical study had been his first attempt to recuperate and upgrade the "primitive" as subverting modern rationalism. Typical of the contemporaneous debate on modernity, involving thinkers as disparate as Wilhelm Hausenstein and Ernst Bloch, he, too, had conducted his arguments on the aesthetic level rather than in sociological terms. His critique had targeted the perspective in the visual arts as a rationalist construct of seeing. The "cubist" deconstructive creation of an experiential, visual "totality" of "successive differences" (W 1:257), informed by the *particular* rather than by the subject's projection of the unity of parts, was to be the antidote against modern rationalism. In the early 1930s, Einstein begins to project his antimodern view onto economic and political forms. In a lecture on "Probleme gegenwärtiger Kunst" ("Problems of Contemporary Art"; 1931), he views socialist movements as a positive expression of an age of a general "Primitivierung" ("primitivization," W 3:582). However, he does not specify how the deconstructive energies of "primitive" art could be retained and work in the modern social sphere. Here, too, Einstein is much more concerned with *attacking* the "bourgeois" institutions.

In his last published essay, "Die Front von Aragon" ("The Front from Aragon"; 1937), Einstein restates his rejection of the aesthetic experience as "art." He defines the "bourgeois" ideal of art as a decorative, ornamental device, criminally masking the vested "colonizing" interests of democratic culture as humanism:

> The "great" democracies hope that Spain as they, these exemplary states, will form a moderate democracy which allows the reconstruction of a subtler colonizing capitalism. (While the Italians and Germans try to rob clumsily and openly; their imperialism is the gangsterism of the over-organized villains.) *The colonization through these cultivated democracies of the literati and art connoisseurs will occur in more humane forms; speculation will be adorned through progressive terminology.* (W 3:466; my emphasis).

Where art as "adornment" ("ornament" had been Adolf Loos's term for the "crime" of turn-of-the-century Viennese styles) takes part in the "gangsterism" of "colonization," original experience must lie in anarchist politics. In its concrete political terms, Einstein's report on the military situation and needs of the anarchists at Zaragoza, dated May 1, 1937, is a desperate but ardent rejection of the politics of Caballero's Popular Front government, which, after the death of Durruti, had even been joined by the CNT leadership against its own principles. It was the hope of the Popular Front that by postponing the issues of the social revolution and by concentrating on winning the war against Franco and the fascists, they would not only secure the continued shipment of arms from the Soviet Union but also gain the support of the Western democracies. Einstein's article, however, unmasks the aesthetic facade of the "bourgeoisie," catered to by the politics of the Popular Front, as a smoke screen for capital- and power-motivated politics. His counterargument, therefore, is that only anarchist political action can generate a "transformation of the real" (W 3:464). Embracing action in itself as an "auratic event," he had written in the Braque essay, "One . . . ought to get used to the circumstance that temporarily artless times are possible and necessary" (W 3:210).

The Dutch journalist Nico Rost, who met Einstein in Barcelona (the armed militiaman had broken into the friend's hotel room after midnight) attests to his personal identification with Durruti's cause: "Nothing of his sarcasm and bitterness was left," Rost writes. In fact, Einstein appeared "much younger . . . I did not know him this way. He hardly spoke about his own life during the past difficult years of emigration, but he again and again began to talk about the Spanish Civil War."[28] Another account of Einstein's enthusiastic commitment to Durruti's anarchists—by Helmut Rüdiger, head of the Deutsche Informationsdienst of the Confederación National del Trabajo and the Federación Anarquista Ibérica—stresses his optimistic espousal of that ominously irrational ideal of *Volk* (which Benn had previously embraced for quite different nationalistic ends): "CE said: You are not a party, you are not an organization, you are a people (*Volk*). For the first time in his life, he thought, had he come in touch with a real people's movement." The armed intellectual's reactions to subsequent negative developments in the political fate of the CNT and the Spanish cause are equally telling of his compulsion to identify with a collective:

> He suffered from the later political turmoil, did not find a place in the militarily reorganized militias, tried to make himself useful in a different way. He remained on the side of the CNT-FAI and stood with it in the hour of the great test during the Communist coup in May 1937. . . . CE was sometimes pessimistic. The Spanish Civil War was the last attempt to save the good cause, he felt. Should the free socialist Spain go under,

one could put a bullet into one's head. He wavered between hope and despair.[29]

This eyewitness testimony reinforces our sense of Einstein's total commitment to *lived* experience, a commitment which Rüdiger assessed as "romantic," even "idiotic."[30]

Thus Einstein continued to be lured by the "primitive," albeit in conflicting degrees of differentiation, from the epistemologically developed discourse of his *Negerplastik* to his "mythical" anarchist position of the period from 1936 to 1937, by polarizing communal experience with modernity's "colonizing" abstract discourses. Einstein's "poor" of 1912 and his tribal African artists of 1915 have undergone a metamorphosis to his anarchist comrades of 1936–1937 as outsiders. Whether it was the lure of the war enthusiasm of 1914, which he initially shared, or the revolutionary turmoil of Brussels between 1918 and 1919, or anarchist action in Catalonia and Aragon, in each case—historical differences notwithstanding—the outsider Einstein commits himself to the collective.[31] At a decisive moment of political crisis, at the point where the political confrontation between fascism and communism for him has made aesthetic revolt historically passé, the fascination with the collective in fact is stronger than Einstein's earlier epistemological drive.

A number of questions have been raised here about Einstein's dilemma-ridden attitude toward the social significance of the artist and art. Was the political stance he took in his pamphlets for an anarchist Spain not a panicked attack on modernity through "metamorphosing" the "poetic politics" (Benjamin on surrealism) of the historical avant-garde into a performance of *acting out* its collectivist myths rather than really breaking with his own avant-garde aesthetics? In *Die Fabrikation der Fiktionen,* Einstein had already been quite aware of the fact that the "dynamic aura" of "things . . . live beings," and the "experience of action," when represented in writing, is always already subjected to a "narrowing" and "deformation" (*FF* 235). That awareness, of course, would have to be set aside by the writing militiaman; it is repressed in his intensely mythical view of action. Writing against the odds of the "deformation" and "narrowing" of all writing, Einstein remains torn between the enduring idealism of literature and an *incomplete* materialist turn toward action since writing the *Fabrikation der Fiktionen*. Hence it is the mythical mentality of his treatise *Georges Braque* rather than the postmodern elements of *Die Fabrikation der Fiktionen* that colored Einstein's subsequent writing in Spain.

In short, contrary to his own program, Einstein was unable to free himself from what he himself had considered the avant-garde's "elitist" aesthetic response to modernity. By contrast, George Orwell's *Homage to Catalonia,* an eyewitness report on the anarchist struggle during the Spanish Civil War, is rooted in a commonsense belief in a language that can unmask the slogans of *newspeak* and communicate a moral truth. By contrast, Andre Malraux's novel *Man's Hope* reflects a commitment to the Republican cause against the Francoists *and* the anarchists; his choice of the genre of the *novel* is to guarantee the "objective" point of view toward a mainstream democratic reading public. Hence Einstein's choice of the political *pamphlet* is proper to *his* cause. Having defined the genre of the pamphlet as a "late" form of writing (*FF* 235), he expects the "new" *after* writing. Conflating action and myth, Einstein, the anarchist speechwriter and pamphletist in Spain, thus only seems to be removed from a position the expressionist had formulated in his essay "Revolte" (1912): "For the revolteur the world could only be justified through the fulfillment of a divine claim, through the realization of a logical axiom. Since that is impossible, he will always reject the world" (*W* 1:123).

In other words, Einstein himself had understood very early on his predicament of being split between his awareness of the impossibility of a transcending experience ("divine claim," "logical axiom") and a refusal to accept a state of metaphysical forlornness. While his *Die Fabrikation der Fiktionen* indeed is the document of an evolving, "early transformation of modernism to postmodernism,"[32] Einstein stays unwilling or unable to fully accept his insights into the condition of modernity that disallows authentic experience. Einstein's revolt remains a revolt against submitting to what he perceived as the futility of aesthetic revolt. In this precarious *post-avant-garde* situation, the "revolteur of the absolute" in Spain surrenders to a politicized "participation mystique."[33]

Postscriptum: Hans Magnus Enzensberger's "novel" *Der kurze Sommer der Anarchie. Buenaventura Durrutis Leben und Tod (The Short Summer of Anarchy: The Life and Death of Buenaventura Durruti;* 1972) consists of a montage of the differing perspectives on the Spanish Civil War as taken by the opposing parties and personalities involved. Interspersed with reflections on historiographic and aesthetic issues, the montage is the case of a review of the ideologies at conflict in Spain that denies any historicist interpretation. The statements attributed to Durruti here appear as one of many possible interpretations of the conflict in the "medium of signs" that cancel each other's claims for truth (which Einstein had wanted to find in the "collective syntax" of the anarchist column).

5. The "Image Sphere" versus Metaphor: Walter Benjamin Debating Expressionism

The Reconstruction of a Critical Constellation
from Surrealism to Film, 1925–1937

Walter Benjamin's antagonistic relationship to expressionism has been alluded to but not yet been discussed as crucial to the development of his
criticism of the avant-garde from his 1929 essay on surrealism to his turn
to Brecht's epic theater in the early 1930s and subsequently film.[2] Furthermore, a review of the stages of his critique of expressionism can provide us with the premise for a new, as it were, defamiliarizing perspective
on the otherwise well-known and in parts somewhat bleak expressionism
debate published by the exile journal *Das Wort* (*The Word*) in Moscow
(1937–1938),[3] occasioned by the case of Gottfried Benn. Nazism had been
supported by highly visible writers of the expressionist generation, such
as Hanns Johst, president of the German Academy of the Arts and the
National Writers' Union; Gottfried Benn, an influential member in both
NS organizations; and Reinhard Goering, Arnold Bronnen, and others.
In his essay "Confessing Expressionism" (1933), Benn had responded to a
mounting high-level National Socialist campaign that characterized expressionism as decadent and "un-German" by attempting to claim the movement as of "exclusively European genetic stock."[4] Benn's racial-biological

arguments suppressed the names of the many Jewish expressionist authors and artists, with some of whom he had enjoyed close and productive relationships throughout the preceding decades. His pretentious welcoming of Marinetti as the representative of the fascist avant-garde in the Berlin of 1934 had been an instance of the aestheticization of the politics for a new European order. In that new order Benn would have liked to see himself elevated to the preceptor of a fascist Germania (see chapter 7). The debate itself opened with Klaus Mann's "Gottfried Benn. Die Geschichte einer Verirrung" ("Gottfried Benn: The Story of an Aberration")[5] but quickly went far beyond his case.

Benjamin had been excluded from this debate; his essay on "Das Kunstwerk im Zeitalter seiner technischen Reproduzierbarkeit" ("The Work of Art in the Age of Mechanical Reproduction"; the second, German version) was rejected in the course of a shift in the Soviet Union's cultural politics toward the Popular Front, which favored what Benjamin called "leftist belles lettres" and showed no interest whatsoever in the mass medium of film. Beyond the intellectuals' stance against the cultural premises of fascism and their focus on expressionism as a paradigm of the suspect international avant-garde, the discussants attempted to reassess the significance of *literary* production for the masses in the age of mass production and mass consumption. My focus on the development of Benjamin's criticism toward this context does reflect our contemporary emphasis on the thinker and critic over Georg Lukács, Ernst Bloch, and even Bertolt Brecht as critics of the literary avant-garde, yet it much more illuminates, in a new light, the historical questions that the avant-garde work of art posed at the time. In the sense that Benjamin's went as far as attempting to even *historicize the literary avant-garde,* I am here not primarily interested in Benjamin's essay as an essay on the *genre* of film, though he clearly addressed it as a timely answer to the crisis of literary culture with which critics had been concerned since the arrival of the new mass medium in the 1910s (see chapter 1). Rather, I consider the artwork essay more specifically as a culmination of his criticism of the subjectivity of *literary metaphor* that determined his interest in "anti-art" surrealism and Dada and is at the roots of his rejection of the idealist discourse of expressionism. Hence I am more interested in its critique of the "image" as a space where conscious experience (*Erlebnis*) fuses with the unconscious (in his terms as *Erfahrung*), a space which for Benjamin is to obliterate also the gap between the metaphysical and physical (the problem of "Ausdrucksdichtung," of the poetry of subjective "expression"). Benjamin's critical pursuit of the *image* in his essays on literary modernism from "The Image of Proust" (1929) to his criticism on Baudelaire in the late 1930s may be much more articulate, much more interesting for contemporary poststructuralist criticism, but these essays have also been amply discussed in Benjamin scholarship. His critique of the historical avant-garde proper, much less exposed, is complementary to that of modernism, but also more radical in the sense that his criticism appropriates some of his subjects' subversive energies as part of the literary struggle in which the critic saw himself involved.

Benjamin's harsh criticism of expressionism actually predates by more than a decade the evolving discussion of the movement in the wake of Lukács's influential essay on "Größe und Verfall des Expressionismus" ("Greatness and Decline of Expressionism"; 1934) up to his "Es geht um den Realismus" ("Realism in a Balance"; 1938). Lukács's criticism of expressionism (and the European avant-garde) on the basis of his advocacy of realism is well known, though I will briefly return to it later. Benjamin argued against expressionism from an entirely opposite point of view, namely, from that of the French avant-garde. Surrealism and the surrealist "image" emerged in the mid-1920s as the basis from which he reviews and critiques the German literary developments in the wake of expressionism up to New Objectivity. At that time, in the early 1930s, Benjamin will attempt to read even Brecht's early epic theater, contrasted in passing with expressionist drama, in the light of the *image* as a constellation of physical/social and metaphysical experience. These terms, which subvert and transcend any normative materialist position, are crucial for a proper understanding of his criticism when compared with Brecht's as most representative of a critique of expressionism that is dialectical in *literary* terms and with Ernst Bloch's philosophical-messianic valorization of the expressionist "archaic-utopian images," later advanced in the expressionism debate. Benjamin's valorization of the visual mass medium film over *literature* (for which he not only continues to downgrade expressionism but now also sacrifices Dada, even surrealism, and, as we shall see, secretly also Brecht's theater) stands out as the most challenging position at his time, as it continues to be the most questionable. Here it is important to keep in mind that his criticism of the avant-garde from expressionism to film is a significant part of a long-standing epistemological quest into the condition of art: "I have tried to form over the years a progressively more exact and more uncompromising concept of what constitutes a work of art."[6]

The Critic as a Strategist in the Literary Struggle

Before we can close in on the stages of Benjamin's critical relationship to expressionism, we must consider his self-understanding as a critic and his views on the work of literary criticism. One can well argue that Benjamin's self-understanding as a critic developed as a result of his rejection of literary expressionism. The aims of his planned journal *Angelus Novus* in 1921, for example, were to be fundamentally based on an "annihilating criticism" of what he considered the corruptive influence of the movement on German literature: "Only terror will overcome the aping of great creativity in the visual arts at the hands of literary expressionism" (*GS* 2:242). And in *Einbahnstraße* (*One-Way Street;* 1928), Benjamin already understood criticism to be an activity that involves yet goes beyond aesthetic interests: the critic is "a strategist in the literary struggle" (*GS* 4:108ff.).

In the early 1930s, the critic Benjamin will apply this self-definition to the task of fighting New Objectivity (which he considered quite broadly an expressionist legacy) as a liberalist stylistic fad. The talk may be "humanity" or "objectivity," the crisis the critic has to face and push toward a decision is at a point where developments can turn either to the Right or to the Left, he wrote. Such crisis at the stage of alarm mobilizes the energies of "polemics" against the "falsche Kritik" (false criticism) of objectivity (*GS* 6:175f.). In contrast to the populist goals of Kurt Hiller or Alfred Döblin, who wanted to take up a public position "beside the proletariat"[7] from which to argue and lead, Benjamin defines criticism as functioning succinctly within the institution of criticism as a contest of critical discourses. For Benjamin, criticism is a specialized form of intellectual production for the expert; it has no direct connection with the public at large. Thus the critic could not claim a privileged mission of intellectual leadership for the masses; this was the "logocratic" attitude of the *Geistige,* believers in the spirit like Hiller. Criticism as part of the "literary struggle" is therefore no longer interpretation of epochal masterpieces; it is an activity that produces insight on its own. We must not forget, however, that for Benjamin criticism, even in its most politicized form, assumes a transitional (in his overall "messianic" view ultimately "redemptive") function in the site vacated by the decline of the work of art as a totality sui generis. Criticism thus retains some of the former's aesthetic qualities as an integral part of the polemics against what he considered to be ideological statements in literary form.

An understanding of Benjamin as a critic thus relies upon analyzing his critical praxis, his language, something that can be done here only on an ad hoc basis. The uniquely intricate fabric of his texts that are most pertinent here will necessitate a close reading. Benjamin's critique of the "decline" of literature as evident in the expressionist literary work, of expressionist "metaphor" as an idealist device that can be no more than fragment, is already topical in the *Trauerspiel* (tragic drama) book of 1925. From here I will follow his turn toward the surrealist "image," in his "Traumkitsch" (dream kitsch) glossary of 1925 and his 1929 essay on surrealism, which uncovers the experience of the "body sphere" that had been suppressed by the idealist tradition. We will see, for example, that his interpretation of surrealism dialectically engages Ludwig Klages's vision of the "archaic" image (an important influence on Benn), both in his 1929 surrealism essay and still in the artwork essay. This may seem to lead us far from our path. But it ought to become clearer than before in Benjamin criticism that, as he writes, the "German observer" of surrealism is significantly determined by his position in the "valley," which is the low point of German literary expressionism. Hence his criticism of expressionism can be understood fully only in terms of his critique of surrealism, and vice versa.

The Dialectical Step, or the Stepping On and Over Expressionism

As has recently been shown, Lukács's turn against expressionism has a long history[8] going back to emerging differences with Wilhelm Worringer during his Heidelberg period in late 1913 and early 1914. After a stage of mutual affinity that had left its imprint on *Die Seele und die Formen* (*The Soul and the Forms;* 1911), Lukács had become aware of their underlying divergence. After all, Worringer's concept of the work of art as the production of a totality that would fill the void of existence was relativistic and thus alien to his own essentialist concept of the totality of art. Benjamin's turn against expressionism was first formulated in the philosophical terms of the preface to his book *Urprung des deutschen Trauerspiels* (*Origin of the German Tragic Drama;* 1925). Unlike Lukács's criticism, it was based on the claim that the strained subjectivism of expressionism was a last attempt to hold on to the totality of the organic work of art. In the preface he gauges the subjective language and mentality of expressionist drama against that of the *Trauerspiel* of the Baroque. Comparing and contrasting Franz Werfel's *Troerinnen* with Opitz's treatment of the same subject at the beginning of baroque drama, he perceives a progressive devaluation of the physical world toward an ineluctably volitional spiritual claim. For Benjamin, expressionism therefore is the stylistic expression of a declining "Zeitalter" (age), where the art historian and theorist Alois Riegl and in his wake Worringer had seen a movement anticipating epochal renewal.

In Benjamin's view, expressionism shares with the baroque a "neue Pathos" and *Kunstwollen* (artistic volition), a term expropriated from Riegl, whom he elsewhere considered as having anticipated the "feeling for style" and the insights of expressionism.[9] Such *Kunstwollen* is opposed to the organic *Kunstübung* (cultivation of art) of classical cultures. In Riegl's as well as Worringer's terms, epochal differences in style were not indicative of varying abilities but were expressions of differing artistic wills. By contrast, Benjamin perceived in expressionist subjectivity a strained, forced, and hence decadent form of artistic volition.[10]

For Benjamin, the poets of both epochs were trying to cover up an irreversible loss of cultural coherence with an arbitrary employment of language marked by neologisms and, most characteristically for expressionism, archaisms. Nevertheless, he warns against the historicist fallacy of an intuitive identification of the present with the past as practiced by some contemporaneous critics. Thus he writes that the literature of the baroque, even if disregarded by the nation, in fact meant a national rebirth, while the twenty years of recent modern German literature characterize a "decline." His critique of the rhetorically inflated language of expressionism thus is based on his understanding of a natural history of styles. In that frame of reference, expressionism represents the downfall of a culture based on the state (*GS* 1:236) and, as he put it succinctly, on the "rounded work of art," "the highest reality of art (as) an isolated and finished work." On the other hand, the expressionist work symptomatizes, though the expressionist dramatists were not conscious of it, "a however preparatory and fruitful decay" (*GS* 1:235f.). Thus Benjamin's perspective here is already dialectical and not evolutionist.[11] It is essentially premised on his messianic view of history as "ruin" and "corpse." History's corpses just as the expressionists' artworks are thus witness to a greater "plan of construction," where origin and goal rest in the theological. The critic's subsequent turn against the legacy of expressionism seems to be so thoroughly secularized and politicized that we may lose sight of its continued underlying grounding in a "messianic" dimension of his criticism as well as of the perceived "preparatory and fruitful" function of his subject's state of "decay."

Benjamin's December 22, 1924, letter to Gershom Scholem had already expressed his waning interest in restoring the "genuine" in German literature against "expressionist corruptions" as a commentator. He conveyed his surprise at having discovered a proximity to "an extreme bolshevist theory" (experienced through his encounter with Asja Lacis in Capri). And he intimates his intention to develop "a politics" from "within himself," before he could concern himself with texts of a different significance and totality.[12] At the very core of the subsequent politicized criticism of expressionism will remain his observation that the poets subjectively forced the *Bildkraft* (image force) of language into the inwardness of the work of art that can no longer express a totality (*GS* 1:236). Redemption must lie elsewhere; in terms of the development of his criticism, he therefore sought to connect the "poetic politics" of surrealism as a form of "materialist inspiration" with his vision of the end of historical experience.

It is probably not too speculative to surmise that the mounting acidity of Benjamin's attack on the expressionists as the *Geistige* through the 1930s may reflect back on his own youthful identification and experience with a culture of *Geist*. As a leader in the academic youth movement, he had made ardent contributions to his group's journal and thereafter to Gustav Wyneken's *Der Anfang* (*The Beginning*). Not only Wyneken but he himself had once contributed to a "logocrat" publication: to Kurt Hiller's first *Ziel-Jahrbuch* (1916).[13] And there had been Benjamin's traumatizing fallout with his spiritual mentor Wyneken over the issue of the war, at the outbreak of which his intimate friend the poet Fritz Heinle had committed suicide.[14] Not even Franz Pfemfert's antiwar *Die Aktion* (sharing the same publishing house with *Der Anfang*[15]) is exempt from his retrospective criticism: It is said to have "exhibited the revolutionary gesture, the steeped arm, the clenched fist in cardboard" (*GS* 3:281f.). In other words, for Benjamin the expressionists had perverted the physicality of the revolutionary "clenched fist" into a reified literary gesture ("paper mock"). While the critic praises Frank Wedekind as an emancipator of the body,[16] the expressionist movement is charged with the suppression of language's correspondence with the physical (which is liberated and redeemed in the surrealist turn against all "belles lettres").

The German Observer of Surrealism in the Valley of Expressionism

With "Traumkitsch" (dream kitsch), a short "Glosse zum Sürrealismus," probably written as early as 1925, after the *Trauerspiel* book as the last instance in his "German production cycle," Benjamin began to turn toward surrealism as an "anti-art" movement. The popular knickknacks of

"Kitsch," the collected daily objects of previous generations, imparted to the critic's touch, as it were, the sensation of a time- and place-shattering dream experience that breaks with subjectivity. The tangibility of these objects thus put to question the "soul" of art. "What we called art," he states already in the past tense, "starts two meters away from the body" (*GS* 2:622).

The avant-garde's turn to the *tactile* experience, as it is also a property of language as sound and sign (as written and *seen*), would greatly interest Benjamin from 1925 on. In the 1930s, he becomes concerned with its function for mass reception in the state of "distraction" as the modern urban environment has erased the privacy of the bourgeois *gute Stube* (best room) of "inwardness" and contemplation. On the basis of such physiological criteria for the modern experience will he even allow a few exceptions to the rule of his dislike of expressionism:[17] Alfred Lichtenstein's and Georg Heym's poetry, "pre-expressionist" poetry (meaning, for Benjamin, developments before expressionism evolved as a movement during the war). The unique character of Heym's poetry may actually help to explain an early split between the poet and Kurt Hiller within "Der Neue Club" (the New Club).[18] With one of its members, Simon Ghuttmann, also increasingly opposed to Hiller's ethical visions, Benjamin had enjoyed close relations through *Der Anfang*.[19]

Heym's "blowing, flaming, rattling images were banners under which poetry readied itself for the last victorious assault on the city" (*GS* 3:182), Benjamin would write in 1929, the year the surrealism essay appeared. In other words, Heym's unruly "rattling" images (as "banners") attack the idea of the city as polis in a humanist sense. In that sense one could call Heym's images *protosurrealist images:* they illuminate the experience of major upheavals in the social body. For Benjamin, Heym's poems opened to view the modern metropolis, "full of omens of impending catastrophes" (*GS* 2:557); they are said to prefigure the condition of the masses in the subsequent war era: suicides, prisoners, the sick, and the insane. Likewise, Alfred Lichtenstein's poems appear to anticipate the triste, bloated figures of the crisis-ridden bourgeoisie. In Benjamin's view, these poems thus articulate insights which the postwar crisis fully brought to the awareness of the bourgeoisie: their function as "human material" on a market, where, as he writes, unemployment was perversely resolved through suicide as a form of "dumping" (*GS* 3:282). It is this very practice of dumping surplus human material that Benjamin will later attribute to Marinetti's aestheticization of modern technological warfare in the artwork essay.

We know about Benjamin's philosophical infatuation with Paul Klee's painting *Angelus Novus*[20] but are less familiar with his esteem for the paintings of Chagall, Kandinsky, and Macke,[21] which corroborates his interest in the visual discoveries of expressionism. Typical of his disdain for most expressionist poets may be his harsh reaction to the personal extravaganza of Else Lasker-Schüler ("empty and sick—hysterical").[22] On the whole, he had already by 1919 rejected the "greater mass of expressionism" as mere documents of a "temporary inner disposition." They could no longer be what they strained to be: "works of art."[23] Hence Benjamin's turn to the surrealists who were no longer concerned with "art." While the crisis of art in Germany was full-blown, unresolved aesthetically and politically, as I have shown in chapter 1, the "German observer" in the "valley" looked up to the French intellectuals. They and the Communist Party in France were much more open to each other than was the case in German lands ("bei uns"; *GS* 2:1039–40).

In spite of having been written in Berlin, the essay "Der Sürrealismus. Die letzte Momentaufnahme der Europäischen Intelligenz" ("Surrealism as the Last Snapshot of the European Intelligentsia"; 1929) seems to constitute a near participation in the French avant-garde project. The German critic Benjamin temperamentally as well as epistemologically espouses the eradication of aesthetic autonomy as it is to take place in Paris. Of course, there were doubts, but they should not be read as the premise of the essay.[24] In the published essay, they are voiced merely in the form of well-placed queries as to the reality of "poetic politics" and the dialectic of ecstasy and revolution. The unresolved questions would not remain in his unpublished notes, however, as the rise of fascism for Benjamin would require a response more effective than surrealist productions for involving the masses, for instance, the medium of film.

The surrealism essay intends to confront the contemporary German critic in Berlin with the fact that in Paris there are activities under way to free the body politic from the culture of inwardness. The surrealists were abolishing the "humanistic concept of freedom" in liberal politics and "belles lettres," the "metaphorical" experience of the subject. As a result of such *avant-garde* activities exemplary for the times, the artist as the "spiritual" authority for Western culture would disappear as well. Hence Benjamin views surrealism as "the last snapshot of the *European* intelligentsia," not just of the French intelligentsia.

Because the text was written with the German critical scene in mind, we ought to revise a scholarly preoccupation with the French context.[25] It becomes obvious that the "strategist in the literary struggle" and observer in the German valley literally displaces a text by one of his opponents in the camp of irrationalist vitalist thought, namely Ludwig Klages's *Vom Kosmogonischen Eros* (1921).[26] The ideas developed therein would culminate in Klages's main work *Der Geist als Widersacher der Seele* (*The Mind as Adversary of the Soul*) the first volume of which appeared in 1929, the year Benjamin's surrealism essay was published.

Klages had had an important philosophical and ideological influence on expressionism, specifically on Gottfried Benn's "archaic images," as Ernst Bloch pointed out.[27] A member of the Cosmic Round and regular contributor to Stefan George's *Blätter für die Kunst*, Klages must be recognized as a major representative of a generation of German intellectuals ranging from Ernst Jünger to Oswald Spengler and Martin Heidegger who repudiated rational analysis in favor of a holistic view of life. Benjamin himself had once invited Klages as a speaker to the "Freie Studentenschaft" in Berlin and still later regarded him as a great philosopher, in spite of criticizing him for his ahistorical rejection of technological modernity. In fact, it can be maintained that his relationship to Klages's phenomenology of space evolved into an affinity of opposites.[28] Such affinity of opposites can be observed in the surrealism essay where the critic "transfunctions" Klages's understanding of the metaphysical nature of the poetic image by turning certain passages from *Vom Kosmogonische Eros,* as it were, into a criticized subtext. In fact, he silences Klages by not even referring to source or author as an authority to be disputed. In the artwork essay, Benjamin will use the same procedure in the discussion of the "aura" (via a central allusion to Klages, who by this time is identified as a precursor to fascist irrationalist ideology).

In the chapter "Vom Wesen der Ekstase" ("On the Nature of Ecstasy") of his book on the "cosmogonic eros," Klages wrote, for example, about the relation of the image to supraindividual experience:

The image possesses a reality independent of consciousness; the thing is being projected into the world by consciousness and exists only *for* an inwardness of *personal* beings. Therefore: for the one who explodes the form of being a persona in ecstasy, the world of facts sinks away, and it arises to him the *world of images* with a reality force [*Wirklichkeitsmacht*] that displaces everything. The vision of the soul is its interior, the envisioned reality its outer pole.[29]

No expressionist could have elucidated the claim for the superiority of an ecstatic "inner vision" or "soul" over experience mediated by consciousness better than Klages does here!

By contrast, Benjamin's analysis of the surrealists' ecstatic debunking of the subject's metaphorical perception focuses on the breaking down of the idealist dualism of an "outer" and "inner," the distinction between a physical and metaphysical realm through the image:

> In all cases where an action puts forth its own image and exists, absorbing and consuming it, where nearness looks with its own eyes, the long-sought image sphere is opened, the world of universal and integral actualities (*allseitiger und integraler Aktualität*), where the "best room" is missing—the sphere, in a word, in which political materialism and physical nature share the inner man, the psyche, the individual, or whatever else we wish to throw to them, with dialectical justice, so that no limb remains unrent. Nevertheless—indeed, precisely after such dialectical annihilation—this will be the sphere of images and, more concretely, of bodies.[30]

In other words, for Benjamin, the surrealist liberation of the body—"the collective is a body, too," he wrote[31]—is total. Yet it is by no means an embrace of raw materialism. The surrealist "dialectical annihilation" frees the body politic from the restraints of sublimation in the praxis of everyday experience, from a life that was previously confined, as it were, to the "bourgeois" interior ("the best room") as a refuge for inner values. As surrealism liberates the body, it simultaneously liberates consciousness from the subjective constraints of inwardness ("the inner man"), of *metaphorically* filtered experience. In Breton's and Aragon's writings, "image and language takes precedence." Thus the surrealist explosion of *metaphor* liberates language; language is no any longer in the service of "art." It is no longer "literature," "artistic" or "poetic," part of the institution of art (a form of "the best room"). Instead, language is freed to engage in the praxis of a "'poetic life,'" of a life that is delivered from the demands of sublimation and rationalist functioning to the utmost possible limits.[32] This life is to coincide with the communist revolution. The surrealist practice of writing or, as it were, the *event* where, as Benjamin writes, "an action puts forth its own image," blends subject and object, conscious and unconscious bodily experience. Such experience (*Erfahrung*) is bringing forth the sublation of the metaphysical into the physical, the end of "meaning," the end of metaphor, the end of "contemplation" in the state of a "profane illumination." In German lands, however, in Benjamin's view, the promises of the "bodily" utopias of Paul Scheerbart[33] and Dada's revolt had remained unfulfilled, while the legacy of expressionism lived on. Thus it is the critic's task to save their legacy for a surrealist renewal. In that sense and context, Benjamin's text dialectically annihilates Klages's vision of the "inner man," of "the soul."

In the context of Benjamin's thought, the surrealist discourse is to overcome the dichotomy of subject and object, which the early essay "On Language as Such and the Language of Man" (1916) still addressed in purely idealist terms. Surrealist writing recaptures and reembodies the "magic of the material" which the early language essay had *separated* from the "pure spirituality ("reine Geistigkeit") of "language as such" that has its origin and goal in "the word of God." There language's "magical community with things is immaterial and purely mental." Nevertheless, the 1916 essay was already opposed to a metaphorical concept of language. It argued against *poetic* language as merely referential (*dinglicher Sprachgeist*) where the subject superimposes itself on the world "through language" instead of uniting with it "in language as such." In which medium "man communicates with God" by "naming" the world of things in "human terms," while the "*creative* word of God" emanates in the "language of the things themselves."[34] Thus the surrealism essay constitutes a dialectical shift in Benjamin's understanding of language. The surrealists' "magical experiments with words," as they fuse with the events of "physical nature," are to put forth the physical world's "own image," opening up the "one-hundred-percent image realm," in an ecstatic moment that Benjamin addresses as one of "materialist inspiration" (synonymous with his messianic idea of a "profane illumination"). On these grounds, Benjamin exhorts the readers of the *Literarische Welt* (1929): "We must understand the passionate phonetic and graphical transformational games that have run through the whole literature of the avant-garde for the past fifteen years, whether called Futurism, Dadaism, or Surrealism."[35] Conspicuously absent from this account is the expressionist experiment with language.

Klages had absolutized the "distance of the image" over the "nearness of the *perceived* object," insisting on the authoritative "untouchability of all images," the result of a metamorphosis of the body into the soul.[36] Benjamin in turn identifies with the surrealist embrace of an experiential *moment* where "nearness looks with its own eyes." This argument returns in the artwork essay as it turns to the technology of film as the medium that offers to the senses a tangible optical unconscious.

Benjamin's Attack on the Liberalist Legacy "from Activism, Expressionism to New Objectivity"

Benjamin's questioning of metaphorical language on the basis of the image continues into the 1930s. The review essay "Linke Melancholie" ("Leftist Melancholy") of 1930, for example, contains his most explicitly politicized critique of the legacy of an expressionist interiority, with a nod in the direction of Brecht's poems as the alternative. It interprets Kästner's as well as Mehring's and Tucholsky's poetry as part of an extremely broadly interpreted idealist legacy that runs "from activism via expressionism toward new objectivity" (*GS* 3:280f.) as he also draws a highly schematic equation between "expressionism and Social Democracy" (*GS* 6:181). His criticism of these liberal leftist writers is most curiously articulated in an imagery of the body. Images of the body pervade the text like a thread that has to be traced closely. Again, the key to understanding the critic's code, as laid open in one of his critical fragments, is his continued polemics against the "terror" of an expressionist legacy of "pathological reaction(s)" to the times. An "expression" stays for Benjamin a mere symptom of a disease that cannot be cured through an "objective" stance of mere intellectual reflection as practiced by the contemporary German intelligentsia. Only a continuation of the dadaist shock tactics into the communist stance of the contemporary surrealist movement of the French generation could have provided the means to cure. The sham of New Objectivity could only be recognized in a comparative contrast to surrealism, he wrote (*GS* 6:177).

The critic's diagnosis of a German "pathology" thus focuses on the *melancholy* of liberal social criticism. He understands its poetry as an expression of a certain *Hartleibigkeit* (hardness of the body), which leads to a blockage of the "fluids" in the "soziale Körper" (body politic) from which the liberal poets have separated themselves. Their melancholy poetry must therefore be seen as the product and symptom of social indigestion.[37] In fact, their poems are commodified: "things" available for consumption by the "bourgeois profiteers" who compensate for their bad conscience in the "sadness of the saturated." Still more poignantly, the critic's eye perceives these poems as creature automatons, "sad and sagging marionettes who walk over corpses." Thus the critic's x-ray gaze, as it were, penetrates the sentimental surface of "belles lettres," uncovering forms of estrangement in these poems. The "hardness of their armor, . . . the blindness of their actions" metamorphose under the critics' watchful eye, into a hybrid militaristic-animalistic form, a phantasmagoric combination of "Tank und

Wanze" (military tank and bedbug). In other words, the reviewer uncovers in poetic sublimation the revenge of the repressed intersubjective physical experience. The idealism of a subject-object separation, the division between inwardness and body, is thus linked to a military deformation of the body politic. The critic makes the same argument against a myth-making mentality that fetishizes technology in "Theorien des deutschen Faschismus" ("Theories of German Fascism"), his review of Ernst Jünger's anthology *Krieg and Krieger* (*War and Warrior;* 1930), and later, in the concluding attack on the aestheticization of war in "The Work of Art in the Age of its Mechanical Reproduction." War is a result of severing the aesthetic experience from collective experience. War exploits technology in the interest of domination rather than exploring its forces in the interest of the body politic. In "Theorien des Deutschen Faschismus," the critic in the literary struggle maintains that the "expressionist avant-garde" has made a significant step in this fatal direction by spiritualizing the experience of the First World War, turning "defeat into an inner victory by means of a hysterically heightened confession of guilt" (*GS* 3:242). The gap between outer and inner experience, art and life, is thus identified as the cultivated—indeed, *aestheticized*—wound through which the physicality of experience is sacrificed. Benjamin levels a similar attack in a review of Kurt Hiller's collection of essays *Der Sprung ins Helle* (*The Leap into the Light;* 1932). His chief argument against these *Geistige* (believers of the spirit) remains that they symptomatize the "pathological blockages" that leave the general body politic itself drained of *Geist* (spirit). In other words, their own spirituality is achieved at the expense of collective experience. Benjamin's criticism of the expressionist legacy thus can be defined as a *physiognomic* critique (fully developed in his writing on Baudelaire) that articulates critical insights into the phantasmagoric entwinement of literary subjectivity and technological modernity. In political terms, the rationale of Benjamin's "Literaturpolitik"[38] demanded that he attack the *Geistige* as a circle of intellectuals who had been arguing since 1918 (then as members of the "Rat der geistigen Arbeiter") for a solution to political problems through a "Logokratie" of a "council of spiritual workers." Lukács's and Benjamin's relentless attacks on Kurt Hiller above all others were a response to the visible position the *Geistige* held in the contemporary intellectual climate of the 1930s.[39]

The core argument of Benjamin's notorious essay "Der Autor als Produzent," ("The Author as Producer"; 1934), namely, that traditional writing only serves a "bourgeois" institution of art, had already been made in the opening passages of his essay "Was ist das Epische Theater?" ("What Is Epic

Theater?" 1931). In fact, Benjamin considered the former a pendant of the latter.[40] The 1931 essay attempted to define the playwright's early epic theater as a *Publikationsinstitut* (Brecht's term) that operates for social change by replacing an idealist notion of *Bildung* (education) with the experience of a nonconceptual totality that is grounded in the sensual realm of the image (*Bild*/eidos). Contrasting Ernst Toller's "theater of the idea"[41] with Brecht's play *Mann ist Mann* (*Man Is Man*), the critic here seemed to seek in Brecht's theater a synthesis between surrealist means (*Bilder*) and a Marxist critique of the theater as a moral institution (which will warrant a separate discussion elsewhere).

Based on Brecht's theory of the epic theater, "The Author as Producer," which was intended as a lecture at the Parisian Institute for the Study of Fascism, was written in the same year Lukács's first attack on expressionism was published in the Moscow-based exile journal *Internationale Literatur*. Nowhere is it more obvious, in outright *political* terms, why Benjamin had so little positive to say about expressionism. After Hitler's coming to power, he reviewed the expressionist legacy in terms of the failure of the Weimar Republic's democratic experiment. The exile's essay, which builds on the arguments developed in his 1930 review of Kästner's and Mehring's poetry discussed earlier, culminates in a sweeping and abrasive indictment of the so-called left-wing intelligentsia. It refers to Heinrich Mann, whom the *Geistige* had at one time considered as a candidate for president of the republic. And it singles out Döblin, who had criticized the KPD (Kommunistische Partei Deutschland) as lacking in spiritual radicalism.[42] Both are harshly addressed as "hack writers" (*Routiniers*) in terms that appear to agree politically with Brecht but are incongruent to the latter's appreciation of, for example, Döblin as a writer.

There were, indeed, extreme professional and ideological differences between the leftist liberal and the Marxist camp already in the early 1930s. They are reflected in Siegfried Kracauer's and now Benjamin's attack on Döblin's, the "hack writer's," appeal to "spiritual leadership" in *Wissen und Verändern* (*Knowledge and Change;* 1931).[43] With 5,000 copies printed, Döblin's call for the primacy of the spirit had a considerable, documented impact on a mostly youthful readership.[44] Unlike Benjamin, however, Brecht would later set ideological differences aside and speak to the issues as a *writer:*

> I have learned more from Döblin about the nature of the epic than from any other writer; his prose and even his theory of the epic have strongly

influenced my drama. . . . I am thinking above all of his decentralization of the epic work so that a whole arises in rapid development, which is formed from very independent units.[45]

When reviewing *Man Is Man* in his 1931 essay on the epic theater, had not Benjamin himself appreciated the playwright's montage of those "very independent units" (*Augenblicke* as "moments" and "gazes of the eye") into a rapid, epic development of a whole? In short, some techniques of expressionist origin to the *writer* in the literary struggle obviously were more useful than an attack on expressionism.

A hack writer, for Benjamin, is a "counterrevolutionary" (at this moment we have an unpleasant recollection of Lukács's verdict on the whole expressionist movement) who "feels his solidarity with the proletariat only in attitude, not as a producer." Hack writers are "bourgeois" specialists in literature who supply the omnivorous capitalist "apparatus of production" without changing it, as Brecht does. In this sense, the authors of activism (i.e., latter-day expressionists like Hiller) and New Objectivity are said to have made "the *struggle against poverty* an object of consumption." With Brecht, Benjamin endorses a "transfunctioning" (*Umfunktionierung*) of the "autonomous" institution of art toward the production of revolutionary consciousness.[46] In terms of his quest for a "progressively more exact and more uncompromising concept of what constitutes a work of art," Benjamin's dialectical approach here has "absolutely no use for such rigid, isolated things as work, novel, book. It has to insert them into living social context."[47] In sum, he formulates a highly politicized interest in a "mighty recasting of literary forms," as the struggle at hand is "not one between 'Geist' and capitalism but between capitalism and the proletariat." Such interest would lead Benjamin toward a position beyond Brecht, even beyond surrealism, to the mass medium film.

Outdoing Brecht and the Historical Avant-Garde; Film: The Production of the "Orchid in the Land of Technology"

Benjamin's relation to *Das Wort* has generally been discussed merely in footnotes, at most in one or two pages.[48] Only the "Pariser Brief I," written during his stay with Brecht in Skovbostrand for the summer, was published in *Das Wort* (issue 5, November 1936).[49] It offers an analysis of a fascist *aestheticization* of technology and war, which obfuscates the functional character of technology by combining a "decadent," aestheticist theory of art with its "monumental practice" (GS 3:490). In other words, the "Pariser Brief" is a sum of his views on a perverted mentality of *Geist* in regard to physical experience, previously articulated in his "Theorien des Faschismus" reviews and of the melancholy poetry of Weimar liberals, the gist of which also informs the conclusion of the essay "The Work of Art in the Age of Mechanical Reproduction." As Benjamin's characteristic luck had it, his sole publication in the Moscow journal, the first Parisian letter, was to be the official cause of his expatriation by the Nazis.[50]

The rejection of Benjamin's artwork essay by *Das Wort* was a mark of the changed cultural-political circumstances in 1937. Moscow had consolidated a consensus against the international avant-garde for the sake of the politics of the traditional aesthetic scope of a broader international Popular Front[51] against fascism. The heritage of a critical realism from Balzac to Heinrich Mann and to *socialist realism* as critical forms of mimesis and representation was proposed as an alternative to the international experiment with language and genre. The debate was centered on expressionism, as it were, as a stand-in[52] for the international avant-garde and modernism from surrealism to Joyce, which the Lukács camp referred to negatively as cosmopolitan formalist literature. With these objectives Lukács wrote his essay "Realism in a Balance." In aesthetic terms, the essay rephrased his earlier criticism that the expressionists "no longer gave form to the contradictions inherent in an objective reality, but more and more to the contradiction between the subject and reality."[53] In other words, for Lukács the problem of expressionism boiled down to the issue of subjectivist formalist techniques (such as montage). Formalism merely duplicated the abstractions of subjectivist experience rather than overcoming alienation and fragmentation. By contrast, the mimetic techniques of a critical realism could detect the gaps between subjective experience and reality and, in a further move, could give expression and form to the manifestations of these historical forces leading toward a new comprehensive experience.

Lukács's "Realism in a Balance" was immediately attacked as a statement of repressive policy by Ernst Bloch, who was supported by the former *Sturm* (*Storm*) editor Herwarth Walden and the expressionist poet and writer Rudolf Leonard. Of course, none of Lukács's concerns as to a *Widerspiegelung* (mirroring) of social reality through the work of art were of interest to the expressionists nor, albeit for entirely different reasons, to Benjamin. The shift in cultural policy toward the consensus of the Popular Front also meant a turn against Brecht's "formalism" as a failure to understand Gorky's humanism and realism.[54] In fact, within the German exile circle, party functionaries like Wilhelm Pieck looked at Brecht's editorship of *Das Wort* with intense distrust.[55] All this is well known and should need no further elaboration here.

What complicates matters is that underlying the rejection of Benjamin's artwork essay may have been Brecht's dislike of the essay's thesis, the loss of the aura of art through the reproducibility of works of art. "Benjamin has discovered this through an analysis of film . . . everything mysticism, while in attitude antimysticism. in such a way the materialist conception of history is being adapted! it is quite dreadful," he later wrote in his journal (*GS* 1:1024f.). Brecht's criticism of the essay's "mysticism" should, however, remind us, positively speaking, of the genuine amplitude of Benjamin's characterization of himself as a "historischer Materialist" or "materialistischer Dialektiker." While provocatively poised against the aberrations of the "Deutsche Ideologie" of *Geist,* he maintained a vantage point for the spiritual in aesthetic production as a technical process, if only by implication. In a suppressed note to the artwork essay, for example, he wrote quite openly: "The laws of cinematic presentation demand from the actor the complete sensualization of spiritual reflexes and reactions; on the other hand, they demand from the filmmakers performances of a highly spiritual character (*GS* 1:1051).

The case of the artwork essay shows that as the exile debate turned to the legacy of expressionism, Benjamin, the outsider, had already moved beyond that controversy into a discussion of mass culture via film. For Benjamin, film had become the medium that most effectively explored and delivered the experience of the "image realm" to the masses. For the participants in the debate, the contemporary cultural crisis also meant the end of "bourgeois" culture. Yet, their very own stake was in *literature*. In other words, for Benjamin the conflict of film with literary culture, which, some twenty-five years ago, critics began to discuss with the emergence of the new medium as resulting in a crisis of the latter (see chapter 1), has reached a point of crisis that must be decisively addressed in favor of film.

As Theodor Adorno maintained, Benjamin's essay may have been symptomatic of an ambition to "outdo Brecht in radicalism."[56] Benjamin certainly meant to criticize what he considered the leftist intelligentsia's outdated preoccupation with "belles lettres." As stated already in his 1929 essay on surrealism and in "The Author as Producer" (1934), he found them obligated "not to the Revolution but to traditional culture."[57] He was, of course, quite aware of his disturbing vested interests as the cultural politics in Moscow continued to define themselves in "leftist belles lettres." The goals of the newly founded *Das Wort,* in which he maintained an unusually close and intense interest,[58] were just such. The radical political expectations he had connected with the Soviet avant-garde[59] during his stay in Moscow in 1925 to 1926 were disappointed: The reading of books had stayed after all more important than the reading of newspapers. Benjamin's double bind was that he considered the Popular Front his political forum, while being compelled to argue against the "strained emphasis on artistic creativity, which is known to us from the cultural debate."[60] In view of the harsh conditions of survival in the literary struggle of the exile period, that position seemed less desirable than it appears today. We now know much more about the Stalinist practices in which Lukács and other debaters in *Das Wort* participated than Benjamin or even Brecht could have known then.[61] Most important, however, his persistence, against the odds, in publishing in the exile journal may have had much to do with the fact that he did not consider his artwork essay a new tendency in his work but a continuation of his long-standing attempt to form "a progressively more exact and more uncompromising concept of what constitutes a work of art."

Since his early criticism of expressionism for forcing language into a work of art, which no longer can be a totality, Benjamin's critique of contemporaneous art has evolved into an assessment of the "crisis of the arts"[62] as the crisis of art, of *literature.*

Like his advocacy of epic theater, his embrace of film is phrased in terms of an aesthetics of production and reception derived from Brecht. Yet it has, indeed, the makings of a latent attempt at "outdoing Brecht in radicalism," which is openly stated in another suppressed note to his artwork essay:

> Among the arts, the theater is the least adoptable to mechanical production, meaning standardization: therefore the masses turn away. From a historical point of view, the most important step in Brecht's work may be that his dramatic production takes a sober and modest, even reduced form, in order to hibernate that way. (*GS* 1:1042)

The various strands of Benjamin's critique of the work of art I have pursued thus far culminate in the "textum" (his term) of "The Work of Art in the Age of Mechanical Reproduction." The essay's radicality can best be gauged by its denial of the validity of the radical experiments of the historical avant-garde, which both camps in the *Das Wort* debate more or less identify with expressionism. Benjamin now takes everything from the avant-garde in order to give everything to film. Yet, the technique of montage did not "become familiar (only) in recent years from film and radio, press and photography," as he maintains.[63] Bloch, Brecht, and Lukács had already discussed it as *the* avant-garde technique in literature and the arts. For Benjamin, however, cubism, futurism, dadaism, and now surrealism (!) are only avant-garde inasmuch as they are *formal* precursors of film.[64] Expressionism, as we shall see, remains his chief target for criticism.

The overwhelming reality of fascism, which practiced an "aestheticization of politics" that would culminate in the powerful nationalist state's art of warfare, called for an irreversible break with all "poetic politics" of small subversive circles. Dadaism, for example, Benjamin's present argument goes, prevented itself from reaching the masses through its esoteric moralism, the boheme's bourgeois inheritance. Yes, the dadaist text, the montage of "buttons or tickets," had already assumed the physical "tactile quality" of a "bullet" hitting the spectator below the level of consciousness that parries and censors shock.[65] Yet, Dada had recoiled from the wider consequences of a loss of the "aura" of autonomous art. It had merely shocked the audience out of its attitude of contemplation. As Benjamin saw it, Dada had been satisfied with being merely useless for a traditional audience.

In Benjamin's scheme, film consequently represents modern technology's fullest capacity to produce intersubjective consciousness. In film, the antiauratic device of montage constitutes the flowing series of images produced by a technical apparatus. Its technology could outperform the human eye and make manifest a visual unconscious (like the surgeon's equipment "penetrating into the patient's body"). In that sense, film produces a "surrealist" image "because an unconsciously penetrated space is substituted for a space consciously explored by man."[66] Like the earlier essay on the epic theater, the artwork essay is concerned with the *concealment* of the montaged nature of the images, here as a *technological artifice.* Brecht's own epic theory and Eisenstein's film, by contrast, were interested in the montage as a device of overt defamiliarization. Benjamin focused, as already in the early essay on the epic theater, instead on "material ideas" as images (*eidota*) in a constant holistic flux (*GS* 2:525). Film in its annihilation of the aura of the symbolic work of art thus *produces* "the sight of immediate reality."

The anti-idealist understanding of the filmed image as a technologically produced "blaue Blume" ("orchid in the land of technology")[67] is a final fruit of Benjamin's surrealist skepticism of metaphor in literature and politics. Based on his surrealist concept of the psychophysiological, tactile "image sphere," his view of the filmed image is again developed against the subtext of Ludwig Klages's tenets of an "*untouchability* of all images."[68]

The immediacy of film is as mediated as it is technologically *produced.* In other words, it is constructed *in* rather than *through* the language of film, due to the *antimetaphorical* grammar of montage. At this point of the essay's argument against "expression as a principle of poetic production . . . and its reactionary functions" (a formulation from his notes; *GS* 1:1049f.), Benjamin cites Franz Werfel's praise of Max Reinhardt's filming of Shakespeare's *A Midsummer Night's Dream* as a paradigm for a mistaken, expressionist notion of film. In his view, Werfel is wrong in understanding film as an organic poetic medium *through* which the outer of the material world is relinquished in order "to bring to expression the fairy tale like, the marvelous, the supernatural" (*GS* 7:363). Only in these long-standing anti-expressionist terms can we start to comprehend Benjamin's often misunderstood assertion that film as film per se produces "a revolutionary criticism of traditional concepts of art."[69]

Benjamin concludes the artwork essay by linking not only futurism but, overlooked in criticism, also expressionism with fascist politics. He is no longer talking about film, as film was the medium through which to analyze the overarching category of the "work of art" to begin with. Fascism is prepared, he writes in a remark, added to the manuscript submitted to *Das Wort,* by a certain false avant-garde: "With D'Annunzio decadence has entered politics, with Marinetti futurism, with Hitler the Schwabing tradition" (*GS* 7:382). Hitler, of course, had spent some time in Munich before the outbreak of World War I, continuing the bohemian ways of his years in Vienna. Schwabing had also been the locale of Ludwig Klages's lectures. More generally, Benjamin refers to the spiritus loci of the amoral, aestheticist bohemian disdain of and self-styled separation from the pragmatic, vital interests of the body politic. At any rate, Hitler here is linked with such mentality that resurfaced in his political practice vis-à-vis the masses. Two years later, in his essay "Ein Bruder" ("A Brother"), Thomas Mann, too, would critically address the phenomenon Hitler as the irrationalist "artist," the self-centered, power-hungry orator and demagogue as a "black magician," as such part of a primitivist expressionist legacy.[70]

Benjamin's political line of attack against artistic countercultures from the point of view of the more advanced film medium in turn is leveled also against surrealism! In other words, at this stage of his critique of literature he *historicizes* also the avant-garde. Surrealism, after all, still a form of "literature," is now linked in a quick move with the audience's "regressive" reaction. His attack on the historical avant-garde culminates in the critique of a futurist aestheticization of war. He quotes a statement by Marinetti: " 'War is beautiful because it establishes man's dominion over the subjugated machinery by means of gas-masks, terrifying megaphones, flame throwers, and small tanks. War is beautiful because it initiates the dreamt-of metallicization of the human body.' " For Benjamin such a proclamation confirms that in war the intersubjective potential inherent *in* technology is perverted *through* technology, turned against the masses whose living social body is turned into an object for war (metallicized). In other words, the dazzling display and the release of the marvelous in technological warfare as an aesthetic experience prevents war from being experienced as a *political* event. Futurist writing, far from its claims for a "parole in liberta," abuses the aesthetic powers inherent *in* language in the interest of power *through* language at the point where for Marinetti the "fiery orchids of machine guns" and "the stench of putrefaction" combine "into a symphony." At that *aestheticized* political moment, the masses contemplate a final grand spectacle: they witness their own destruction as physical beings. "*Fiat ars — pereat mundus,*"[71] Benjamin writes (transforming Ferdinand I's famous motto concerning the sacrifice of the world for the principles of "iustitia").

A subtext of Benjamin's critique of Italian futurism, I maintain, remains his critique of the metaphorical poetics of expressionism and its politicized legacy. After all, from the German translation of Marinetti's futurist manifesto in *Der Sturm* in 1912 to Benn's welcoming speech for Marinetti in 1933, some expressionists had cultivated a particularly close affinity to futurism. While its early reception in Walden's journal was a case of a purely aesthetic influence, Benn had unequivocally embraced futurism in the interest of his concept of a European fascist order. Due to these circumstances, it is altogether plausible that the German literary and political context rather than the Italian is of primary interest to Benjamin in the writing of the essay.[72] The reference to Marinetti is, of course, topical, as his movement presents the actual case of the avant-garde as an actor in a fascist war. But these arguments were prepared earlier, as we have seen in the case of Benjamin's long-standing critique of expressionism.

Since "Theorien des Faschismus" (1930), focused on Ernst Jünger's adventurous prowar writings, Benjamin had attacked militarism as a politically perverted form of idealism that operates by destructively "dumping" the human body. Evidently the *Ausdruck* (expression) of a totalized *Erlebnis* (experience in a volitional sense) as separate from physical experience is the basis for the fascist totalitarian state as a monstrous and murderous "Gesamtkunstwerk" ("total work of art") spectacle. Thus Benjamin's critique of fascism does not argue against nationalism or racism on an ideological level. It addresses instead the politically manipulated dichotomy of *Geist* and body, the blockage of their correspondence and communication in social interaction—in art as in war.[73]

Echoing such an argument in his *Passagenwerk,* Benjamin reflects on expressionism as a significant "eruptive" turn toward "inwardness" in advance of C. G. Jung's "esoteric theory of art." He refers to Gottfried Benn's (and Döblin's) "specifically medical nihilism" as an aesthetic deflection of the shock experience of the "interior of the body," a topic he had plans to write about.[74] Whether or not Benn's early provocative *Morgue* poems, shocking the reader with images of cancer patients and corpses, or Döblin's analyses of physical phobia (as in the novella "The Assassination of a Buttercup") would really have corroborated his assumptions about the origins and consequences of inwardness may remain a question here. At any rate, on such grounds he defers to Lukács's arguments in the expressionism debate from which he had been excluded: "Herein one cannot disregard the connections which Lukács has established between expressionism and fascism" (*GS* 5:590)).

Offside: Brecht, Bloch; Benjamin

A major issue in the expressionism debate conducted in *Das Wort* was the production and communicability of literature in terms of "popularity" (*Volkstümlichkeit*).[75] Benjamin's embrace of film with just that question in mind, of course, was opposed to the belief in literature shared, in spite of all differences, by Lukács, Brecht, and Bloch. In an amendment to the second version of the artwork essay meant for publication in Moscow, he had placed his own faith in the popularity of an image from the collective dreams of technological modernity: "earth-orbiting Mickey Mouse."[76] Clearly, the cultural politics of the forum he wanted to address were far removed from such argument. Benjamin had placed himself squarely offside.

With his peculiar antiliterary stance on film, he was intellectually also removed from the writer and critic closest to him. Appreciating the significance of expressionist techniques for his own work, Brecht concurred with Bloch's indictment of Moscow's cultural politics in the matter of expressionism as comparable to Hitler's.[77] Brecht's views, for his own sake as well as for that of an antifascist solidarity cunningly reserved to the memory of his desk, placed Lukács's power motives "into the most dangerous proximity to 'Blood and Soil' and an indecent metaphysics of the organic."[78]

His dialectical relation to expressionism was that of a *literary* critic who, after all, had himself written quite a bit about the timeliness of film, however, arguing for an interaction between the different media. The poet's and playwright's relationship to expressionism is dialectical in the terms of *literature,* not dialectical in the sense of a radical self-critique of art as attributed by Benjamin to surrealism. In other words, Brecht is not interested in "language as such," which is Benjamin's concern we have traced from his early critique of expressionism in the *Origin of the German Tragic Drama* (1925) to the essay on surrealism and the early essay on the epic theater.

For Brecht, expressionism stands in between "revolution" and "evolution;" it is a putsch, as the expressionists "only liberated themselves from grammar, not from capitalism." Nevertheless, the critic as writer has a place for the subjective expressionist effort at liberation, as he "take(s) seriously any attempt of liberation." On the other hand, he is firmly opposed to a purely formalist enterprise, in which case "the avant-garde . . . can march so much ahead that the majority cannot follow." For Brecht, the technique of montage, then, is not the miracle weapon per se but may merely supplies "solutions *on paper*": "*Naturalism* and a certain *anarchic montage*" may be rendering mere "symptoms of the surface" (this was, in fact, Lukács's objection against expressionist formalism). Obviously Brecht, in opposition to Lukács in the debate, does not want to talk about "*den* Realismus,"[79] nor does he totalize expressionism like Benjamin. He prefers, instead, to consider individual writers and their specific techniques for solving specific *literary* problems.

Brecht singles out individual expressionists who influenced his early plays. For example, *Baal,* his response to Hanns Johst's *Der Einsame* (*The Solitary One*), or his play *Trommeln in der Nacht* (*Drums in the Night*), are marked by a kind of worked-through expressionist legacy, as "Kaiser, Sternheim, Toller, Goering provided the spoils for the realist."[80] Benjamin himself records in a diary entry of June 17, 1931: "Brecht appears to think of, besides Strindberg, Georg Kaiser as the greatest technician among the newer authors; he regards especially his 'Alkibiades Saved' as a major instance for understanding the epic theater" (*GS* 6:439). Just a year before, in 1930, Benjamin had written about Döblin's *Berlin Alexanderplatz* as the very last (and therein already vanishing) instance of the "bourgeois" educational novel. The real hero there is not the human persona but the metropolis of Berlin itself, speaking authentically in multiple montaged discourses. For Brecht, at least according to Benjamin, the expressionist playwright Kaiser may have had a comparable significance for the understanding of

cultural paradigm shifts: "He characterized Kaiser as the last idealist dramatist, whose theatrical technique had already reached a standard which made
it useless for the purposes of idealism. He is the dramatist before the turn"
(GS 6:439).

It should be noted that Brecht's earliest criticism of expressionist drama,
as recorded in his notebook in 1920, had voiced the very same reservations Benjamin would maintain throughout his critical campaign against
expressionism. The expressionists, Brecht wrote, had embraced the "idea"
but had had "no ideas"; they had "embodied" the "soul" instead of demonstrating *Geist* in the body. He singled out Georg Kaiser, in particular,
for his strained rhetorical pathos as the "verbose Wilhelm of the German
drama."[81] Later, however, he would refer to Kaiser and Döblin as his "two
extramarital fathers."[82]

And Ernst Bloch, of course, thoroughly identified with expressionism. In
"Diskussionen über Expressionismus" ("Discussing Expressionism"; 1938),
his response to Lukács, Bloch stressed a specifically *volkstümliche* (popular) tradition of expressionism. For him, the movement's forms, images, its
"revolutionary imagination,"[83] were rooted in folk art as a collective expression. Simultaneously he stressed the "productivity"[84] of the artistic *subject*,
its ability to receive and express the messianic "images of a purer world"
and to remove the barriers between art and life, between the metaphysical and physical realms. The expressionist work of art, for Bloch, was a
product of the creative *subject's* "daydream," which mediated the "not-yet"-
experienced through "archaic-utopian" images—the emphasis is on *utopian*—as collective expressions. Prominent in Benjamin's correspondence
with Adorno since 1934 had been the concern with the "archaic" image as
a collective phenomenon within the *individual* psyche as defined by Klages
and Jung. The concern was to be resolved in assessing the site of collective
dreams (in recourse to Freudian terms) within the material conditions of
the social body, where the constellation of the "archaic" and the experience
of technology, the physical and, ultimately, the metaphysical, shows itself
in the form of "dialectical images."[85] By contrast, Bloch attempted to solve
the problem of the regressive dangers of the "archaic image" on the basis
of a subject-centered creative experience that projects into the future. For
him, expressionist art and literature was *the* "avant-garde."[86]

As for Gottfried Benn, the expressionist philosopher had campaigned
against the poet even before the expressionism debate in the exile journal was triggered by the poet's embrace of Nazism and Klaus Mann's reaction to it. In the essay "Songs of Remoteness," written no later than

1933 and included in *Erbschaft unserer Zeit* (*Legacy of Our Times*), Bloch had targeted Benn's antimodern escapism, his "thallasalic regression" to the "Urbilder." The essay had placed the poet in the intellectual company of Ludwig Klages leading into the political camp of Adolf Hitler.[87] In these terms Bloch moved on the same grounds that made Benjamin draw a connection between Klages and Jung, "who has signed himself over to fascism."[88] Benjamin otherwise showed (like Lukács) little developed interest in the Benn scandal itself.[89] Yet, Benjamin must at least be credited with having hinted at the problem with his "Pariser Brief" published in *Das Wort:* criticism before 1933 had failed to pay sufficient attention to Gottfried Benn and Arnolt Bronnen.[90]

The underlying differences between Bloch and Benjamin[91] during these years were perhaps best expressed already in Bloch's review of Benjamin's *Einbahnstraße* (*One-Way Street*) in the *Vossische Zeitung* in 1928: "No subject, hardly a *we* can be perceived here. . . . Nothing of the births of the subject, of Klee's and the expressionists' 'self-crystal-forest.'"[92] This passage fully manifests Bloch's inherent dislike of the distanced intellectualism of Benjamin's "surrealist philosophy" and his aversion to expressionism.[93] It is suppressed in the review's revised version in *Heritage of Our Times* (1935) for the sake of preserving an intellectual front against fascism. For Benjamin, in turn, it was Bloch's unchanged idealist position that, in his eyes, left the advocate of expressionism without a concretely identifiable forum in the literary struggle as a political struggle.[94]

As here traced in terms of the chain of commentaries, essays, and reviews from 1916 through 1937, explicitly or implicitly debating expressionism, Benjamin had consistently grounded his critique of "art" in his affirmation of "language as such." There is, of course, another group of essays that deal with high modernism. They reach from "The Image of Proust" (1929) to his critically nostalgic essay on Baudelaire (1938–1939) as the "poet without a halo." These essays are on the other side of, yet complementary to, his questioning "literature" in terms of the avant-garde's experiment with language. Devoted to the question of language and narration, literary language and the unconscious, they, too, pursue "a progressively more exact and more uncompromising concept of what constitutes a work of art," (*GS* 1:1023) a concept that, beginning with the book on the *Trauerspiel*, was based on his critique of expressionism. Here we have focused on his most radical tendencies: Haunted by the idea of the end of the authority of individualist art and, on the other hand, the rise of the totalitarian masses, he had sought to find an answer—via surrealism, in Brecht's work, and subsequently in film—to the failure of a "humanist concept of freedom."(*GS* 2:295)

Benjamin's theoretical extremism, culminating in his ardent attacks on "belles lettres," may have blinded him to the practices of the massive output of Nazi film productions effectively *aestheticizing* propaganda (though the Parisian exile was, of course, removed from witnessing its effects on the German masses). From the point of view of today's experience of Hollywood's earth-orbiting visual culture, Benjamin had to fail, of course, in his critical quest for an alternative experience of a collective subject. A critique of the avant-garde's legacies today must be conscious of the impossibility of finding and defining such experience. In an age of voracious commercialism, the boundaries between art and advertisement are instantaneously erased, as the expressionist Yvan Goll had already adduced in his play *Der Unsterbliche* (*The Immortal One;* 1918–1920), film being the paradigm (see chapter 8). Clearly, however, Benjamin has more consistently and with greater intensity than other contemporaneous critics of the avant-garde articulated the "crisis of the arts" as the problem of "art." The specter that haunted the expressionism debate in the 1930s has left its critical traces in a future that is our present.

6. The Avant-Garde against Itself

George Grosz and Bertolt Brecht from
Postexpressionist Berlin to the American Exile
and the Postwar Cold War Aftermath

While the expressionism debate in exile revealed the conflicts between the
critics of the avant-garde, among them Bertolt Brecht, the changing relationship of the painter George Grosz and the playwright can be regarded
as an example of the crisis of a politically involved avant-garde exiled from
the country and culture in which they had developed their positions. Such
a predicament is reflected on the personal, on the political, and, significantly, on the level of the artistic discourse. Changes in the patterns and
forms of the avant-garde's literary texts or in its iconography often consciously correspond to major upheavals in the sociopolitical context; they
are more conspicuous than the reflections of mainstream writing and art on
changing times. In this case a growing discrepancy between two erstwhile
closely allied critics of German society and politics since World War I culminated in the American exile. Their differences had become symptomatic
of a schism within the German avant-garde in exile, differences concerning
the political viability of writing and art which carried over into their formal
practices and resulted in their opposition in the immediate postwar cold
war era. At that time, Grosz was still in the United States, while Brecht had
resettled in East Berlin.

This is how the story could be told on the biographical level: The painter, realizing a lifelong dream, had left for the United States only a few weeks before Hitler's rise to power. He immediately set out to make his art an expression of his newfound home and devoted himself to capturing, acquiring, and developing the new code[1] of the American city, New York, and the American landscape, Cape Cod. Contrary to the stereotyped assessment maintained in art criticism (now thoroughly refuted by Kay Flavell's 1988 biography), Grosz never became a completely apolitical artist of landscapes and nudes. In his core work, the satirist of the "Wilhelminian Republic"—the derisive term he and John Heartfield coined for Weimar Germany—continued to comment on the monstrosity of Nazism. His first caricature of Hitler as a barbarian dated back as far as 1923, when it was published in the dadaist journal *Die Pleite* (*Bankruptcy*). For his postcommunist critique, informed by an unending series of conflicts with party-line positions on art and a disillusioning visit to the Soviet Union in 1929, he returned to the form of allegory, which was, as in the case of the 1936 *Interregnum*, equally applicable to the condemnation of fascist and communist totalitarian practices. He thereby knowingly disappointed and alienated the American leftist art world that had welcomed him as an avant-gardist of exemplary political art. For the longest time, the American Left simply refused to admit that Grosz no longer was the committed leftist satirist he had been in Weimar Germany by continuing to stage him as such. Only with the Hitler-Stalin pact of 1939 did the American Left gradually begin to shift from political art to the forms of an international abstract modernism, which would become the dominant culture of liberal democracy in the postwar era. This turn constituted a reversal that Grosz was to resist at a high cost to his international career. His work in exile was altogether eclipsed by the dominating influence of Paul Klee, Picasso, and French surrealism in the United States as well as in Europe.

The painter's isolation from the radical Left in America had been deliberate. Deliberate, too, was his growing isolation from the German exile groups, with whom he felt he had little in common to begin with. He expressed this, for example, in a fairly compromising letter to none other than Gottfried Benn, dated June 1933, in which he attempts to walk a tightrope between Klaus Mann's attack on the supporter of National Socialism and Benn's haughtily irrationalist "Antwort an die literarischen Emigranten" ("Answer to the Literary Emigrants"). The letter sets out this biographical premise: "By God, I do not belong to those quarreling emigrants—because I did not come here in January for 'political' reasons—at that time General Schleicher was still in power, and it did not look like such a near victory

of Hitlerman yet. I think, I really left for so-called economic reasons—
mixed with the desire for adventure and travel . . . in order to get to know
this unknown country, which is still big in becoming."[2] Yet, Grosz never
succeeded—even if he occasionally chose to think otherwise[3]—in blend-
ing into a genuinely American economic, artistic, and intellectual climate,
either. In this particular personal context, and in the overall political constellation, Grosz ultimately embraced a version of modernist absurdism,
exemplified in his 1947–1948 series "Der Maler des Lochs" ("The Painter
of the Hole"),[4] which I will discuss subsequently.

Brecht, of course, was a genuine exile in the United States. He never for
a moment lost sight of his goal, shared with other exiled intellectuals, to
return as soon as possible to a Europe liberated from fascism and brought
closer to communism. The Marxist writer was uncompromising in the matter of art and politics to the degree that his notion of a revolutionary theater
was unable to penetrate Broadway and his film projects failed in Hollywood. His own isolation from much of the American Left stemmed from
different causes than Grosz's: For him, the Left was not leftist enough in
matters of art, and his image of America was that of hell made in Hollywood. Furthermore, very much contrary to Grosz, Brecht's position vis-à-
vis the Soviet Union remained, at least officially, sympathetic.[5]

In these rough terms, the Grosz-Brecht split seems to be well explained
by the story of the renegade versus the hard-liner. I would like to offer an
alternative story, however. Only when the focus on the exile period is en-
hanced by a review of the times of their cooperation will we gain a much
more precise view. The painter's oscillating affinities to the playwright and
his ultimate embrace of a quasi-absurdist point of view ought to be understood as stemming from an individualist anarchist mentality that seeks
political alliances and commitments only in times of revolutionary potential. Hence also his oscillation between aggressive political satire and consciously ambiguous allegory.

The Painter between Benn and Brecht

In the early years of expressionism, the artist and the writer shared an anarchist mentality. At that time, it was possible for Grosz to develop a foun-
dational relationship not only with Brecht but also with Gottfried Benn,[6]
while Brecht, of course, defined his work against the grain of expressionism.
Grosz's affinity to Benn expressed itself specifically in a series of "night-
cafe" sketches, one of them bearing the title "Dr. Benn's Cafe," and a poem

with the title "Kaffeehaus" (1918), to which Benn responded with a series of "night-cafe" lyrics, written during the period from 1912 to 1921. It is not at all surprising, then, that some of Benn's "dramatic scenes," written in occupied Brussels as grotesque antiwar satires, for example, "Die Etappe" ("Home Front"; 1916), have the making of a literary adaptation of Grosz's sketches ridiculing the "pillars of society." Some of the poems of the "poor B.B." collected in the *Hauspostille* (*Manual of Piety;* 1927), specifically Brecht's earlier lyrics like "Vom ertrunkenen Mädchen" ("Of a Drowned Girl"; 1920), even have much in common with the pessimistic themes and mood of Benn's *Morgue* cycle of 1912. In 1927, Kurt Tucholsky could still refer to Benn *and* Brecht as "the greatest lyrical talents . . . who live in Germany today." Not much later, of course, the two were to become outright antagonists. In the same essay, Tucholsky compared the tenor of the poems of Brecht's *Hauspostille* with the poems of the young Grosz.[7]

World War I is the watershed event in which the bohemian Grosz begins to turn away from Benn and toward Brecht. The cooperation of Grosz and Brecht as severe critics of German affairs begins with the latter's adaptation of Grosz's sketch "K.V." (A l) in the "Ballade vom toten Soldaten" ("Ballad of the Dead Soldier"; 1918). Grosz's well-known antiwar drawing of 1916–1917 depicted a worm-eaten skeleton being given a physical before it is sent back to the battlefield. The sketch was later included in Grosz's collection *Das Gesicht der herrschenden Klasse* (*The Visage of the Ruling Class;* 1921), for which Brecht had ample praise. The former coffeehouse bohemian, since 1916 a member of the Spartacus League and then of the Communist Party, had turned activist.

It is significant that Brecht included the Grosz-inspired "Ballad of the Dead Soldier" in the appendix of the 1929 Propyläen edition of *Drums in the Night.* He had amended the stage directions to the fourth act to have the schnapps dealer Glubb sing it to the guitar. In these years, and still in the early 1950s in the German Democratic Republic (GDR)—when he considered the introduction of Glubb's nephew as a "positive hero," fighting and falling for the revolution—Brecht was belaboring what he considered to be the reactionary nature of his 1919 play. In 1953, he would continue to draw a direct connection between Grosz's sketches and his own plays. In a note introducing his commentaries "Bei Durchsicht meiner ersten Stücke" (Upon reviewing my first plays), he points out that his early plays and Grosz's sketches had been looked upon "not as depictions of an evil world but as the works of evil people"; they had been called "undermining . . . because they had demonstrated the general dissolution of morality and of the old institutions." The "Ballad of the Dead Soldier," he remembers, had been viewed as an example of his "low mentality" and had led to his exile, as it supposedly had "insulted the soldier of the world war."[8]

In light of this declaration of solidarity, it is altogether startling that in the following "Vorwort zu *Trommeln in der Nacht*" ("Foreword to *Drums in the Night*") and in an imagined "Gespräch mit George Grosz" ("Conversation with George Grosz"), Brecht should subject his former companion to a severe critique. It appears that the playwright, now living and working in the German Democratic Republic, is bent on rejecting the painter, still in the United States, as a "bad influence" on his early work. Altogether forgotten seems to be, for example, Grosz's cooperation with Erwin Piscator's Schwejk staging in 1927, for which Brecht had been invited to help revise the manuscript of the dramatized Hašek novel. After all, Grosz had transcribed Brecht's concept of the "defamiliarization effect" into his live, on-stage illustrations, as one critic observed. After all, Brecht himself had had plans to transplant, as it were, the "blasphemy" trials from 1928 to 1930 of the Weimar government against Herzfelde and Grosz (because of his sketch "Christus mit der Gasmaske" ["Christ with Gas Mask"]) onto the stage in the manner of a political "happening." Furthermore, Grosz had at that time illustrated Brecht's *Die Drei Soldaten* (*The Three Soldiers;* 1932) and had planned to illustrate the playwright's collected works. Now, however, in his fictitious "Conversation with Georg Grosz," Brecht denies that his former collaborator was at all politically engaged:

> I do not believe, Grosz, that one day you felt the urge—out of insurmountable pity with an exploited human being, or from anger against an exploiting man—to sketch something pertaining to this matter onto the paper. I rather believe that sketching was a sort of entertainment for you, and the physiognomy of people your stimulation. I imagine that one day you discovered in yourself a strong, irresistible fascination with a certain face as the great occasion to cater to your whims. It was the "Visage of the Ruling Class."[9]

Denying Grosz any class-conscious position, the GDR playwright Brecht goes as far as to undercut his "urge to protest" as "economically" satisfying. In short, Grosz' art is amoral, aestheticist, and capitalist.

It is obvious from the context of Brecht's remarkable self-criticism of "Der Erfolg von *Trommeln in der Nacht* bei der Bourgeoisie" ("The Success of *Drums in the Night* with the Bourgeoisie") that the playwright chooses to condemn the Groszian anarchist elements of his play at the expense of the partner, whose influence on his own early work he now regrets. And, indeed, the play's milieu—the interior of the bourgeois Balickes and Murk's Picadilly Bar, the metropolitan street scenes with its bourgeois, petit bourgeois, and lumpenproletarian types—is clearly indebted to the visions of the painter. Through his attack on George Grosz, the playwright has more than prepared the way to criticize his own bourgeois-anarchist attitude at the time he wrote the play: "The revolution, which had to supply the milieu, did not interest me more than the Vesuvius is of interest to a man who wants to place his pot of soup on it."[10] The rejection of his own disposition, and Grosz's implicitly as well, is, of course, not strictly personal but a rigid Marxist critique of art as a bourgeois enterprise. Brecht's self-criticism of 1953 is as schematic as his remarks about the political dialectic of the avant-garde, which the exile in Denmark had jotted down in his notebook:

> the avant-garde
> dadaism
> expressionism
> new objectivity
> the contemporary play
> canned music, concert music, "music for communal use," the songs for the masses, the "learning play" [*Lehrstück*], the "revue," . . . the staged aphorism, the enacted slogan. we criticized the times, and the times criticized us.[11]

Already in 1930, Brecht had written a devastating materialist polemic against the historicist art historian who interprets "all historical epochs as equally close to God." Here, in these critical, ultimately self-critical, lines, he proves himself a dialectical materialist historian who does not stop short of his critical goals, even if his own person and work seem to be in the way of a politically progressive assessment and development of art: "We criticized the times, and the times criticized us."[12]

In a letter of August 1934, Grosz had asked Brecht for a copy of *Three Soldiers* and had praised his "choruses of the house painter" ("Anstreicher-chöre"; a reference to Hitler, the former house painter). The same letter had questioned, however, the writer's rigid view of the world in his poem "New York," calling it a lifeless "Marxist wishful image" ("marxistisches Wunsch-bild") of one who had not experienced the American reality.[13] Two months later, Grosz would express his enthusiasm about the prospect of illustrating Brecht's plays and his willingness to follow Brecht's instructions. He concludes that letter with a reference to his involvement in "a topical painting,

a series" ("aktuelles Bild [mehrere]"), such as the critical allegories "Assassination of a Dictator-King," "End and Decapitation of a Freedom-Fighter,"
and "Reunion with Party Friends and Oath" ("Attentat auf einen Diktator-
könig," "Ende und Enthauptung eines Freiheitshelden" and "Wiedersehen
mit den Parteifreunden und Schwur").[14]

Personal discrepancies based on perhaps not yet fully analyzed, certainly
not yet openly admitted, ideological differences begin to surface in Grosz's
letters to Brecht as early as May 1935. Thus he gives the playwright in Denmark, who five months later will visit New York in order to supervise the
proposed staging of *Die Mutter* (*The Mother*), a full account of a meeting with Eisler in that city. The composer of the music for *The Mother,*
promoting the play in New York, is mercilessly ridiculed for his Brechtian
speech mannerisms and what Grosz refers to as the "Chinese method" of
argumentation: "He maintained that this method compares to a kind of
"television" [*Fernseher*]; for the one who uses it, everything suddenly becomes comfortably flat . . . like a dish . . . Yes, that's what he said. . . . Then
all riddles would be solved. Wonderful. Altogether wonderful. Of course,
he rendered the death-blow to my romanticism." Grosz here implicitly alludes to Brecht's concept of *Gebrauchskunst* (art for communal use). The
main target, however, is the doctrine of "socialist realism," promoted since
the First Congress of Soviet writers in 1934 — by Shdanov and other Soviet
mandarins of cultural politics such as Radek — as the only true avant-garde.
In other words, the object of ridicule is the "Chinese method": "A flat dish
is really beautiful and useful at the same time. . . . For the adored masses
the most stupid and the flattest is the best. . . . Please do not fool your-
self, dear Bertie . . . your stuff is to the masses (except perhaps for a few
poems) nonsense." Obviously, Grosz could be reminding Brecht of the previous failure of his *Die Dreigroschenoper* (*The Threepenny Opera*) at New
York's Empire Theatre in April 1933, and of *Die Mutter* (*The Mother*) in
Berlin to genuinely arouse the interest of the working classes. The ensuing fiasco of the short-lived performance of the latter play by the Theatre
Union in New York, which in spite of Brecht's notorious tantrums and legal
threats watered down the notion of the epic theater beyond recognition,
had brought about his falling out with the Left. The scandal was to confirm
Grosz's realistic appraisal of the situation. His letter from New York is also
an affirmation of the complex vitality of American society. It ends in a critical swipe at Wieland Herzfelde, whose prediction of the immanent collapse
of the Ford empire is registered as another example of the propagandistic,
ideological aberration of the "Chinese method."[15]

It is the postscript[16] to this letter which gives away that Grosz's attack on Eisler and Wieland Herzfelde was nothing but a pretext for an implied criticism of Brecht himself. Grosz's grotesque self-criticism is nothing but an inverted form of criticism of the addressee. Tongue in cheek, Grosz refers to his own opinions as "mistakes of the petit bourgeois: lack of orderly attitude, bourgeois mindlessness, anarcho-fascist tendencies. . . . Disrespect for the taboo. Probably maintains contact with counterrevolutionaries (the worst), probably with Trotzky personally." And the postscript ends on a heightened note of Dada-like mockery: "No medals. Sentenced three times for disorderly mentality. May not publish anymore. Concentration camp. Paper for sketches only once a month . . . at good conduct. May dress by himself." Such a pose of a self-criticism is, of course, a mask that allows him to show his true face and thereby to ridicule Brecht's "television"— rationalism as nothing but ideologically blinded utopianism.

More than ten years later, after the defeat of Nazi Germany, Brecht would once again try to enlist his sketching collaborator of the late 1920s and early 1930s, now a fellow exile in the United States, in the service of his plans for the regeneration of the "alte Kulturland" (seasoned land of culture). He asks Grosz to accompany a poem—most likely "Der anachronistische Zug oder Freiheit und Democracy" ("The Anachronistic Procession or Freedom and Democracy"), written early in 1947—with some sketches for a provisional edition to be sent to Germany. Wieland Herzfelde was to prepare a solid issue later.[17] Grosz, who had so eagerly contributed his illustrations to *Three Soldiers* (1932) and who, at the end of 1934, had agreed to illustrate Herzfelde's planned edition of Brecht's *Gesammelte Werke,* now flatly declines: "By the way, the labor of illustrating political slogans (even if in the form of poetry) is one of the greatest and most strenuous in the world." For such a task he would need to succeed in his efforts to develop a "machine" (meaning an equivalent to Brecht's "television" already referred to more than a decade ago). More significant for the assessment of a split between the two artists as a schism within the avant-garde is Grosz's refusal to get involved in a cultural reconstruction of Europe: "By the way, I was surprised about the sentence 'seasoned [*altes*] land of culture.' There you hit the nail on the head . . . Exactly, that's what it is."[18]

The Painter of the Hole

In short, now Grosz openly refuses to share Brecht's program of promoting cultural political changes. Instead, at the conclusion of the same letter, he emphasizes his involvement with, and indeed, his identification with, a series of paintings called "Wanderer ins Nichts" ("Wanderer into Nothingness"):

> Not after Radek . . . dedicated to Sartre and Heidegger: one painting bears the title "the painter of the hole" (Maler des Lochs), the other "the musician of the hole," a third, "the poet of the hole" . . . they consist of thin (but firm) lines but do not give any shadow, they are grey in grey . . . their insignium (as the Romans called it) is a real torn hole of canvas. Incredible. That man has around himself hundreds of hole-like sketches . . . however, he is nevertheless interested also in "beauty," that he remembers darkly but accurately, for example, he means the intricately fine- finest nuances in grey . . . everything, really is grey there. The rats, well, you are thinking something, and at that very moment a rat runs into the corner.[19]

Wieland Herzfelde attributed his friend's turn toward a form of existentialist absurdism, also found in Grosz's 1946 autobiography, to a growing cultural pessimism after the deployment of atomic bombs by the United States.[20] That interpretation has its merits, but it is much too narrow in light of the continuity of grotesque and absurdist elements in the painter's work from one world war to the other. In 1949, Grosz would once again write Gottfried Benn a telling letter, in which he comments on one of the darkest, most resigned and least appreciated works the poet ever wrote: "I read *The Three Old Men*. Would like to tell you that for me you are one of the greatest poets alive. That's what you are."[21] In a sense, then, as documented by other letters both from the pre-Nazi and the post-Nazi era,[22] Grosz has returned to those origins that Brecht, on the other hand, had become so eager to criticize in himself.

It is quite significant that Grosz should have been so "invisible," not only to the American Left but also to Brecht, during all these years. How could Brecht, after the war, ask Grosz to cooperate with him as if nothing had changed between them since the late 1920s? Grosz's need for clowning and posing in contradictory attitudes, fully acted out only during his Dada phase in Berlin, had apparently never been fully identified, even by his closer associates, as a genuine expression of his anarchic mentality. By the same token, one cannot understand Grosz's self-identification with the "painter of the hole" as an unequivocal stance, for the reference to "Sartre and Heidegger" is contradictory, of course. However, he had by this time identified with a broadly defined existentialist position where Kafka's work was "always on [his] nightstand."[23]

His early work, too, had been an expression of division and tension, marked by a kind of aborted dialectic: "In reality I was at that time everyone I sketched . . . I therefore was split into two parts. In other words, I participated in life."[24] Grosz's paintings then and thereafter can thus be considered portraits not only of his audience but also of himself, even if we are led to view them as a distancing critique of the former.

By comparison, the playwright had always insisted on *Wirkungsaesthetik* (aesthetics of effect) as a precondition for art production that makes a difference. In a literary sketch, "Portrait des Beschauers" ("Portrait of the Viewer"; 1920), the author of *Drums in the Night* describes in a series of instances the development of a painter of historical subjects. In his first phase, the artist serves the traditional "spiritual education of the . . . bourgeoisie," then becomes an avant-gardist who wants the audience to take a "critical stance." Brecht's painter had established his reputation by glorifying the historical deeds of Hannibal, Napoleon, and Bismarck; now he fails to satisfy the expectations of his audience and critics. They insist on the cathartic function of representing the tragic, and the refuge from the historical experience the "true work of art" renders by virtue of its "singularity" (*Einmaligkeit*). Brecht's painter, however, becomes more and more interested in the depiction of history as a dialectical collective process, which encompasses both art and audience. His emphasis turns to involving the audience, "for its own benefit," in the subject matter through techniques that point to the medium of paint and cardboard as the material means of representation. In short, he develops what Brecht will later programmatically call the "defamiliarization effect" of "epic" art. The bourgeois establishment, of course, judges such technical orientation as "experimental" in the sense of ephemeral, as the "end of art."[25]

Brecht's historical materialist artist, however, here sees the beginnings of a new form of art. Brecht's "Portrait of the Viewer" provides an example (and is an example) of this new form of art in presenting an apocalypse à la Breughel, or for that matter, à la George Grosz. Grosz's paintings like "Pandemonium," dedicated to Oscar Panizza (1917–1918), as well as central images of *Interregnum* (1936), are admittedly indebted to Breughel, for whom Brecht himself had nothing but admiration. Brecht depicts his literary icon of apocalypse, Duke Karl der Kühne, after the battle of Murten as a lonely corpselike rider. Without a face, he appears as a pale green, translucent specter reflecting an inflamed sky; his bent-over posture is mirrored by a landscape of bent and broken trees. The duke's prominent hands, ominously swollen, are compared to those of a murderer, strangling the reins of the frightened horse. The rest of the body is described as in total decay, bloated and worm-infested below the waist. To top it off, Brecht, as it were, installs a stark and yet paradoxically complementary contrast into his imagery: Like the proverbial pearl in the sick oyster, the duke's heart, isolated in the caved-in chest, shines in "beautiful light vermilion."[26] On the "wirkungsaesthetische" level of the image, the heart functions as an equivalent of the technique of "defamiliarization," which Brecht already employed (rudimentarily) in the play *Drums in the Night*. Besides the play's dialogues, which commented on the personae and the action, a "paper moon" was switched on or off at strategic dramaturgic points. The paper moon served as a visual device to prevent the romantic "gawking" of the audience. In Brecht's "historical painting," the design of the duke's "beautiful light vermilion" heart, as it were, illuminates the compensatory function of aesthetic beauty. Aesthetic beauty is grounded on the sacrifice of life; it is the product of the catastrophe of history and offers respite from it. In light of the devastation of the First World War, the end of which was also the end of the Hohenzollern monarchy, Brecht's piece thus thematizes the duke's bodily degeneration as the political dissolution of feudalism. The rendition of dissolution is politically progressive for Brecht—this he will restate in his remarks about the "Defamiliarization Effect in the Narrating Images of Breughel the Elder"—as long as it has the tendency to change "the relationship of the viewer of his pictures to the subject matter depicted."[27] In that critical sense, the portrait of the duke is a "portrait of the viewer" in 1920.

For a time, George Grosz's work no doubt satisfied this requirement for Brecht. When he becomes convinced, however, that the dialectic of the avant-garde also implies a criticism of the criticism of the times in the context of changed political constellations, he will call outdated that which in its own time had been dialectical. In this fashion he reevaluates, for example, in 1938, his own early poems, the poems of the *Manual of Piety* (1927), in comparison to his class-conscious Svendborg poems: Compared to his earlier poetry, the poems written in Danish exile constitute for Brecht, from an aesthetic point of view, a "decline." From a political point of view, however, they are valued as a progressive stage. Two years later he would write about the poems of *Manual of Piety*:

Literature here reaches that degree of dehumanization which Marx perceives in the proletariat and at the same time the finality which inspires him with hope. . . . Beauty establishes itself on wrecks. The sublime writhes in the dust, the absurd is being celebrated as liberation. The poet is not even with himself in solidarity any more. Risus mortis. But this is by no means weak stuff.[28]

In this dialectical sense, all of these remarks could have been made about Grosz's *Visage of the Ruling Class* as well. In fact, Brecht had praised this collection of sketches when it was published in Moscow. The reason why, in 1953, he chooses to criticize the "painter of the hole" for a work previously praised must therefore lie in the changed historical context. Brecht's change of mind is related to the development of a global split that Grosz's letters beginning in the mid-1930s had contained in personal overtones. Only during the postwar period would it become clear to the former collaborators that an irreversible schism was taking place within the ranks of the avant-garde.

As early as 1934, Grosz had become aware of the fact that America was moving toward a "flowering of the arts" in which surrealists like Salvador Dali and Georgio de Chirico played a major role. Grosz continues to observe these developments closely through 1953, when he realizes that postwar America has evolved into the "art center of the world." Abstract painting, which Grosz abhors, is now en vogue; Paul Klee is noted as having the greatest success. What impresses Grosz most is that "our great master Dali," whose craftsmanship he emphatically admires, had succeeded — to no small degree through anarchist clowning — in capturing the American popular imagination,[29] something which his less "painterly," more cerebral, after all, more politically rooted work had mostly failed to accomplish. For Grosz, the trend toward an existentialist absurdism, which he had adopted early on and which would become a dominant expression also of postwar Europe, represented a global intellectual and artistic awareness of the fact that the times criticized the cultural and political efforts of the artists not merely as utopian, but as futile. This assessment is shared by other exiled intellectuals, as I have amply discussed in chapter 3.

It is this awareness of the era that Grosz demonstrates in "Painter of the Hole." The image is re-presented in the painter's self-interpretation in his letter to Brecht. The "insignium" of the "torn canvas" is to forcefully signify to the viewer a critical denial of the political potential of art. Such a denial is paradoxically implied by the term "Roman" as a historical refer-

ence to the fall of the most powerful empire and culture of classical antiquity. This, not the "bourgeois" ideal of "beauty," is his major concern:
"However, he is nevertheless interested also in 'beauty' that he remembers
darkly, but accurately," he wrote to Brecht.[30] Thus the painter Grosz, just
like Brecht's painter of the "Portrait of the Viewer" (1920), is fundamentally interested in an aesthetics of a "critical stance." He has forgone the
ideals of "bourgeois education," of the eternal value of beauty and the "true
work of art."[31] He proceeds to explain to Brecht the function of the painting's means of presentation, his use of the color gray: The painting is to
demonstrate the technical process of creating "beauty," namely in "intri-
cately fine-finest nuances in grey." Gray is not a familiar color for unfolding
beauty to the viewer, he seems to point out to Brecht in the letter. Thus its
subject matter is the creative process as the reflection of the medium itself,
which thus defamiliarizes the creation of "beauty" (in which he is "also
interested").[32] His goal is to involve the viewer in the artist's reflections on
the limits of art in a political as well as in a metaphysical sense. It is as if
Grosz has translated into the medium of painting Hegel's dictum, "When
philosophy paints its grey in grey, a form of life has become old. Minerva's
owl only begins its flight at dusk."[33] In other words, through "grey in grey"
life cannot be rejuvenated but only recognized.

Thus George Grosz is not one of the "bourgeois" painters whom Brecht
—in his comments on "Volkstümlichkeit und Realismus" ("Popularity and
Realism"; 1937) in the context of the expressionism debate in *Das Wort* (*The
Word*)—refers to as mindless artists on a sinking ship "who still in the very
moment of sinking are occupied with the invention and perfection of paintings." But Brecht, choosing to be unaware of the unique complexity of the
painter and his work, frames him as such in the German Democratic Republic of 1953. Fully aware of the contemporary cosmopolitan dominance
of abstract art as sanctioned in the Western part of Germany by his antipode
Adorno, and falsely identifying the painter with this trend, he indignantly
writes in his fictive "conversation with Grosz": "the position of art in our
days is indeed yours."[34] The struggle and schism within the avant-garde had
turned into its postwar phase (to be discussed in terms of the contemporary significance of Brecht and Benn in the second part of my concluding
chapter) and deteriorated into the official cultural battle positions of the
cold war in which Brecht appears to reveal a crisis of writing of his own:
the dilemma of writing that has turned ideologically rigid.

Part Three : **The Avant-Garde at a Standstill**

7. Gottfried Benn and Nietzsche, 1937–1938
The Aporia of Writing History
in "Wolf's Tavern"

It would be quite inviting to further reflect on the affinities and differences between Gottfried Benn's and Carl Einstein's "hallucinatory-constructive" aesthetics, their commitments to political extremism, albeit of opposite ideological persuasions, in the distinctly different topography of home and exile already touched upon in chapter 4. Yet, my main interest here consists in a close reading of "Weinhaus Wolf" ("Wolf's Tavern"; 1937–1938) in terms of its discursively constructed philosophical ruminations and reflections rather than its "hallucinatory" images. "Wolf's Tavern" is a text that, more tellingly than any other, articulates the contradictory nature of Benn's reversal vis-à-vis National Socialist ideology and of his changing reception of Friedrich Nietzsche's thoughts on the relation of history to life. The narrative is a watershed in the poet's development; claiming a "bio-negative" essence of art, it rejects any form of utopianism in a totalizing gesture of withdrawal into a wounded interiority and protectively reverts to a rigid solipsism.

One of the questions that arises with this extraordinary many-layered text relates to the issue of a disillusionment of avant-garde writing under totalitarian regimes initially supported with conviction. The question is whether a renegade, what is more an author who turned against Nazism only after he was attacked by its functionaries, can be considered a representative of the "inner emigration," as Benn himself elected to view his decision to join the army as a medical officer—quite flippantly—an "aristocratic form of emigration."[1] Clearly, one has to reserve the otherwise too fluid designation of "inner emigration" to those writers who stayed in Nazi Germany but refused altogether to collaborate with the regime, who were not tainted by the *völkisch* ideology but rather opposed it openly in their work, whether published at the time or not. Though Benn cannot be excluded from the discussion of those who sooner or later saw the light during these dark years,[2] there is obviously no comparison with authors like Elisabeth Langgässer or Ricarda Huch, who from the very beginning, at great personal costs, resisted any temptation to collaborate and tangibly expressed resistance. After all, Ricarda Huch was one of the writers who voluntarily resigned from the Preussische Akademie der Dichtung (Prussian Academy of Poetry) when asked to express her loyalty to the new state in response to a circular of which Benn had been a principal author: "What the present government prescribes as national conviction, is not my idea of what it means to be German."[3] Clearly, the case of Benn in 1933–1934 represents a chief paradigm of the dialectic of totalizing utopianism that has turned into totalitarian terror. In terms of the overall issue of how the German avant-garde since the 1910s views its own relations to political and cultural changes, specifically in regard to the status of literature, it is thus instructive to outline our understanding of Benn and his work as a case that most problematically represents its story from its beginnings.

At the beginning of my study, I already tentatively placed the discourse of his Rönne prose (1914–1916) within the expressionist agon of art over art as a most radical example of expressionism's break with representation, thus with historical experience. The poet considered the cycle of experimental "novellas" his breakthrough to "absolute prose," which the medical officer, stationed during World War I in occupied Brussels "in the eye of the hurricane,"[4] experienced as a release and refuge from history. Our discussion of Weimar culture as a productive crisis of literary culture that was faced with the growing impact of the mass media reviewed Benn's attempt to compete most effectively with Brecht in the arena of the musical *Lehrstück* (learning play) and radio. It brought out the poet's continued aversion to the idea of change and telos through history. Thus Benn's embrace of and essayistic contribution to National Socialist ideology in 1933 and 1934 is a radical break from his previous position, as it meant the espousal of a *political* direction, even though a yearning for deindividuation and the surrender of the self to a primitive totality had already characterized much of his earlier writing. Benn now attempted to close ranks with the expressionist playwright and high-ranking NS functionary Hanns Johst, with a vision to mastermind the cultural affairs of the Third Reich. The poet may already have seen himself as the future president of the ideologically reconstituted "Deutsche Akademie der Dichtung" (German Academy of Poetry). The move failed because of NS cultural politics. His desire to become for the "new state" what Marinetti (whom he had personally welcomed in Berlin in 1933), in his eyes, was for Italy at the time failed when Hitler failed to accept expressionism as a legitimate expression of the "new order" in Germany. Benn's representative advocacy of expressionism would result in a attack on his person and work in the National Socialist journal *Das Schwarze Korps* (*The Black Corps*) in 1936; thereafter, in 1938, he was barred from publishing.

In "Wolf's Tavern," written in 1937–1938, the poet appears to altogether repress his personal views in the first hours of the Third Reich; instead, he overcompensates by an attack on any and all historical thought. Benn's near-cultist reception in postwar, educated West German circles, beginning with the 1948 publication of his *Statische Gedichte* (*Static Poems*) in Switzerland, is a case of unique empathy and projection. It is not a case of empathy with a poet of the "inner emigration," however, but rather with a poet who has presumably—like oneself—participated as agent *and* victim in the barbarism of German history. Thus Benn gives expression to what many felt to be a last remaining transhistorical value, the value of absolute, "static" art as refugium from history, as consolation and absolution. What is more, he begins to be regarded as a foremost modernist voice of the times, is compared to T. S. Eliot or Auden, and is viewed by eminent conservative critics and scholars such as Max Rychner and Ernst Robert Curtius as a "European" phenomenon, though his reception in non-German-speaking countries still is, and remains to the present day, controversial or marginal.[5] It should not be forgotten, however, that in the late 1920s and early 1930s, Benn had been given the chance to receive recognition with a wider English-speaking audience as he came to share an internationally highly visible forum, the avant-garde journal *transition,* together with James Joyce, Gertrude Stein, André Breton, and Samuel Beckett. In fact, the editor Eugene Jolas, upon the recommendation of Carl Einstein, translated and published Benn's narratives "Die Insel" ("The Island") and "Der Geburtstag"("The Birthday") in *transition* (vols. 2 and 5; 1927). These translations were accompanied by the editor's essay "Gottfried Benn," which clearly recognized the writer's fundamentally solipsistic disposition but also his search for new means of expression as representative of "a few of the advanced spirits in almost every country today."[6] Benn's quasi-surrealist "Urgesicht" ("Primal Vision") was translated and appeared in the very year of its German publication (*transi-tion* 16–17; 1929). The poet was consistently invited to respond along with major modernist writers and critics to inquiries concerning the "Spirit of America," the "Crisis of Man," and the "Malady of Language." And Jolas's 1932 translation of "The Structure of the Personality (Outline of the Ge-ology of the 'I')," an essay which viewed the modernist poetic experiment as an exploration of the bodily unconscious, was a landmark for the jour-nal's program, which still in 1935 (!) referred and deferred to Benn's ideas about the relation of the primordial to metaphysical expressions.[7] In his autobiography *Man from Babel*, reviewing Benn's engagement for National Socialism, Jolas attempted to take back some of Benn's significance. For example, he remembers the occasion of meeting the poet in Berlin during 1930, "his repetitive insistence on the 'bankruptcy of the antithetical struc-ture,' " meaning of the idea of a progressive spiritual development through poetry, so dear to Jolas himself. Yet Jolas's critical retrospective cannot but express the satisfaction that "He agreed with me as to the poet's right to a new vocabulary and syntax." While Jolas admits at this point that "Benn has undoubtedly written a few of the great poems in modern German," his postwar reappraisal of Benn in the latter parts of *Man from Babel* criti-cizes his embrace of "Hitlerism with lyrical exaltation," aptly finds his ex-planations of "his 'double life' . . . unconvincing, and his clandestinely pronounced 'no' unheard by all except himself."[8] Jolas's judgment can be considered a fair example of Benn's artistic and political estimation in rep-resentative Anglo-American criticism from the 1950s through the 1970s, if not up to our very own days.[9]

My concluding chapter will place Benn's precarious postwar reception by Hans Magnus Enzensberger into a constellation with the influence which Brecht's work had on the German avant-garde in the 1950s and 1960s. Both writers were of equal, if conflicting, importance to a new generation that attempted to come to terms with German history and the significance of history as such. In other words, the work of Gottfried Benn, besides that of Carl Einstein, has been and is throughout this study a measure of re-flection for the aesthetical and political trajectory, of the conflicting dis-courses of the German avant-garde. A central concern of this chapter is that Benn after his involvement with National Socialism will claim or reclaim an aesthetic space of utmost "privacy" and untouchability.[10] As this aesthetic space is *meant* to be an *apolitical* or suprahistorical space, it cannot be con-fused with the *political* notion of "inner emigration" as a form of resistance. The writer's withdrawal into this solipsistic space is already fully articulated in his philosophical narrative "Wolf's Tavern." It constitutes a further step in the development of his "absolute prose," corresponding to his new self-image of a "Trappist" monk altogether removed from the historical realm. While Benn's involvement and fallout with National Socialism have been amply discussed as a political affair,[11] I here would like to address his reversal as a unique example of a wavering reception of Nietzsche's visions of aesthetic autonomy and utopianism. Benn's relations to Nietzsche are the case of an unparalleled affinity of literature and philosophy, and ultimately politics.

"Wolf's Tavern"; Benn and Nietzsche, 1937 to 1938

Gottfried Benn's aesthetic views are a unique case of the significance of Nietzsche's thought on art and history for the historical avant-garde and modernism. Except for a brief moment in occupied Brussels during the First World War, before he withdrew from Carl Sternheim's and Carl Einstein's project of an "Encyclopedie zum Abbruch bürgerlicher Ideologie" (Encyclopedia for the Destruction of Bourgeois Ideology),[12] Benn understood his affinity to expressionism as being fundamentally a question of artistic expression. He never identified with its activist program for change. Still after the Second World War, Benn would emphasize Nietzsche's crucial importance for expressionism. In "Nietzsche nach fünfzig Jahren" ("Nietzsche after Fifty Years"; 1950), he writes:

> Everything that my generation discussed, confronted in reflection, one can say: suffered, one can also say: popularized—all that had essentially already found its expression and its exhaustion and its definitive formulation in Nietzsche; everything else was exegesis.[13]

His own relationship to Nietzsche's thought was fundamentally a matter of "reflection," "expression," and "formulation." Bruno Hillebrand thus could write of Benn's "language-bound" reception of Nietzsche: "What is philosophy with Nietzsche has become style and form with Benn."[14] Hence the question arises as to what aspect of the philosopher's thought, as we shall see, so consciously contradictory in itself, may have influenced the writer the most. It is Benn's solipsistic disposition, which began to evolve in reaction to his experience of World War I in occupied Brussels,[15] that sets him apart from the mainstream expressionist revolt, from the generation he addressed still in 1950 as "my generation," and its often "popularized" Nietzsche exegesis.

The mainstream of the expressionist movement, indeed, embraced Nietzsche's Zarathustra as a prophet of a new era, a cult figure, as the guru of a cultural revolution to be brought about by the "new man." In its literary realization, this "new man" appeared frequently as a fairly bizarre construct mixing Nietzschean with Christian (!) features, for example, as the sons in Georg Kaiser's or Walter Hasenclever's plays, whose youthful cosmic visions were much too big for the father's narrow but stronger reality but were also too big for themselves. Thus Nietzsche was invoked, as here by Hiller: "Nietzsche . . . our powerful and devotedly loved master, as whose disciples we feel ourselves in each line that we write."[16] The Nazis, of course, would deliver the ultimate perversion of the literal reading of the philosopher's symbolic figures by forcing "the blond beast" from his texts into their racist context. On a critical note—as if attempting to exorcise his own problematic Nietzschean heritage in retrospect—Thomas Mann saw in the "Overman" the very incarnation of the devil ("this faceless and shapeless fiend and winged man"), a "non-figure staggering at the borderline of the ridiculous."[17] Benn, too, when coping with his Nietzschean legacy after 1933, as to be elaborated shortly, understood the figure of Zarathustra literally, if critically: "Zarathustra . . . what a child of nature, what evolutionary optimism."[18]

Thomas Mann's polemical reference to Zarathustra as a "non-figure," "faceless" and "shapeless," may, however inadvertently, have touched upon a central issue, which readings by Derrida's students have fully explored. Such readings build on the insight that Nietzsche's "concepts" and "signifiers," though they appear clearly delimited and determined, do not have a stable identity. Nietzsche's texts, "uprooted from any truth, in which the classical text found its rest and security,"[19] thus constitute a field of oscillating reversals in which difference of meaning, for example, of the oppositional pairs Dionysus and Apollo or Overman and herdsmen, is deciphered as a figure of speech. The modernist text is based on seeming self-contradictions that emanate from the core of a cognitive "blindness," an aporia of linguistic intentionality as well as the potentiality of linguistic play. The *Zarathustra* text thus consists of a series of nonidentical relations, for instance, the notions of "truth" and "lying" or the immediacy of "life" and the distance of "history" as elements of forgetting and remembering.[20] The endless reversibility of such terms is a function of the subjectivity of language, that is, of the metaphorical nature of language, its capacity to create illusion as well as to concede defeat and deceit in absence of any absolute truth. Of course, these insights are not original insights of deconstructionist practice but are already fully stated in one of Nietzsche's earliest texts, "Über Wahrheit und Lüge im außermoralischen Sinn" ("On Truth and Lie in an Extramoral Sense"; 1873).

In his essay "On Truth and Lie in an Extramoral Sense," Nietzsche contrasted the man of "ratio" with "intuitive man," the "frivolously gay hero." In subverting normative grammar and semiotics through iconoclastic linguistic play, the "frivolously gay hero" can offset the confining historicity of language: all concepts are shattered as linguistic conventions. However, these creative acts of intuition, in which experience is released from the conceptual, are not to be misunderstood as totalizing mythical projections. Rather, they are acts in which the word creates the "appearance" (*Schein*) of origin, of being (the timeless) versus becoming (the historical). For Nietzsche, intuitive creativity acts on the awareness that linguistic signification reflects the mere subjectivism of a twofold "awkward imitative translation into a totally strange language": sense stimuli into images, and images into sounds. "Intuitive man" is not irrational man; after all, he has the *insight* (Latin *tueri*) that the metaphorical, thus rhetorical, process ultimately schematizes all "experience" into a hierarchy of rigid conventions, of concepts claiming (anthropomorphisms as) "truth."[21] It is only as "appearance" that art can express the totality of the moment. By the same token, art is neither static nor absolute (as for Benn in 1937–1938 and thereafter). As Nietzsche implies in this early essay, art remains part of the life of a whole culture, in which it may ideally (as it supposedly did in ancient Greece) dominate the sociopolitical realm. While the romantics and later also the expressionist movement gave to art such mythical power, the aesthetic experience itself has limitations. It translates, as it were, all experience into temporal relations—"relations of succession" (*Successionsverhältnisse*),[22] in Nietzsche's terms, mere "representation of the present." Art thus maintains its distance from life, a distance which the experience of the telos-oriented historical avant-garde illuminates the more drastically it attempted to eradicate it, as Habermas has argued.[23]

Benn's postfascist development, which ultimately sets him apart from Nietzsche and brings him closer to Spengler's cultural pessimism, merits closer critical attention. What makes tracing Benn's affinity to Nietzsche difficult and interesting is not only the seemingly contradictory aspects of the philosopher's work but more so the contradictions of its reception by Benn. Benn's postfascist reception of Nietzsche is marked by a reversal that appears to follow his political turnabouts. His politicization of Nietzsche's utopianism and of expressionism in the interest of the "new state" and the "new Europe" is, after his growing skepticism of the NS movement and after his fall, countered by an acid turn against such politicization. Once rejected by the Nazis, he attempts to attribute the rise of National Socialist ideology to the author of the *Zarathustra* and his "popularizing" interpreters, from whom he excludes himself by now identifying his views with the Nietzsche of the late lyrical fragments. An initial strategy of making Nietzsche the spokesman for the "breeding" of strong life had informed his pro-Nazi speeches and essays, such as "Answer to the Literary Emigrants" (1933), the response to his former admirer Klaus Mann, his speech for Marinetti (1934), and the essay "Züchtung I" ("Breeding I"; 1933). In these texts, a Nietzschean "inner vision"—which also informs his defensive "Bekenntnis zum Expressionismus" ("Confessing Expressionism"; 1933) from which he programmatically purged all Jewish expressionists—was twisted, forced outward, as it were, into what he obscurely called a "militant transcendence." Benn regarded such collective "militant transcendence" as a primordial expression of a fundamental mutation of history itself. He saw it manifested in the antinaturalistic style of German expressionism and the international avant-garde of the European "white race." The subsequent strategy, one of recoil from National Socialist ideology and a turn toward solipsism and the later Nietzsche, is employed in "Züchtung II" ("Breeding II"; 1940) and "Kunst und Drittes Reich" ("Art and the Third Reich"; 1941). These later writings would not be published until after the war.[24]

His falling-out with the Nazis and the continued attacks on his person and work caused Benn a trauma to which he would not admit but which discloses itself "between the lines" of his prose "Wolf's Tavern" (begun in Hanover in 1937, finished in Berlin in 1938),[25] as I will attempt to show as through a close reading (that will legitimate such inference). On the level of its literary philosophical discourse, this text contains highly idiosyncratic reflections on his expressionist legacy, which could well be read in relation to the expressionism debate in *Das Wort* (1937–1938), for which Benn himself was the cause. In his many reflections on expressionism, Benn never even mentioned this indictment of his person and work. And in "Wolf's Tavern" he admitted only to those aspects of his expressionist legacy which he could claim to have contributed to his self-avowed status as a "suprahistorical" poet; the "rest" was discredited accordingly.

"Wolf's Tavern" delivers a complexly politicized misreading of Nietzsche. Benn now focuses critically on the utopian dimension of the philosopher's early work and casts him, on these grounds, as a prophet of Nazism. On the other hand, he develops an insightful reading of the philosopher's underlying fundamental epistemological skepticism, which he claims only the *late* Nietzsche admitted to. The Nazi essayist Benn had turned into the poet-monk (a "Trappist," in his own term). As if to justify his retreat into art as a realm sui generis, Benn would now disallow every connection between life and art as a social *or* vital form. The move implicitly means the totalization of a "suprahistorical" realm. Hence it is quite different from Nietzsche's ideas of a dialectic of complementary historical perspectives arising from the relations between a "monumental," "antiquarian" and the "critical" experience of history, the subject of the second "Unzeitgemäße Betrachtung" ("Untimely Meditation"), "Vom Nutzen und Nachteil der Historie für das Leben" ("Of the Use and Misuse of History for Life"; 1874). Benn's reversal is most openly expressed in the text's philosophical reflections, which reject the "breeding optimism" of Nietzsche's Zarathustra, the "idealistic Antinous": "what a child of Nature, what evolutionary optimism, what shallow utopianism about the spirit and its realization!"[26] Benn thus embraces the cultural and epistemological skepticism of Nietzsche's last stage, of his *Ecce homo* and the lyrical fragments, a stance he will maintain through his postwar essay "Nietzsche nach fünfzig Jahren." That essay emphasizes the significance of the philosopher's skepticism, once again in reflection of the *Zarathustra,* the "Bible" of the utopian expressionist movement.[27] However, Benn here embraces Zarathustra as Nietzsche's "man without content": "Everything about me is lying . . . but that I break asunder, this breaking apart of mine is true."[28] And he invokes Nietzsche's consciousness of the world as aesthetic form as the essence of his own "Artistenevangelium" ("artist's gospel"). This reading of the *Zarathustra* fully discloses Benn's ability to read "what is hidden behind the rhetorical devices,"[29] behind Nietzsche's figures of speech. It recognizes the philosopher's understanding of the metaphorical nature of language. What becomes obvious, then, is that Nietzsche's textual play, his setting up and simultaneous undercutting of idols, is the ruse in which the poet-critic's vested interests get entangled. Benn's attack on Zarathustra's "Züchtungs-optimismus" (breeding optimism) in "Wolf's Tavern" is not only an attack on the NS appropriation of Nietzsche, which only a few years ago had been his own; it is ultimately an attack on any naive "futurist" reading of the philosopher as practiced by the expressionist and futurist movements. The attack thus implies a criticism of that aspect of the philosopher's work that seems to have set itself up for a "popularizing" reception.

The philosophical narrative allows such a reading in terms of the author's views and experiences not only in its manifest reflections but even more so in terms of its narrative strategy. It constitutes a process of memory in which a remembering self (the narrator) reflects on the remembrances of a remembered self in a topography and a context of historical problematics. This context is not "fictional" but constructed, if defamiliarized, thus not "autobiographical" in a naive sense, as the author's in Hanover (1937), as we shall see. After all, Benn's intimate correspondence with Oelze suggests such interpretation, particularly the letters of "the last two years (in which) we have talked about certain topics that we should really summarize and conclude," as Benn writes on May 17, 1938. And he will send Oelze a typescript of "Wolf's Tavern": "It really is only a composition of our correspondence."[30]

The narrator-protagonist of "Wolf's Tavern" seeks refuge in a remote corner of the establishment. The "Weinhaus Wolf" was by Benn's own accounts his favorite pub during his stay in Hanover. The narrator's reference to his professional affiliation with the "colonial sphere and the world of the consulate" is, however, a defamiliarizing construct that allows him to assume the attitudes and perspective of a widely traveled cosmopolitan man of the world (which Benn himself missed so much in his own experience when comparing himself with his correspondent Oelze, the "gentleman" from the Hanse-Stadt Bremen). Isolated from the other clients, absorbed in self-reflection, the remembering self views himself in contrast to the "Kulturträger" (pillars of civilization), to the "Gegenwartserwählte" (deputies of the present) of a provincial town in Germany. In its petit bourgeois mentality, the town (Hanover was and is a civil service center) represents for the narrator the "historical core" of modernity. Dissociated from the outside, in a "Weinhaus" which brings him closer to the reach of an inner, as it were, Dionysian experience, the loner's reminiscences freely float the images of his "Wanderjahre," his years of educational travel, of his mythical experience of the cultures of China, the South Seas, and Asia ("sectors of the wheel of Sansara in the whirl of infinite possibilities, with interpretations in all the directions of everlastingly inscrutable creation and of dreams").[31] These ruminations and musings, which implicitly reflect Benn's fascination with the literature of French ad German cultural anthropology, sometimes of questionable scholarly quality, thus lead the narrator to question the legitimacy of the Western world's, "the white race's," hegemony over mankind. The narrator from now on becomes, more and more obviously, Benn's constructed (not "fictional") alter ego, "the 'logical' form of such representation resembling that of a statement of real conditions."[32]

The notion of "history" is the narrator's cue for an outrageously provocative diatribe that ultimately conflates Western rationalism with any form of utopianism and contemporary National Socialist ideology! The narrator faults the rationalist belief in progress as responsible for the hypertrophic aberration of Western culture. Through his fictive alter ego, Benn thus intends to counterattack the liberals and leftists who had assailed him since the late 1920s (Kisch and Becher)[33] for his irrationalism, since 1933 (most prominently Klaus Mann, and Ernst Bloch) questioned and condemned him for his commitment to National Socialism. For the tavern philosopher, the dialectic of the Enlightenment has in fact culminated in fascism, in the fascist type as a corrupted image of Nietzschean prophecies ("the jaws of Caesar and the brain of troglodytes, that's their type!"): "Recently they have talked much of their history. . . . They also pointed to their masterhood— master race—all right then, who were these masters?" The tavern patron, emotions surging, goes on to now parry the NS ideologues's (such as Börries von Münchhausen's) personal charges and the attacks in the *Schwarze Korps* (*Black Corps*) and the *Völkische Beobachter* (*People's Observer*), both on May 7, 1936, against the author's work: "What speaks out of me is disintegration, I was often told. . . . You're trying to disintegrate Nature— that's the limit! The blood and soil of us all." Barely able to cloak his hurt feelings and resentment in philosophical terms, Benn's narrator goes to the extreme of denying that historical thought can be at all useful for experience: "Anyone who has nothing at all to offer to the present day talks history!"[34] In a "monumentalist" historical "review of cultures," the brooding guest, intoxicated with Nietzschean ideas, now tracks the decline of the West from a heroic age to modern mass democracy. He finds the roots of the "historical sickness" in the excesses of rationalism: "No conviction, no art, no religion, no science. Everything must conform to the yardsticks of clear logic: premise, assertion, proof."[35] The ideas of progress and rationalist subjectivity thus are pinpointed as the source of Western decline and perversion in contrast to the "infinite possibilities . . . of inscrutable creation and dreams" with which his inner vision connects the non-Western experience. However, the narrator is as far from projecting any utopian remedies as he is from sentimentally deploring the loss of such mythical experience for modernity. Instead, he asserts that the path of Western culture must be resolutely faced as a dead-end street, signifying nothing but the finality of the Western *Kulturkreis* (culture cycle). Thus, as much as Nietzsche's essays on art and history, discussed earlier, are a subtext (or *intertext*) for "Wolf's Tavern," the text refers to them with distinct reservations and qualifications. Benn's essay "Nietzsche nach fünfzig Jahren," written a decade and a half later, will, in spite of its resounding endorsement of his aesthetics, explicitly point out certain limitations of Nietzsche's thought: It refers to the philosopher's flirtation with utopianism as an expression of monolithic European thought fixated on the generative model of Greek culture. Instead, Benn adopts Spengler's "Kulturkreislehre" ("dogma of cultural cycles") as the Archimedean point from which to view human history and review Western history at the end of its cultural cycle. In this sense, "Wolf's Tavern" already develops a typology of "truth" in apparent reference *and* opposition to the early Nietzsche's contrasting of "rational" man and "intuitive" man. In "On Truth and Lying in an Extramoral Sense" (1873), the philosopher had based this contrast on a unique complementary affinity, as neither type can ultimately be—in the sense of the textual play with difference—the standard-bearer of "truth." Quite unlike Nietzsche, for whom "lying" is ultimately a universal principle, Benn's text endows a "central" and "profound" type with the truth of "absolute spirit," whereas the "active" Western historical type merely gropes about in the fog of never ending delusions.[36] While for Nietzsche history is the bridge for transcending history, for Benn history thus culminates in an unbridgeable rift.

One here senses an ominous similarity to Horkheimer and Adorno's *Die Dialektik der Aufklärung* (*Dialectic of Enlightenment;* 1947), also derived from a reading of Nietzsche as well as against the historical background of the experience of fascism (linked with a totalized criticism of modern capitalism). Benn's view that the Western idea of progress has unmasked itself as the terror of rationalist, exclusionary subjectivity is comparable to an extent. In both instances, scientific thought is conflated with instrumental rationality—this is Habermas's broad criticism of "avant-garde consciousness" in the wake of Nietzsche, whom he addresses as "the first to conceptualize the attitude of aesthetic modernity before avant-garde consciousness assumed objective shape in the literature, painting, and music of the twentieth century."[37] The crucial difference is that Horkheimer and Adorno's pessimistic reaction to contemporary history is to work as a negation of "thought that has lost the element of self-reflection,"[38] while Benn absolutizes his categories of "truth" ("central," "profound") and finality. In "Wolf's Tavern" Benn shuns the ideal of a "spirit (*Geist*) in the service of life," here sarcastically quoting a standard slogan of messianic expressionism as the romanticized epitome of the mentality of progress. And his narrator goes on to point out that such mentality has obviously brought about its own refutation through the technological developments of modern warfare—of "the machine-gun, the tank, and poison gas"—which the medical officer had witnessed in action during World War I. "The mind is there to serve life. Cultivation they call it," the narrator mutters. Railing against what he perceives as the intertwinement of rationalist and utopian excesses in historical thought, he concludes, "There's no more realizing of the spirit in life."[39]

In his second "Untimely Meditation," Nietzsche had charged art with creating the paradox of the "appearance" of "life" as "being," engaging in a play of displacement the uprooting movement of "becoming" in history. Benn, however, having turned toward the *late* Nietzsche and Spengler, undercuts any art-life relation by adopting the formula of art as "absolute" and "monologue." Benn's readings of Nietzsche's works from "Über Wahrheit und Lüge im außermoralischen Sinn" ("On Truth and Lying in an Amoral Sense") to *Also Sprach Zarathustra* (*Thus Spoke Zarathustra*), thus shift, arrest, and petrify, as it were, the play of difference rendered by Nietzsche's figures of speech into what he wants to see in "Wolf's Tavern" as the definitive skepticism of the late Nietzsche:

> Only in the last stage, with Ecce-homo and the lyrical fragments, did he *allow* that other datum surface into his consciousness, and that, one may suppose, brought about his collapse: that brown night when he stood on the bridge staring down into the abyss, beholding the abyss—late— too late for his organism and his role as a prophet.[40]

The implication of Benn's statement, of course, is precisely that Nietzsche was never *un*aware of that "other datum," which he now "allows" to "surface." The author of the early Rönne novellas, the army doctor stationed in Brussels, in the "eye of the hurricane"[41] of the uprooting experience of World War I, had found a uniquely intoxicating sense of *jouissance* in the endlessly shifting play of language. The narrator of "Wolf's Tavern"— isolated in a room that has "a suggestion of sinking, its shape and paneling like the interior of a ship," a "torpedo speeding into the depths"— has lost all sense and science of gaiety. The author has now elected to be *unaware* of the function of Nietzsche's play with differences. For Benn, the poetic word has become "monologue"; it has nothing at all in common with the "words and concepts" of human communication, not even as play. Benn now chooses, quite idiosyncratically when compared with the romantics' use of it, the term "cipher" as the synonym for his poetry. The "cipher" of his poetry articulates an "extra-human truth." It is not only severed from life, as "bio-negative,"[42] but is indeed hostile to life as much as it cancels the experience of the present moment. Such are the words of the narrator: "We are no longer concerned with breeding for a future we can neither await nor utilize, but with our own bearing in an eschatological present that has become an abstract experience only." [43] (Benn's terminology, though meant as distancing, here remains tainted by his NS experience, since the phrase "bio-negative" merely negates a racial-biological ideology of "Züchtung" [breeding], and the term "Haltung" [bearing] stems from a shared Prussian-National Socialist mentality.) The finality of this pronouncement of the absence of presence and the end of the future transcends mainstream modernism's consciously subjective critique of the relation of life to history. In contrast to an avant-garde inspired by a "naive" reading of Nietzsche's early essays and his influential *Zarathustra*, a distinct countertrend had emerged from within modernist culture. A literature that comprises developments from Kafka to, broadly speaking, the writers of the absurd takes back or reverses the historical avant-garde movement's vision of an "unspoiled presence." However, Benn's stance goes beyond Kafka's perceptions of the spontaneous gestures of physical experience and even beyond Beckett, who endows the play of difference between words and silence, words and gestures of the body, with a sense of the senses. Benn's refusal of life is based on the claim of insight into the soliloquy and blindness of language (as "cipher" or the "black letter"); [44] his poetry articulates "abstract experience." Thus he denies the possibility of art to "represent the present" (in Baudelaire's term) [45] or at least inform "by contrast" a dialogue between art and life, in terms of Habermas's critique of what he sees as the mythical closure of the late Benn [46] *and*, without much differentiation, Nietzsche. [47]

Benn's trauma, incurred in his relations to National Socialism, at least contributed to a compulsively undifferentiated conflation of the fascist myth with the utopianism of expressionism *and* modern rationalism, as I have shown. No other "dark" writer of the age lapsed into such a disturbingly chilling mentality of anger and denial. The NS prohibition of his writing on March 18, 1938, coincided with his revisions of "Wolf's Tavern," finished in Berlin on May 17, 1938, begun in spring 1937 in Hanover. The "Trappist's" claim for his philosophical narrative to break with life as a form of presence *and* historical experience meant a much more rigid development of his previous Nietzschean vision of art's metaphysical transcendence of history. [48] This claim becomes transparent in the writing of "Wolf's Tavern"—through and beyond the fictive references to his situation in Hanover's "Weinhaus Wolf"—also toward his personal history within German history.

Much of what may be hidden in the philosophical reflections and the structural perspectivism of "Wolf's Tavern" comes to the fore in Benn's previously cited correspondence with Oelze. Benn's letters from 1937 through 1938 deal prominently with "the problem of history" from a Nietzschean point of view and refer to his fiasco with National Socialism. He insists that "the whole affair" with National Socialism is of "no significance" for his productivity. Thus he feels free to turn to Nietzsche's "Lebensproblem" (problem of life), the subject of previous letters. From time to time, however, he needs to assure his partner that his own views are untainted by his political experience: "I ask myself daily, if it is resentment, weakness, aestheticism that causes me to devote to the problem of life little attention." He insists that his interest in the "Gestaltungsproblem" (problem of form) over the "Lebensproblem" is the consequence of "something constitutionally genuine, solidly rooted in my way of thinking" that makes him see "today's problematics" rather in Nietzsche's terms of "the justification of the world *only* as an aesthetic phenomenon."[49] Hence Benn proceeds to state his view of the insignificance of historical and political events in ways resembling those of "Wolf's Tavern." In previous letters to Oelze, Benn had intensely questioned the validity of Nietzsche's preoccupation with life in the terms of his *Zarathustra,* going as far as to maintain that the thinker's "collapse" was the result of "a sudden shame for his Zarathustra, of his breeding optimism, his hopes for a realization in the sociological and physiological." Suddenly "it was too late; he had bred and thundered too long, and indulged in S.A. premonitions," he writes. And Benn repeats his view that *Geist* (spirit) and life are "two different circles, two forms of expression" united only by a force standing far behind both, and he restates the verdict made in the novella: "Spirit *does not* serve life."[50]

All this is more consistent with Benn's aesthetic views before 1933, and incongruent with the essays written during his pro-NS phase, which put so much stress on the leadership by history's "great men" (Napoleon, Hitler), above all, the unity of the German Volk ("People means much!") with its leader.[51] This ideological layer protrudes ominously, briefly but clearly in his correspondence with Oelze when he links the question of "Nietzsche und les juifs" (Nietzsche and the Jews) with an "elitist" anti-Semitic sentiment (rarely expressed elsewhere): "I personally do not believe that he loved the Jews very much. For that he had too much of an aristocratic feeling."[52] Otherwise his letters abound with a conspicuously strong contempt for the Germans as "the lowest and disgraced people, the most stupid, the most un-European. A pitiful fatherland, dear Herr Oelze!"[53] Such anti-German sentiment, though plausible in view of the development of German affairs at the time as a form of German "self-hatred," is not quite as credible as Benn's insistence on his fundamentally aesthetic disposition is. After all, we must not forget, his stance for National Socialism had also been an aesthetically derived (corrupted) position, an *aestheticization* of politics. In that sense, he had been fascinated with the Nazi torchlight parades, the unity of the NS movement with the masses, the totality projected by the daily radio propaganda, and so on.[54] His reversal now may be part of his own "shame for his breeding optimism, his hopes for a realization in the sociological and physiological,"[55] his very own "S.A. premonitions," part of *his* "collapse," *his* trauma caused by hindsight, late, if not too late, but complexly expressed in "Wolf's Tavern."

My aim here has been to make a transparent case for understanding the major philosophical, aesthetic, and political issues involved with Benn's writing of the narrative in the context of the years from 1933 to 1938. Given that, I have tried to stay away, as much as a focus on a writer's embrace of and retreat from a political and moral phenomenon such as National Socialism and its strong impact on his work allows, from a monocausal explanation of the status of "Wolf's Tavern" in Benn's work. Hence I would like to, in conclusion, once more recall the incisive significance that his early prose, written during the heyday of expressionism, had on the development of his work. Here the incisive "bio-negative" view of poetic language taken and practiced in the philosophical narrative well exceeds his long-standing solipsistic discourse. That disposition may indeed manifest (as Jean-François Lyotard has attempted to assess the expressionist mentality as such) a "nostalgia for presence," leading to a "melancholia" reflecting "on the powerlessness of the faculty of presentation."[56] Benn's solipsistic disposition had first come to the fore as a response to the singularly personal experience of the poet and medical officer in occupied Brussels. Removed from the front, with few working hours and duties in a hospital for prostitutes, cared for by his orderly, he was mostly left to himself and to writing in the privacy of a spacious mansion. To these circumstances he attributes the "birthday" (the centerpiece of his Rönne novellas is consequently entitled *Der Geburtstag* [*The Birthday*]) of his seminarrative, semirepresentational prose, which centered on the experience of the protagonist's loss of social persona and the discovery of an unbounded "self." The text *Gehirne* (*Brains;* 1914) was a first step toward his "absolute prose" (for which Carl Einstein's early prose experiment *Bebuquin* stayed a significant reference). And "Wolf's Tavern" represents an intermediary stage toward what is fully developed in his 1944 "Roman des Phänotyp," an "abstract" montage of reflections without a self. To those months of a fulfilled creativity in Brussels Benn will look back in intense yearning throughout his life: "I lived at the edge, where existence wanes and the self begins. I often think back to those weeks; they were life, they will not return, everything else was fragment and waste."[57] Nevertheless, he stayed fixated on such conditions of a creative isolation. He sought to reconstruct such creative moment whether retreating into writing (with limited hours for his practice as a doctor) in his abode in Berlin, overlooking the shabby courtyard of the apartment dwelling, or escaping in 1938 from his treatment by the Nazis ("I wanted out of Berlin") into the army as an "aristocratic form of emigration," as he put it so glibly.[58] His experience in Hitler's army gave the medical officer and writer, on singular occasions, a sense of remoteness from history in the midst of history, as during his months in a fortress ("Block II, room 66") looming high, like a "blimp," above the Eastern town of Landsberg an der Warthe in 1944. These were instances of a repetition of his "Urerlebnis" in Brussels during World War I, "in the eye of the hurricane."[59] The niche of the "Weinhaus Wolf" in Hanover after his falling-out with National Socialism, however, was a much more problematic space of creative isolation than the others. The postwar reception of Benn's poetics and discourse of withdrawal by two of the most significant, albeit opposing, postwar poets and critics, Helmut Heißenbüttel and Hans Magnus Enzensberger, to be discussed in the overview of the concluding chapter, will attest to the fascination as well as the alienation that is tied to this poet's unique aura and pose of melancholy privacy, wounded untouchability, and singularly heightened awareness of the word as a "cipher" and "black letter" ("Probleme der Lyrik," 1951])[60]

8. Utopia/Dystopia: From Expressionism to Hans Magnus Enzensberger

The Avant-Garde at a Standstill

Revolution, a 1913 painting by Ludwig Meidner, foregrounds a flag-waving combatant on the barricades. His head bandaged, he grimaces in pain yet in seemingly steadfast defiance. Behind him, a town square erupts in gunfire and fiery explosions; bodies fall from the rooftops of collapsing buildings. In Meidner's *Apokalyptische Landschaft* (*Apocalyptic Landscape*) of the same year, a nude male figure lies supine in the left foreground as if unconscious. The fire beside him is turning to ashes, while the horizon is simultaneously lit and darkened by the impact of a comet that shakes the rows of build-ings, scattered on mountaintops and in valleys, in their foundations. For Joan Weinstein, the painter herewith seems to offer "revolution as the alter-native to apocalyptic destruction."[1] The catch, however, is that these two paintings were placed on opposite sides of the same canvas. As these two images form the two sides of the same coin, as it were, their unusual con-stellation may be emblematic of the Janus-faced tensions of expressionist discourses and of the bipolar nature of the crisis of the German avant-garde in the long wake of the expressionist movement.

The constellation of these early, prewar expressionist paintings appears to self-consciously articulate an insight into a precarious affinity of utopian-to-dystopian discourses. The entwinement of an avant-garde utopian desire with a deep-rooted, often premodern, archaic cultural pessimism, even a longing for a final catastrophic crisis that ends all crisis, opens an indeterminate space of reflection between revolt and recoil, which I have at the beginning of my study already addressed as eminently characteristic for the expressionist movement's precariously unstable idealism. I will here thematize the agon and ultimate intertwinement of utopian and dystopian discourses as uniquely marking the history of the German avant-garde from expressionism up to the post–World War II era and, in the aftermath of the student revolt in the late 1960s and 1970s, its entering a distinctly postmodern phase. This trajectory may be understood as propelled by a crisis caused not only by externally changing conditions but ultimately brought about by the critical, demystifying nature of the human mind, about which crisis Paul de Man writes that "literature finally comes into its own, and becomes authentic, when it discovers that the exalted status it claimed for its language was a myth."[2]

The opening section of this chapter will retrace the Janus-faced nature of the utopian expectations of expressionism from the prewar to the post–World War I era as a crisis of signification in aesthetic and political terms, reaching a climax of a *post-avant-garde* "negative aesthetics" in the period of political exile. The emergence of a "negative aesthetics" marked a fundamental review of the authority of art in Western culture and constituted a crucial historical step of the German avant-garde toward postwar postmodernist productions. The second section will point out the legacy of Carl Einstein's language pessimism and his denial of representation, considered by Helmut Heißenbüttel already in the 1960s as a postmodernist "turning point" for the development of "experimental" poetry in the Federal Republic of Germany (influenced by Gertrude Stein, Kurt Schwitters, and Ludwig Wittgenstein's philosophy of language). The legacies of Carl Einstein, as I will show also in the instance of Paul Celan, or of Benn are more important for postwar avant-garde developments than the short-lived, if powerful, resurgence of expressionism with the work of Wolfgang Borchert, foremost his play *Draussen vor der Tür* (*Homeless;* 1947). Their resonances are more important than the postwar flood of minor parables of the absurd written in the vein of Franz Kafka, whether, for example, Friedrich Dürrenmatt's "Der Tunnel" or Ilse Aichinger's radio play *Knöpfe* (*Buttons*).

Postwar Western Germany, reconnecting after the dark years of Nazism with the culture of the Western democracies, shared, reinforced, and, in fact, exemplified the transatlantic "cultural miracle" of a transformation of the formerly adversary culture of high modernism and the avant-garde into the representative culture of Western individualism and democracy under American hegemony.

Such development was the more possible and even plausible for German postwar culture as this move was based on a traditional authority of art that, largely discredited under Nazism, was needed for an overall cultural reconstruction. In falling back on the German idealist tradition, modern art, "abstract art," was, in fact, now endowed with a similar quasi-religious aura as once literature and art in the heyday of the expressionist generation during the First World War. While America may have experienced for the first time in its cultural history an institution of art,[3] in Western Germany the official culture of the free world found a still familiar space. It was restored in a familiar space, though at first it startled, provoked the public at large (and still angered unrepentant Nazis as "degenerate art"); and to the new elite it appeared to provide a new start. Such familiarity and newness in one seems to have provided an extraordinary, powerful energy for the dominance of modernist productions in Germany that lasted throughout the 1970s. In this era any changes stayed within the overall paradigm of modernism as there was, for example, a shift from an interest in Benn to Brecht. The student revolt in the late 1960s and early 1970s began to switch the focus of attention away from high modernism to avant-garde productions, including agitprop street theater, and thus in effect appeared to revive avant-garde traditions. Benjamin's "film essay," "The Work of Art in the Age of Mechanical Reproduction," became a cult text, and in its wake Brecht's media essays regained some attention; these were concrete signs that the Left was no longer satisfied with Adorno's dialectic of an aesthetic of negation, no longer content with a critical theory of modernism averse to the praxis of life. There was, however, besides a temporary appropriation of pop art enlisted by the New Left as a form of avant-garde postmodernism against high modernism,[4] no significant intrusion of mass culture onto the intellectual and artistic German scene. By contrast, America had seen high modernism attacked by pop art since the 1950s, which attack from the "below" of popular culture here opened the doors to a specifically American brand of postmodernism, albeit soon of global significance. In the wake of the demise of the student rebellion, however, doubts of German intellectuals concerning the political function of also the avant-garde became dominant. Typical for a certain continuity of German culture from expressionism onward, these doubts were, in the extreme, once again raised in apocalyptic terms. A variety of dispositions toward the "meaning" of art, ranging from pessimism to despair in the work of Peter Weiss or Heiner Müller, and less well-known writers, was not only concerned with an "exhaustion" of the forms and language of modernism but freighted with or coping with *Endzeitstimmung* (moods of an epochal end). By contrast, in American postmodern literature, as John Barth pointed out in an attempt to tackle the concept of the "postmodern" as a writer, the awareness of a modernist exhaustion stimulated the invention of and play with new forms and experiences, liberated for a literature of "replenishment."[5] Evidently there was no paradigmatic shift, a radical "postmodern breakthrough" in German literature. Gerald Graff even attempted to deny such rupture for American literature as he constructed a continuity of the apocalyptic and the visionary dimension of high modernism with the literature of the 1950s and 1960s.[6] German postmodernism, however, clearly evolved as a critique of modernism from within the agon of conflicting discourses of the avant-garde. This intrinsic trajectory limits and defines the approach to postmodernist aspects of German literature in the late 1970s taken here.

The focus on postmodern discourses resulting from within the "crisis of the modern"[7] excludes later developments, for example, in feminist or minority literatures which have been and are increasingly being addressed in an alternative postmodern context of critique and resistance.[8] The context of the critical constellations I have chosen in this study paradigmatically narrows our attention to the most significant transitions of a single writer of international stature. I will thus turn in the final section of this chapter to Hans Magnus Enzensberger's poetry from the late 1950s through the mid-1970s, which engaged the whole tradition of modernist poetry as *Weltsprache* (universal language) and is marked by a paradoxical reception of Benn's late "static" poetry *as well as* Bertolt Brecht's poetry for social change, both on the level of ideas as well as in terms of his very own *experimentation* with their concepts of language. Pursuing Enzensberger's twists and turns through the mid-1970s, I will focus on an aporia of writing poetry, such as the cycle *Der Untergang der Titanic. Eine Komödie* (*The Sinking of the Titanic: A Comedy;* 1978), which has raised the very experience of *aporia* — beyond the dualism of the utopian/dystopian discourse of the historical avant-garde — to a vantage point for continued creativity in *post-avant-garde* conditions.

Looking Back on Expressionism, or Post-Avant-Garde Self-Parody: The Memory of a Spiritual Vision Lost

"Expressionism does not create germ cells of new life, but shows the atoms of the old," Friedrich Gundolf, never a friend of the movement, wrote in 1921, "ancient Egypt, early China, Gilgamesh, negroes, Maya . . . not as historicism but as narcoticum . . . because one intuited the gaping hole."[9] The same could be said from a conservative point of view, the great indifference as to the "meaning" of art in the 1980s and 1990s notwithstanding, of our present postmodern condition in the arts. Not only the enemies of expressionism but the expressionists themselves awoke to the realization that their *Aufbruch* (awakening) had been more of an ending. Wilhelm Worringer, too, had to revise his vision of expressionism as the harbinger of a new epoch. In a lecture given at the German Goethe Society in Munich in 1920, he reassessed it as the "great final panic of an art losing all faith in itself," marked by "empty gestures" in the "hollow space" of the "awareness of futility."[10] Many of the artists and writers cited at the beginning of this study as an example of the expressionist pathos of a *Zeitwende* (turning of the times) would engage in a litany of self-depreciating cynicism that differed from the dadaists' brutal attack on expressionism only through its underlying mood of anguish. In "Der Expressionism stirbt" ("Expressionism Is Dying"; 1921), Yvan Goll made the overstatement that the "Browning" (revolver) in the streets of the German Republic of 1920 "makes a louder bang" than the sound of the tuba of Ludwig Meidner's European prophecies, and demanded: "Away with your sentimentality, you Germans, what is the same as: you expressionists. Because, let's bet: even Ludendorff is, after all, an expressionist."[11] Even Kurt Pinthus or Kasimir Edschmid, expressionism's former impresarios, begin to see "kitsch," "mannerism," "faddism," and "commercialism" where they once had seen "a new ethos of life."[12]

On the whole, the prewar expressionist "revolutionary" attitude had been, in the original sense of the term (*re-volvere*), inspired by the desire to return to a primordial state, in the extreme, through the destruction of a decadent age, through "Holocaust . . . mass deaths, hence the birth of a new man," as described by the expressionist poet Johannes Becher.[13] Such a mentality of archaic, anarchic violence, coupled with a pervasive longing for the "New Man," obviously projected the resolution of cultural and social conflicts onto a mythical level. In retrospect, the expressionist literary and artistic production revealed to the movement's erstwhile participants and their advocates, regardless of their postexpressionist politics—conservative, liberal, or communist—a fundamental dilemma of signification in a metaphysical, cognitive, artistic, and political sense. The crisis of modernity, as these writers, artists, and critics experienced it now, does not forebode or anticipate, as in a conventional crisis situation, a critical "turning point in an unfolding sequence of events"; rather, it fundamentally "produces uncertainties in assessing the situation and in formulating alternatives in dealing with it,"[14] which may also define a postmodern condition.

The crisis of the avant-garde becomes altogether evident at the moment of the inevitable demise of its totalizing futurist, utopian visions in the course of the powerful events of war, civil war, revolution, restoration, and ultimate commercialization. Yet this crisis was always already immanent due to an ineluctable intertwinement of the "new" with tradition. I would like to put it this way: The avant-garde is a prime paradigm for a crucial mark of cultural modernity, for the phenomenon of the "Gleichzeitigkeit des Unzeitgemäßen" (the contemporaneity of the untimely), as Ernst Bloch assessed it.[15] On the whole, in spite of its radical posturing, it reveals a secret relation, or, better, a more or less hidden complicity, with traditional thought. The avant-garde thus can be viewed as symptomatic not just of a "crisis of the arts"[16] but of a "culture of crisis." If we want to designate a space for the avant-garde, it would be the opposite of what Peter Bürger proposed: Instead of breaking away, the latent function of the avant-garde was to cope with the age's wavering between traditional society and its myths (recessive) and the functionalism of modern mass society (dominant). Compared with the other relatively unified avant-garde movements, expressionism may be the most telling, most symptomatic paradigm of such indecision. It can be equated neither with decadence (as Benjamin and Lukács claimed) nor with renewal (the claim of Ernst Bloch and many expressionists themselves).

Where the potential for change appears to have been replaced by the permanency of crisis,[17] what happens to the creativity of the writers and artists who had considered themselves part of an avant-garde? What about their artistic production in times of disillusionment, self-doubt, self-incrimination, increased introspection and retrospection? The salient characteristics of a memory and skeptical remembrance of the expressionist revolt range from sarcastic absurdism to self-parody as forms of an *intertextual* reflection, *intertextual* in the sense of referring back to the production of the expressionist heyday. As prefigured by the constellation of Meidner's pre-World War I paintings pointed to at the beginning of this chapter, expressionist utopianism typically reverses itself to absurdist dystopian visions as the flip side of exaggerated expectations. We can observe these reversals, for example, in the postwar plays of Kaiser, Toller, and Goll. Goll's two-act playlet *Der Unsterbliche* (*The Immortal One;* 1918–1920)[18] raises issues that Walter Benjamin, nearly two decades later, would attempt to address in his essay "The Work of Art in the Age of Mechanical Reproduction." However, unlike Benjamin, Goll does not indulge in any collective hopes that could be connected with the emergence of the new medium of film as replacing literary culture (cf. chapter 5). On the contrary, he attributes the loss of the "aura" (in Goll's terms, the "soul") of the unique work of art to an omnivorous process of commercialization. Contrary to Benjamin's later illusions, Goll here points out a false sublation of the artist's creativity into a corrupted collective: Sebastian's, the individual's "soul" is "immortalized" in the medium of photography ("soul photography one mark twenty per dozen copies") and film by *mortification*. The apparatus of the film industry has merely transferred the aura of the artist's work of art onto the phony aura of the film star, who is nothing more than a commodified mass idol. Whether Goll is conscious of it or not, he here reflects the high-culture preference of the liberal political camp (which also was Meidner's).[19] Goll's *Methusalem oder der ewige Bürger* (*Methuselah or the Eternal Bourgeois;* 1922), illustrated by George Grosz, thematizes another such recoil. The grotesquely surreal and sharp-witted satire charts the metamorphosis of a revolutionary student into a business tycoon who, instead of ideas, produces shoes for the masses.

The consciously thematized transformation of high hopes, which expressionism as a movement had previously connected with change, into an awareness of their commercialization appears to characterize a *post-avant-garde* experience. At this point, there cannot be any return to a "naive" modernism that would be unaware of its critique as always already "defused by the autonomous institutionalization of its artistic practice."[20] And there is obviously more than just submission to a self-absorbed skepticism. The boundaries of modernist writing seem to have been expanded, thematically and formally, made translucent to the previous attempts to break out of the constrictions of the "art world."

Indeed, as Paul de Man noted, "the literary mind espouses the pattern of a demystifying consciousness."[21] My point of departure for establishing a transitional status of certain forms of expressionism to consciously postmodern writing is, most basically, based on the criterion of an awareness of art as an "institution": The more the expressionist author becomes aware of art as an institution that conflicts with avant-garde visions of creative originality and the authenticity of language and style, the more the work articulates a "post-avant-garde" experience, which informs the "postmodern" experience once these insights have been accepted and become the premise for aesthetic productions. The progression of this chapter from a discussion of the expressionist avant-garde to post-1968 literary developments takes its departure from such a point of view.

Furthermore, forms of self-parody such as Goll's surpass the ironic distance of individualist, modernist self-reflection. They may thus be viewed as an important element of a post-avant-garde consciousness, characterizing an evolving awareness of the limitations of artistic creativity for projects that aim beyond the aesthetic domain proper. It may be said that postmodern writing will displace the discourse of parody and self-parody, which, after all, has always served as a critical part of the literary and artistic tradition. In the vacuum that arises with an increasing erosion of the potential of innovation in terms of styles and literary forms, pastiche, a chief characteristic of postmodernist productions, merely imitates, mimics voices and styles now dead.[22] Pastiche appears to equivocally oscillate between nostalgia for the past and affirmation or critique of contemporary cultural and social conditions in the age of mechanical reproduction and mass consumption. As epitomized by Andy Warhol's serial images of Marilyn Monroe, the experience of ubiquitous, mass-produced images erases the difference between the authentic, original image and the simulacrum. In this sense my understanding of the postmodern is largely informed by Fredric Jameson's notion (as also addressed by Andreas Huyssen) of a particular trajectory from modernism and avant-garde to postmodernism, where the latter is viewed as a process of relativizing, playing with, or emptying out the formers' claims in indifferent or equivocal terms. Hence it may be said that the postmodern condition is marked by a forgetting of history, in Jameson's terms, a "transformation of reality into images, the fragmentation of time into a series of perpetual presents."[23] If postmodernism thus can be understood as "the endgame of the avant-garde,"[24] then the *post-avant-garde* phase of expressionism may be the beginning of such an end in the context of modernist German literature and the visual arts, questioning along with the usefulness of history the meaning of art for life. The intensity of the expressionist agon of art over art, its quasi-experimental turn to a variety of conflicting aesthetic forms, may have already illuminated, at least by implication, the relativity of the work of art and its claim of totality (see chapter 1). We also recall Worringer's 1920 reference to the movement's efforts as the "great final panic of an art losing all faith in itself."[25] An intense mode of tormented self-reflection in the aftermath of a movement's demise is, of course, the farthest from the coolly insightful aesthetic "indifference" epitomized by Marcel Duchamp's ready-mades in the early years of the avant-garde. In view of the contemporary fervor of cubism, the furor of futurism, of expressionism, and, a few years later, of Dada in Zurich and Berlin, Duchamp's shifting of trivial objects of daily usage, such as a bicycle wheel or a bottle rack, into the realm of the art exhibition was a precocious self-critique of art as an institution. At any rate, the expressionist self-critique, however emotionally performed by an individual voice, will warrant further research as critics relate the legacies of expressionism to the postmodern experience.[26] Clearly, the experience of the expressionist avant-garde laid bare the conditions of art as an "institution" not only for aestheticism but also for its very own productions.

In extension of my focus on expressionism's implicit relativization of "styles" and the "work of art," I have discussed in the instance of George Grosz's paintings and the novels of Hermann Broch, Alfred Döblin, and others a post-avant-garde turn to what has aptly been addressed by Lützeler as a form of "negative aesthetics," "an aesthetically beautiful condemnation of the aesthetically beautiful" as a most salient mark of literary production in political exile.[27] Indeed, as my case studies have illustrated from chapter to chapter, a mode of writing and painting that questions the meaning of the subject's aesthetic creativity in the era of wars and revolution, mass production and mass consumption, marks a certain continuity of discontinuities from the Dadas in the exile of Zurich to Berlin dadaism and the literature and art of the era of political exile in the 1930s and 1940s. My interpretation of the case of Carl Einstein (chapter 4) was to show that the intellectual in exile often felt compelled to unmask the avant-garde and the entirety of modernist developments, including his own work, as engaged in the "fabrication of fictions" (ideology), in the self-interested manipulation of signs. It is tempting to reconsider such "negative aesthetics" (and there is no better term for these extreme critiques of the production of aesthetic experience) as a historical step toward a postmodern awareness, as has been shown by Jochen Schulte-Sasse in the instance of Carl Einstein's *Die Fabrikation der Fiktionen* in the 1930s.[28] In the following section, I will attempt to explore the potential of understanding a break and transition from *within* modernism to a postmodern awareness via forms of a "negative aesthetics" (meaning *aesthetics,* nevertheless) for the specificity of the German avant-garde. In the case of the reception of Einstein's late poetry by the postwar experimental writer Helmut Heißenbüttel, we are dealing with a postmodern critique of modernism from within the realm of modernist art. Heißenbüttel's experimental project reflects on the conditions and limits of linguistic subjectivity, the metaphorical processes of language as communication or the "poem," while his "texts" attempt to reproduce or produce the intersubjective perception and experience of the world as constituted by linguistic materiality and functions. His project thus differs substantially from the terms of an avant-garde "anti-art" project of outright break and discontinuity that subjectively marked Einstein's essays before and his activities during the Spanish Civil War.

From *Poem* to *Text:* "Design of a Landscape": Carl Einstein, Paul Celan, and Helmut Heißenbüttel

The most extreme response to the demise of the expressionist, humanist vision to "change the world" through aesthetic means is the denial of the capacity of the language of art to express an authentic experience of the self, the result of a denial of language as representation. Such insight had been incisively formulated by Nietzsche, whom the expressionist mainstream chose to misread in its messianic zeal. The dadaists in the exile of Zurich, later in Berlin, reacting to no small extent against the expressionist "pathos" of renewal through art, marked the first avant-garde instance of such denial. Carl Einstein, once a member of Berlin dadaism, wrote his long poem "Entwurf einer Landschaft" ("Design of a Landscape"; 1930) in response to his isolation in the Parisian exile and his inability to transform the transcendental doubt of his *Bebuquin* (1907–1909) into a language of intersubjective experience (*BEBII*). The poem questions, in the vein of Nietzsche, language as a medium for articulating "truth."[29] Einstein's last poem is, indeed, a final expression of a dying individual voice that articulates its impending death by endlessly repeating its *awareness* of language as "narrow grammar," a stenographic "grid."[30] While Rosalind Krauss is focused on the avant-garde's illusions of "originality as an unconscious 'grid,'" Einstein's poem is an example of the avant-garde's post-avant-garde, postmodernist insight into an underlying prefigurated "grid" of language as a lifeless texture that *obliterates* the presence of a natural landscape (as in this excerpt):

> Du verhallst in geeiste Wolke
> Enger Grammatik,
> Strauchelnd gehetzt
> In hochstaplerisches
> Dich bestehlendes Wort.
> Strick über bodenlosem See
> des Gefühls.[31]

(You fade away into icy cloud / Of narrow grammar / Stumbling hunted / in swindling / Word stealing from you / Rope over bottomless sea / Of sentiment.)

Eugene Jolas, from whose translation I here quote, published the poem of his "advisory editor" in *transition. An International Quarterly for Creative Experiment* 19–20 (June 1930), though it really did not fit the journal's idealist program of the "Revolution of the Word" (in which section the translation appears). It is questionable whether Jolas really understood the epochal significance of his friend's last poem, as much as his translation of *Gefühl* as "sentiment" instead of "feeling," for example, fails to capture the connotation of *Gefühl* as a prelinguistic, rudimentary act of apperception. Einstein shared such understanding of "feeling" with Benn, whose Rönne prose had exploited this dimension under the influence of Semi Meyer, "the work of an unknown Jewish doctor from Danzig, who had said verbatim about feelings that they reach deeper than the mind."[32] Hugo von Hofmannsthal's "Chandos Letter" (1902) had expressed a comparable negation of language as representation. Yet, while its concepts turned for the self into "rotten mushrooms," constituting a "text-scape" of mortification, the self still found through intuition as a primary, prelinguistic response to the world ("feeling," in Einstein's lines) an avenue toward the experience of the "silent language of things." Einstein's "feeling," however, is inextricably tied to *and* separated from linguistic concepts that displace the existence of an other; "feeling" here is also a feeling of anguish. His language pessimism, a late development in his writing, may be said to go beyond an ontological, epistemological crisis at the turn of the century.

While von Hofmannsthal had written the fictional "Chandos Letter," addressed to Francis Bacon, really as a pretext for an inquiry into a "total forgoing of literary activity,"[33] Einstein's poem was, in fact, his last. It inherently reflects on his personal experience of writing within the history of the rise and fall of the avant-garde, expressionism, Berlin dadaism, and surrealism. Such language skepticism was completely alien to Italian futurism or French surrealism. It leaves behind any trust in linguistic as perceptual innovation, as it articulates an awareness of the instantaneous "institutionalization of semiotic praxis in modernity."[34] Were it not for the *feeling* of anguish and agony expressed in this poem, such awareness could indeed be addressed as fully articulating a paradigmatic shift in experience beyond a modernist dissociation of sensibility. In fact, Helmut Heißenbüttel has assessed Einstein as the least known and yet most important poet in the

German language for understanding such a shift. He regards the poem "Design of a Landscape" as a "turning point" from a modernist belief in the fulfillment of the aesthetic experience to an awareness of its being emptied out into mere signs. Heißenbüttel himself will make this awareness productive for his experimental language *texts*. His texts ground themselves on the recognition and very acceptance of language as a system of signs, while they attempt to "demonstrate" productive transgressions of the limits of language in a "meditative" play with its constituents. In the sense that the "text's" intersubjectivity differs from the subjectivity of the "poem," the "experimental" writer knows his own work removed from Einstein's historical situation, yet he understands Einstein's poem as standing before the "threshold" of the "new." The gist of Heißenbüttel's interpretation of "Design of a Landscape" is that here "a self that has become historical in its grammatical independence addresses itself."[35]

> Bilder höhnen
> Zeichen verzaubern
> Entleben uns
> Ich-ein Bild-
> Müde des Namens
> Und deine Augen
> Monotonen
> Flachen in kreidige Blindheit
> Bist mir erloschen im Griff
> Staunender Trauer

(Pictures sneer / Signs bewitch / De-live us / I-an image- / Weary of the name / And your eyes / monotones / Flatten into chalky blindness / You've become extinct to me in the grip / Of amazed sorrow.)

Here, again, Jolas's translation of *Bilder* as "pictures" should be replaced with "images," as Einstein's text also puts into doubt the intuitive dimension of the *image* as valorized from the romantics to the surrealists. For Heißenbüttel, these lines point to the speaking subject's awareness that "something new is in the offing, but it can only reach out toward it by suffering that which is no more, no longer at service, no longer available to its speaking."[36] While the expression of suffering from language determines the content of the poem, its "vaguely constructive principles" point beyond suffering, a result of the insight through suffering ("amazed mourning," or, better translated, mourning as *thaumazein*). Indeed, different from

Gottfried Benn's "hallucinatory constructive" creation of an inner realm, and from the surrealist externalization of such a realm, Einstein's text already shifts the words from their reference to objects and a subject's inner state toward referring to themselves in semantic clusters. These may—as Heißenbüttel put it—point to an "unknown, new world of things."[37] Thus words become signs in a realm without a self, an experience that comes after the experience of the "I—an image—weary of the name."

Heißenbüttel, of course, knows that Dada in Zurich, Merz in Hanover (Kurt Schwitters), had already, with anger and joy, gone beyond the self suffering from itself in the naming of itself. Thus he defines his own work as going beyond Dada's "anti-poetic demonstrations" and Einstein's *linguistic despair*. He invokes as new points of departure Ludwig Wittgenstein's philosophy of language, his concept of the "limits of language," of "language games," and that which *shows itself* beyond the threshold of language, as well as Gertrude Stein's linguistic meditations.[38] Heißenbüttel's claims mark a new stage in the history of the German avant-garde. His experimental poetry, in fact, becomes part of a changed critical constellation, where Heißenbüttel and Hans Magnus Enzensberger are, as we shall see, the major contestants in an agon of competing discourses. They both invoke, in disparate ways, besides Benn and Brecht as the most influential writers during the postwar period, the formal achievements of European modernism and the avant-garde. For Enzensberger, however, programmatic literary experimentation in the early 1960s has turned into an empty formalism without risk that caters to the demands for novelty.[39] For Heißenbüttel, on the other hand, the "anti-aesthetic polemics" of the New Left were not radical enough, as they failed to address Walter Benjamin's concerns with the potential of an aesthetic production of collective experience.[40]

Heißenbüttel's *text* "Entwürfe für Landschaft" ("Sketches or Designs for Landscape") refers, by virtue of its title (significantly in the plural) to Einstein's poem. Its distance from Einstein's "Design of a Landscape" is highly calculated in terms of a *pastiche*. A form of literary quotation, the pastiche is neither parodistic nor nostalgic, rather a point of departure, of departure also in the sense of leaving behind. As an overly programmatic *Entwurf* (design), it may also be one of the language poet's most sterile texts. It "begins":

> eine Möglichkeit ob das müßte schiefgehn und einer mit einer
> weißen weiß überhaupt ganz in Weiß der Gute denn er ver—
> liert ja nichts und dabei eine. . . .[41]

(a possibility whether this should fail and someone with a white knows altogether in white the good fellow because he does not lose anything and therein a . . .)

The "constructive" dimension of this (really untranslatable) text here is based on the contiguous phonemic associations of *weißen* (white) and *weiß* (knows)—vaguely reminiscent of Hans Arp's play with that semantic difference in his "Strassburgian Configuration." And the text explores logical aspects expressed semantically—*Möglichkeit* (potentiality)—and grammatically: the subjunctive of *müßte* (should), etc. The text progresses in the third "stanza," better "text phase," into a word-field stereotypically constructing a romantic literary "landscape" ("moon blue") of a past ("that is already long," "evenings"). The subjective projection of that *literary* space is simultaneously deconstructed by textual self-reflections ("who knows," "white . . . a small invention"):

> das ist schon lange wenn Mond blau ein unveränderlich im Bohnen-
> gestrüpp wer weiß was sehr warm noch und abends
>   eine kleine Erfindung bergaufwärts[42]

(that is already long when moon blue an unchangeable in the thicket of beans who knows / white what very warm still and evenings a small invention up the hill)

There is no longer anger or joy (Dada), no suffering (Einstein), while a form of liberation from the constraints of subjectivity articulates itself as a process of metonymical linguistic relations. The montage produces a space in which the *chance* of antimetaphorical associations and traces of subjective control coalesce (. . . "the good fellow because he does not lose anything" . . . / "that is already long when moon blue").

Paul Celan's "Entwurf einer Landschaft" (from the collection *Sprach-gitter* [*Speech Grille;* 1959]) is less hermetic than his subsequent work. It is a *poem* which—unlike Heißenbüttel's *text*—articulates the progression of an evanescent subject's *seeing* and somehow still *speaking* for *uns* (us):

> Rundgräber, unten. Im
> Viertakt der Jahresschritt auf
> den Steilstufen rings.
> Laven, Basalte, weltherz—
> durchglühtes Gestein.
> Quelltuff,

wo uns das Licht wuchs, vor
dem Atem.[43]

(Round graves, below. In / the four-stroke of the year's pace on / the steep
steps around. / Lavas, basalts, worldheart—/ red-hot glowing rock. /
spring-tuff, / where the light grew for us, before / the breath.)

Celan's poem speaks also in an intertextual sense. It is situated, it appears, in
a historical literary space between Else Lasker-Schüler's poetry, evoked with
the adjective *weltherz-durchglüht* (worldheart—/ red-hot glowing; potentially, however, also "burned through" in the sense of burned-out), and
T. S. Eliot's "Waste Land" imagery of rock (*Gestein*). It attempts to approach a prelinguistic point of epiphany and illumination: "wo uns das
Licht wuchs, vor dem Atem" (where the light grew for us, before the breath).
Celan's memory is intertextual in citing the exact title of Einstein's poem
but also opaquely referential in *constructing* a landscape in traces that may
remind the reader of the landscape of the French Pyrenees where Einstein
(like Walter Benjamin) committed suicide in 1940 ahead of the advancing
German army. The poem begins with evoking a view from above onto the
"Rundgräber unten" (round or circular graves below), in which context the
"us" of the second stanza may very well be the "us" of the Jewish experience of the Holocaust. Like "Todesfuge"("Death Fuge"; 1952), "Design of a
Landscape" seems to inherently jar with Theodor Adorno's well-known (if
mostly misquoted and misunderstood) 1949 dictum that "to write a poem
after Auschwitz, is barbaric" (thus not "impossible," as its sloganized corruption maintains). Adorno does not fail to add, however, that cultural
criticism (including his own) is not autonomous but rather is subjected
to the same "dialectics of culture and barbarism": "and that corrodes also
the insight, which states, why it has become impossible, to write poems
today." Adorno's point rather was that therefore poetry and the "critical
mind/spirit," after Auschwitz, can no longer rest in "self-sufficient contemplation" as *traditional* poetry does.[44] Celan's "Death Fuge" thematized the
barbarism of Nazism and its perverse infatuation with German culture,
while it reflected on its very own status as a "fuge" constituted (*gefügt*) by
victimization and death, thus, indeed, jarring the poem's traditional contemplative constitution. "Design of a Landscape" does not evidence quite
such a pronounced dialectical understanding of its own composition, yet—
like all of Celan's poetry—it reflects on the temporality, historicity, and dialogical potential or aporia of its language, which undermines its reception
as an *organic* totality sui generis.

Celan's poem "Entwurf einer Landschaft" paradoxically traverses an "unbetretbare Stunde," an hour, the time and experience of death, that cannot be entered. It does so by way of entering, in the *temporal* sequence of its steps, the center of the landscape as an image-scape. A "saddle of stone," resembling the "forehead of an animal," is marked by the traces of violence (*gebeult*) and devastation by fire (*verkohlt*):

> Ölgrün, meerdurchstäubt die
> unbetretbare Stunde. Gegen
> die Mitte zu, grau,
> ein Steinsattel drauf,
> gebeult und verkohlt,
> die Tierstirn mit
> der strahligen Blesse[45]

(Oilgreen, seasprayed the / hour that cannot be entered. Against / the middle, gray, / a saddle of stone on top, / dented and charred, / the animal forehead with / the blaze of rays.)

Celan's poem "Design of a Landscape" echoes Einstein's final poem by repeating its title, yet it is an answer,[46] or better, *Gegenentwurf* (counterdesign). It responds to the former's "amazed mourning" about the loss of self, the "blindness" of signs and images in *evoking* the illuminating experience of the image realm "before the breath" that precedes its linguistic articulation (a major leitmotif in Celan's subsequent poetry, as in *Atemwende* [*Breathturn;* 1967]). It is the poem which creates in self-reflection of language that *metaphorical* space of insight within language. This space is simultaneously also an unspoken (nonmetaphorical) space, the "breathing" space between "before" and "the breath" ("before / the breath"). It is suspended between silence and speech, as marked by the slash (/), yet in the process of *conflating* with articulation. By contrast, and it is the specific contrast which points to the singular significance of the poem for Celan, Einstein's "Zerfiele das Wort, wir atmeten enteist" ("If the word would disintegrate, we would breathe freed from Ice") despairs in the metaphorical "grille" of speech. Speech is a "grille" ("wandering/shifting cages"), the word "impales us / Into the smiling lie / Of petrified trees." Speechlessness would be a state of integration and the integrity of "breathing" *after* language. In Einstein's poem, the names of the self, of nature, and God are tautological to death: "Nähren die über dem Tod / Geschwätzigen" (Nourish those chattering over / death). Celan's "design of a landscape," however, is a "language-/image-scape" oscillating between solipsism and referentiality. In terms of referentiality, it may also point to Benjamin's suicide near Portbou by the "oilgreen, seasprayed" Mediterranean seaside, thus extending the design of the historical landscape across from the region around Pau in the western part of the Pyrenees, where Einstein drowned himself in a river. In terms of its reflection on language and image, Celan's poem, albeit from the divergent point of view of its *metaphorical* language, invites a comparison with Benjamin's early understanding of language as a medium *in* which (not *through* its consciously *referential* use as a tool) "man communicates with God." Man does so by "naming" the world of things in "human terms," while the "*creative* word of God" emanates in the "language of the things themselves" ("On Language as Such and the Language of Man"; 1916). Yet, Celan here allows more space for the subjective dialogical creativity of language. The poem's "us" appears to reach from the ultimate historical Jewish experience of death to a messianic vision of man at the *moment* (in German *Augenblick*) that always already underlies and is not separate from the course of human history (and the historicity of language): "wo uns das Licht wuchs, vor / dem Atem" (where the light grew for us, before / the breath). This luminous vision grows as it is refracted and reflected by death's "strahlige Blesse" (blaze of rays) with which the poems ends.

By contrast, referentiality—intuitive, subjective, or historical—is, at least *by design*, undercut by Heißenbüttel's *text*, which opposes the open *reproducibility* of its linguistic performance, a mixture of chance and pattern, to the *poem's* aura of singularity. Different from Celan's, the experimental writer's interest in Einstein's poem is exclusively formalistic, as it projects literary history as progressive consciousness of language over personal and historical experience. Einstein's "Design of a Landscape" was still constituted by a subject that mourns in language the loss of the "content" of language due to its subjectivity. Yet it maintained that experience as a content expressed in a mortified language/landscape. By comparison, Heißenbüttel's text goes beyond what Hegel addressed as "the end of the romantic form of art" (meaning the end of romantic subjectivity as the end of an identity of inner and outer in classical art).[47] It attempts to *cancel* (the intertextual reference to Einstein's final poem is "aufheben," more in that sense than in the sense of preserving) the "romantic form of art" in its final modernist phase and thereby articulate what we now address as the postmodern experience.

Aporia: Hans Magnus Enzensberger's Muse

The student revolt in the late 1960s and early 1970s brought back some of the utopian energy of the historical avant-garde, in lifestyles and political activism that targeted the institutions of the state. In the mid-1970s, however, a *Tendenzwende* (turn of tendency) occurred: Intellectuals began to renounce the visions of a leftist political culture, a development which the conservative critic Hans Egon Holthusen attempted to assess with a shift from the "Benn-Brecht-alternative" of the early 1960s to a "victory of the principle of 'Benn' " over the "principle of 'Brecht'."[48] The always puzzling development of the poet and critic Hans Magnus Enzensberger, seen by many as an heir to Brecht's poetics and criticism,[49] albeit an anarchic inheritor who had simultaneously appropriated the techniques of European modernist poetry, specifically of Benn, seemed to provide a case in point for such a turn of tendency.

In 1968, the year of the student "revolution," the eloquent spokesman of the literary New Left and editor of the radical *Kursbuch* (schedule of trains and handbook for directions), had been part of an alliance of writers that confidently pronounced the "end of bourgeois literature."[50] Enzensberger joined the discussion, which favored documentaries and reports as means to unmask the class conditions of Western societies. In those days, such declarations were stunning but could be expected, besides being quite familiar from the historical discussions in the late 1920s, when Kisch and Becher debated Benn. Inexplicable, however, seemed the publication of a collection of Enzensberger poems only two years later, among them thirty-three new poems that were of a subtle romantic anarchic character.[51]

The appearance of Enzensberger's poetry cycles *Mausoleum. Siebenunddreißig Balladen aus der Geschichte des Fortschritts* (*Thirty-Seven Ballads from the History of Progress;* 1975) and *Der Untergang der Titanic. Eine Komödie* (*The Sinking of the Titanic: A Comedy;* 1978) then came as the ultimate surprise: this was the turning point. For a conservative critic like Hans Egon Holthusen, these poems were evidence for a "recantation" that relinquished the principles of the leftist "movement" (the "New Enlightenment") resulting from a clash of the poetic imagination with political experience.[52] Thus Holthusen attempted to characterize Enzensberger's changed outlook in reference to the tone and themes of Benn's poetry, admittedly without being quite successful in identifying the contemporary poet with the latter's cultural pessimism and artistic credo.[53]

Holthusen's review of these poetry cycles speaks of a "victory of the principle of poetry" over historical experience, if in the terms of an "aesthetics of the absurd": For Enzensberger, "poetry and history . . . invent each other (as) lies." Yet the critic does not attempt to clarify the contradictions inherent in such a phyrric "victory" of the poetic principle. After all, Holthusen is mostly interested in Enzensberger's change, his forgoing of the "principle of hope" and his turn to a different, Benn's, image of mankind: "the human being as Zero."[54] The critic's evaluation of the poet's "changed" view of humanity hence is clearly more ideologically motivated than the otherwise close, fascinating reading of his poetry would justify. Holthusen would have done much better had he focused instead on the fact that there has always been an element of indeterminacy in Enzensberger's work. The Benn and Brecht scholar Reinhold Grimm—intensely provoked by Holthusen—subsequently set out to explain the contradictions in Enzensberger's poetry as a constitutive part of his work. He continues to see the poet of the mid-1970s and the early 1980s, with whose work he had occupied himself periodically since the late 1950s, as an anarchic poet, who never could end up in the arms of restoration: Enzensberger "has, in effect, never ceased to fight, both as an author and a citizen, for the enlightenment and thus betterment of the human race and condition. . . . Enzensberger (though he may grow pale like Brecht's Herr Keuner upon reading this) has not changed." For Grimm, the anarchist poet has stayed subversive, changed has merely the expression of his poetic anarchism, from the "gay, exuberant anarchy" of the 1950s to his "gloomy chaos and anguish" since the mid-1970s.[55] Nevertheless, Grimm, whose first essay on Enzensberger's "Montierte Lyrik" ("Montage and Lyric Poetry"; 1958) had demonstrated the closest affinity to Benn's montage techniques, does not fail to mention that the gloomy poetry of *Die Furie des Verschwindens* (*The Fury of Disappearance;* 1980) "explicitly approves of Benn's poetic existence," citing also an earlier 1973 letter in which Enzensberger had informed him of a "half-secret come-back" of Benn ("One is quoting him again."). At the same time, Grimm points out, Enzensberger "plans to exclude from (his new journal) *Transatlantik* . . . all poetry and fiction alike! He is determined . . . to accept and publish nothing but reports based on hard facts."[56]

What both critics apparently failed to read closely in their antagonistic involvement with each other—as a latent context for Enzensberger's poetry since the mid-1970s—is his oracle, formulated in his contribution to the 1968 discussion in *Kursbuch:* "Whoever produces literature today, can neither be justified, nor refuted."[57] In my view, Enzensberger had already then *split* himself, as it were, into the activist critic and the poet who continues to write poetry. Hence he continues to write poetry fully aware that poetic creativity is not autonomous, not privileged in the sense of romantic or symbolist poetry, rather an experience to be exempt from any and all classification ("cannot be justified, nor refuted"). Herein lies the blind spot of both critics: neither Holthusen's ultimate identification of Enzensberger's position with a nihilistic stance nor Grimm's insistence on Enzensberger's paradoxical, anarchic Benn/Brecht heritage realizes that the poet himself has definitively moved out of the horizon of a dualistic utopian/dystopian perspective (which may be linked to the "Benn/Brecht" constellation), characteristic for the history of the German avant-garde. In my view, Enzensberger has changed at the point when he raises the very *aporia* of writing poetry to the status of a creative principle (however different from Heißenbüttel's linguistically reflected principle of aporia).

To understand this change, we will want to return to Enzensberger's early work of the 1950s and 1960s before turning to an interpretation of *The Sinking of the Titanic* as a paradigm of a poem that no longer can be understood as "modernist." In an early essay contributing to a discussion of poetry in the 1950s, collected under the title *Mein Gedicht ist mein Messer* (*My Poem is My Knife;* 1961), Enzensberger had defined poetry, in the well-known Brechtian terms of *Gebrauchsgegenstand* (object for use), as a *Produktionsmittel* (means of production) for demonstrating and changing certain conditions of awareness, in short, and quite boldly, as a means for the "production of truth." On these Brechtian grounds, he had turned against Benn's poetics as the poetic doctrine dominating postwar German poetry: the idea of *Ausdruckswelt* (world of expression) that denies the object, the idea of autonomous form, of poetry as "monologue . . . directed at no one" except the "lyrical self," and so on. Thus we have Enzensberger's question that also applied to Heißenbüttel's "experimental" poetry, which he disliked, if "language itself (be) really the only material of the poem?"

Yet, Enzensberger is not as Brechtian as one might assume, since he simultaneously declares himself, against any global visions of change, as a poet of the *Einzelfall* (the singular): "As poems are finite, limited, and contingent, one can only produce through them finite, limited and contingent truths."[58] His contemporary essay "Poesie und Politik" (1962) expands on the significance of the singular: "Poetry renders future . . . it reminds us of the 'Selbstverständliche' (obvious/self-understood), which is 'unverwirklicht' (unrealized). . . . It is anticipation, and be it in the mode of doubt, cancellation, or negation."[59] In short, Enzensberger, in writing a poem, is concerned with that which negates experience as presence, with the alienating effect of ideology. In that sense, the poem's interest in the *particular* anticipates "presence" as a latent "future." Hence his paradoxically political unpolitical insight into poetry: "Its political task is to refuse all political task and to speak for all, still when it talks of no one, of a tree, a stone, of that which is not."[60] In one of his poems, published two years later in *Blindenschrift* (*Braille;* 1964), a beacon at the seashore will thus signal "nothing" except *presence* (an experience beyond the horizon of utopian/dystopian projections of the historical avant-garde):

> weiter bedeutet es nichts.
> weiter verheisst es nichts.
> keine lösungen, keine erlösung,
> das feuer dort leuchtet,
> ist nichts als ein feuer,
> dort ist der ort wo das feuer ist,
> dort wo das feuer ist ist der ort.[61]

(it does not mean anything further / it does not promise anything / no solutions, no salvation / the fire there shines / is nothing but a fire / the place is where the fire is / where the fire is there is the place.)

In a "manual" for the reading of his poetry collection *Landessprache* (*Indigenous Speech;* 1960), Enzensberger had already declared in point 4 that his poems were "not meant for spurning, deepening, and spreading anger." Hence Enzensberger's provocative turn against both Brecht and Benn, while, paradoxically, both poets continue to influence his work, when he situates the poem beyond the alternatives "here party calendar, there timelessness."[62] Hence his insights in the "Aporien der Avantgarde" ("Aporia of the Avant-Garde"; 1962), his critique of the historical avant-garde as a collective project of "anticipation" of sociopolitical experience within the aesthetic domain. What the avant-garde "anticipated," Enzensberger states, was merely its success over the resistance of modern society against modern art. The avant-garde's real risk, namely, its assimilation by a market-driven system, was, however, not mastered. The surrealist "pure" action, for example, was no more than "blind action," fitting quite well with the empty dynamics of modernity. And the philosophical quasi-scientific claims of contemporary "experimental" literature run no risk at all, he states with writers like Heißenbüttel in mind, being no more than a "language game" without obligations. For Enzensberger, contemporary attempts to continue or revive avant-gardist futurist models over the real risks of the *individual work of art* are "anachronistic," "regressive" illusions, since the "law of increasing reflection is relentless."[63] In sum, already in 1962 we may sense that Enzensberger is only a (crucial) step, however short or long in terms of the progression of his work, away from an *outright* valorization of *aporia* itself that comes in the wake of his valorization of the paradox of poetry and politics, of negation and critical doubt that faces aporia. Aporia will be the name of his muse, the more the insightful blind spot itself, in which the *Blindenschrift* (braille) of poetry is written, becomes the very creative principle for Enzensberger. At that point, the "relentless law of reflection" has led him to the poem as an act of reflection in language on language, language not as "pure material" (in the vein of Benn and Heißenbüttel) but as a "gestus" (in terms of his Brechtian heritage).[64] For this understanding of language, the *Gegenstand* (object) is no longer as close at hand for the subject as in the early poetry (though not as removed from language as in Heißenbüttel's *texts*). For Enzensberger, the poem remains a *poem* as much as it stays an expression of a subject against all odds, as much as it recognizes and thematizes these odds from an epistemological distance that is beyond Einstein's suffering from the abyss between the subject, language, and the object. At that point, where *aporia* has become the point of departure for the aesthetic process, Enzensberger has changed, after all. He has not, however, switched from Brecht's gestic poem to Benn's "bio-negative" *absolute* poem as a "black cipher" (see chapter 7). This we shall see in the context of his later poetry put into its contexts.

By the mid-1970s, in the wake of the demise and assimilation of the student revolt, the editor of the *Kursbuch* saw that the spectacle of revolution was over. For Enzensberger, the concept of revolution had turned into an escapist metaphor for a global civilization and its discontents. Terms like "Third World," or "First World" "capitalist" or "communist," no longer expressed substantive value distinctions. The contemporary "avant-garde" event represents an accelerated worldwide commodification process. It involves a battle of all against all for a share of the pie. It it this pie, Enzensberger writes, that the underdeveloped nations really mean when they cry out for "revolution."[65]

In this vein, more and more German intellectuals in East and West alike rejected a Marxist critique of ideology as ideology. A common culture of skepticism replaced the leftist credo with what appeared to be a reemergence of a Nietzschean critique of ideology, a modernist critique of modern rationalism. As it often bordered on Kafkaesque visions, this new mentality typically displayed less of a postmodern *jouissance* of liberation from ideologies than a resigned sense of loss. In his play *Der Auftrag* (*The Mission;* 1979), the East German writer Heiner Müller, for example, unmasked the concepts of freedom and revolution as a cyclical series of masks of treason. The true "revolutionary" is the doomed victim; revolutionary poetry has always been the poetry of futility, the play asserts. By 1980 Peter Weiss had completed his monumental *Ästhetik des Widerstands* (*Aesthetics of Resistance*), a three-volume case study of the relevance of the arts from antiquity to surrealism for twentieth-century political activism. Enzensberger's ideological opponent on the left, the author of the activist plays *Vietnam Diskurs* (*Discourse on Vietnam;* 1967) and *Gesang des Lusitanischen Popanz* (*Song of the Lusitanian Bogey;* 1974), in which the cause of the so-called Third World was emphatically embraced, here retracts his previous views. In writing political history as art history and vice versa, Weiss forces himself to admit that the attempts of the avant-garde to integrate aesthetics with the social life-forms have been doomed to failure. Political resistance can only be *aufgehoben,* sublated, saved, and conserved, in the realm of art, or in the death of the martyr, for which Auschwitz remains a universal symbol. On the other hand, in the midst of mutual destruction, art maintains a locus of resistance—critiquing both the silence of speechless resignation and the shrillness of ideology. As Weiss affirms, because every future is instantaneously filled anew with torture, arson, and murder, "Utopia would be necessary."[66] These German literary developments from the 1960s to the 1980s clearly constitute a *Tendenzwende.* However, this turning should ultimately be addressed within the context of sociopolitical trends that had a larger scope than Germany, then still divided into East and West.

In his play *Das Verhör von Havana* (*The Havana Inquiry;* 1970), Enzensberger still shared Weiss's optimism, derived from his initial Cuban experience, that the Third World offers the possibilities of "art being part of life," as Weiss had claimed in his Angolan play *Song of the Lusitanian Bogey.* But Castro's persecution of dissident writers and intellectuals in a Cuba increasingly dominated by the geopolitical and economic interests of the Soviet Union, and Vietnam's imperialist incursion into Cambodia, lead Enzensberger to become disillusioned with the intellectual and political identity of the Left. He expresses these feelings of dislocation in his poetry, specifically in *The Sinking of the Titanic.* This work is, in critical and aesthetic terms, far superior to a whole trend of a contemporaneous "doomsday" mentality and literature. It resists the regression to a well-known German apocalyptic tendency, articulating in an inimitably light mode, compared with which

Peter Sloterdijk's *Kritik der zynischen Vernunft* (*Critique of Cynical Reason;* 1983) is a Sisyphean task, a postmodern argument for a continuous labor on positive and negative myths.[67]

The Sinking of the Titanic sets forth a self-reflective hermeneutic argument concerning the relationship of utopia and dystopia in history. The poetic cycle attempts to define the nature of history from the point of view of a supposedly lost but now creatively remembered poem, written a decade earlier in Castro's revolutionary Havana, about the *Titanic* catastrophe in 1912. It does so by discussing its own heuristic function, that of a work of art. The long poem invariably returns, after numerous episodes either relating the sinking ship — the *Titanic,* of course, is a symbol for the supposed indestructibility of progress — or the Cuban revolution, to its own status, articulated by a lyrical I: "In reality, nothing has happened. The sinking of the Titanic has not taken place; it was only a film, an omen, a hallucination." This is so because what happens, happens "all or nothing in my head of forty-six thousand gross registered tons." This consciously solipsistic, if ironic, position is *critical* in that it makes its own solipsism as well as the utopian/dystopian visions of history the *Gegenstand* (object) of the poem: "At that time we still believed in it (who: 'we'?) . . . We still believed in an end at that time/when? ('at that time'? 1912, 18 45 68?) and that means: in a beginning."[68]

Aside from a Nietzschean digression on the truth and lies of language itself, the paradigms for such reflections are taken from the visual arts. The examples range from "Apokalypse. Umbrisch, etwa 1490" ("Apocalypse: Umbrian, about 1490"), a lyrical icon thematizing the artist's paradoxical pleasure at expressing images of the *Weltuntergang* (end of the world), to "Die Ruhe auf der Flucht. Flämisch, 1521" ("Rest in Escape: Flemish, 1521"), a Breughel-like tableau. In the cycle's four poems dedicated to the problem of art via paradigms from the visual arts, the relationship of the idyllic and the catastrophic is defined as an existential entwinement of idealization processes and social power. The argument also addresses the oppression that language as a means of communication *and of art* exerts on the phenomena. In the last poetic icon, this condition is finally pointed to as the relation of "blindness" and violence.

The poetic tableau, the haunting opaque beauty of which can here only be suggested, begins:

Ich sehe das spielende Kind im Korn,
das den Bären nicht sieht.

Der Bär umarmt oder schlägt einen Bauern.
Den Bauern sieht er,
aber er sieht das Messer nicht,
das in sein em Rücken steckt,
nämlich im Rücken des Bären.[69]

(I see the child playing in the corn, / who does not see the bear. / The bear embraces or strikes a farmer. / He sees the farmer, / but he does not see the knife / that sticks in the back, / namely in the back of the bear.)

In the face of the deeply comprehended inexplicability of phenomena, of their quasi-monadic appearance, the dualistic ideas of utopia/idyll and dystopia/catastrophe thus are viewed as projections of the self. They are perceived as tautological constructs reacting to the impossibility of the knowledge of truth and to the immutability of violence. The impenetrability of the world appears as relative to the subject, which, after all, acknowledges its very blindness to its own condition. The subject understands through reflection, although it is a reflection that admits—in an aporetic *gestus* of knowing—to the impossibility of knowing: "I have seen all this except for the knife in my back."[70]

Enzensberger's images function quite differently from the "dialectical images" of Benjamin (whose "Über den Begriff der Geschichte" ["Theses on History"; 1940] constitute one of the "intertexts" of the poem). Benjamin, after all, continued to cling to the messianic vision that one might intuit, after discarding the illusion of evolutionary "progress" ("wie er sich in den Köpfen . . . malte" [as visualized in the mind]), a certain knowledge at the moment of what he calls a "dialectic at a standstill." Benjamin's moment was the moment of "Jetztzeit" (now-time) in which the subject surrenders its identity to a constellation that deconstructs the boundaries of the subject/object dichotomy: "In this structure does he recognize. . . ." Beyond that, Benjamin still insisted that it was possible to experience a certain profoundly intersubjective epiphany (as it were, a "profane illumination") from the work of art, which is "revolutionary" to the extent that it explodes the historicist interpretation of events: "In each work of art there is a locus in which the absorbed viewer is touched as if by the cooling wind of an incipient dawn."[71] The goal for both Enzensberger and Benjamin is the unmasking of the idea and ideal of *Fortschritt* (progress); for both, "progress" and "decline" are merely two sides of the same coin, namely, of the concept as a rational device. "Progress" and "decline" are mere *metaphors* for an event that cannot be normatively signified. Enzensberger, however, denies any possibility of an alternative vision beyond the open-ended reflection constituted by the text-reader relation. By contrast, Benjamin's critique of *metaphor* in literature and politics, which we have traced via his criticism of expressionism and its legacies, was based on his belief in the totality of the image, expressed *in* language. After all, he attributed to the "dialectical image" "redemptive" energies in terms of a greater "plan of construction," where "origin" and "goal" rest in the theological. While the image is the alternative mode to conceptual language from Schlegel's "Gespräch über Poesie" ("Dialogue Concerning Poetry") to Hofmannsthal ("Chandos Letter") and to Benjamin, Enzensberger attempts to deal with the instant reification of the aesthetic sign (including the image) through power relations rooted in the subject's (as his own) relation to language. In other words, he insists on the subject's capacity to expresses itself, however aporetically, *through* language. Thus, and here he has not changed, Enzensberger, after all, insists on the experience of the subject, albeit as an experience of *aporia,* to which the "gestus" of his poetry points. By contrast, to return to the constellation discussed earlier, Heißenbüttel attempts to overcome the aporia of the subject (epitomized by Einstein's poetry in the 1930s) in turning to the a priori of language, which his *texts* articulate as an intersubjective phenomenon.

With Enzensberger's aporetic insistence on the subject, manifest in his poetry since the mid-1970s, the German avant-garde may have come full circle in its agon for an "authentic" relation between art and life. The avant-garde of the mid-1970s and 1980s confirms, in its own way, the historical experience of the expressionist avant-garde of the prewar, war, and postwar era that projected its dreams and fears in the images of utopia and dystopia, of revolution and catastrophe, as we have seen in the case of Meidner's paintings and Jakob van Hoddis's doomsday poem. If the sons have returned to their fathers or grandfathers, they have, however, critically absorbed the older generation's experience. After two world wars, the atom bomb, and numerous full-fledged wars in Asia and the Middle East, Enzensberger, in a 1978 essay on the theme of *Weltuntergang* (doomsday) reevaluates the collective "images of catastrophe" as "realistic" inasmuch as they emerge from social life-forms. Are they not, he asks, an expression of the unconscious reacting to our daily exposure to the mass media, which show that we are in a continuous state of war, in hospitals or jails? In a critique of the ideologies of the political Right and the political Left—his sympathies still rest with the Left—he criticizes the latter's anachronistically naive utopianism in a sobering attempt to refine its analytic capacity. He decries the left's dogmatic "academic exorcism," its fearful and undialectically defensive attempts to ban the power of myths through edicts. He reminds his friends that classical Marxism itself has for a hundred years exploited the mythical mode by equating collective images of catastrophe with the immanent collapse of capitalism. And he attacks as a leftist taboo the stereotyped assertion that any comparison between natural and societal processes be a "reactionary" design to undermine the idea of revolution: "The elementary force of the imagination teaches millions of people consistently to break this prohibition. Our ideologues make fools of themselves when they try to eradicate inextinguishable images like flood, fire, earthquakes, and hurricanes." For Enzensberger, the images of the apocalypse and doomsday thus also contain a cognitive potential: "The idea of the apocalypse has accompanied utopian thinking since its beginnings; it follows it like a shadow, it is its flip side . . . without catastrophe no millennium, without apocalypse no paradise." In that omnipresent sense, the catastrophe has not taken place; it is not "real," but "a second reality, an image that we form, a production of our incessant imagination, the catastrophe in the head."[72]

Thus "negative utopia" has its own reality. A product of the collective imagination, it reflects the daily experience of crisis metaphorically, therein constituting a challenge to modernity's rational discourse. The compulsion to conjoin events in an imaginary totality, albeit a negative one, thus is a symptom of the deficiency of rational experience. As a compensatory experience, the mythical mode legitimately challenges conceptual analysis and systematic theories, and it invites reflection that may free toward the apperception of phenomena. In this sense, reflection for Enzensberger is not Habermas's "metapower," which grasps and dissolves all other powers.[73]

While Habermas attempts to salvage the enlightened project of modernity in the midst of a "neue Unübersichtlichkeit" (new opaqueness), for Enzensberger, it seems, one must be absolutely postmodern. The postmodern witness of the mid-1970s and 1980s writes against the grain of the mentality of the late 1960s and early 1970s in which ratio attained a quasi-mythical status, a mentality that had been also his own.

The Austrian Alfred Kubin had already posed a comparable critique of rationalism in his paintings and in his 1909 novel *Die andere Seite* (*The Other Side*). Kubin provocatively rendered the images of the indissoluble entwinement of reason and myth, of enlightenment and terror, of the conscious and the subconscious, of life and death, of utopia and dystopia, as a unity beyond categories. Some seven to eight decades later, marked by the conflicts between the avant-garde's visions and historical events, which

I have traced throughout this study, Enzensberger would attempt to salvage certain traces of enlightenment from the mythical mode of experience, previously the target of his own Marxist-inspired political criticism. In this sense, the revolutionary Enzensberger may have been a modern-day version of the rationalist Herkules Bell who set out to defeat Patera, the archaic tyrant of Kubin's dystopian community, the "dream state," before we detect that modern rationalism (Bell) and irrationalism (Patera) are but the two sides of the same coin. Had the rationalist in Enzensberger not been deceived by the leftist visions of a "dream state" of modernity? Had he not been aware of the fact that every dream is the product of the opposing forces of the rational and the irrational? How then should one, once more, interpret his 1968 statement that "whoever produces literature as art can neither be justified nor refuted any longer"? This was an argument of his "revolutionary" days, yet it seems to have retained a unique validity for Enzensberger. Was it an indictment of the raison d'être of art, or did the author give art a uniquely indeterminate status? Clearly, his statement went beyond totalizing the decline of the power of the artist and intellectual in the state, as it also did not assert art's freedom from all ideology and external authorities. Rather, it gave art an equivocal status in the modern state. That the significance of art is beyond definition is the explicit theme of his later *Sinking of the Titanic*. These are merely some of the questions provoked by Enzensberger's poetic and essayistic work. His is a consciously indeterminate project of enlightenment that takes its departure from one prominent tenet of an early insight: "the law of progressive reflection is inexorable."[74]

The agon and crisis of the avant-garde we have traced is ultimately a matter of our language, of our concepts, which Nietzsche had perceived at the roots of the modern crisis of interpretation. Beyond that, the avant-garde pushed this crisis of interpretation toward the edge where the modern concept of art as an autonomous aesthetic phenomenon is questioned and "art" becomes questionable as a social institution. Enzensberger's insight that art articulates an indeterminate relationship of utopian desires and dystopian fears had already, in the first decade of the century, informed seemingly esoteric, apolitical, yet analytical artists and writers such as Alfred Kubin and Franz Kafka or expressionist poets like Jakob van Hoddis or Georg Heym, whose work deconstructs the experience (*Erlebnis*) of the Cartesian subject. In other words, in the hermeneutic light of the decentering text, the event of modernity lies neither in the utopian project of revolutions nor in the dystopian reversals of cultural pessimism. Rather, for the creative individual, a permanent crisis makes itself felt in view of the immutability of man's unconscious and of the relative immobility of modern institutions. Against this seeming impasse, however, the avant-garde opened the understanding of art to heterogeneous voices. These go beyond the myth-making mentality of revolutionaries inspired by the myth of rebirth and the mentality of those whose imagination is captured by the primordial phenomenon of decay and death. The postmodern dialectic of the avant-garde in the vein of Enzensberger is an indeterminate dialectic that continuously negotiates the desire for wholeness and the insight of reason with the awareness of the "blindness" of language—at a standstill. At this point there may be no return to historical forms of utopianism.

Notes

Throughout this book, in cases where there is no acknowledged translator of a foreign-language work, the English translations are mine.

Introduction

1. See Andreas Huyssen and David Bathrick, eds., *Modernity and the Text* (New York: Columbia University Press, 1989); Bronner and Kellner, eds., *Passion and Rebellion* (New York: J. F. Bergin, 1988); Bernd Hüppauf, ed., *Expressionismus und Kulturkrise* (Heidelberg: Carl Winter Universitätsverlag, 1983); and most recently Richard Murphy, *Theorizing the Avant-Garde: Modernism, Expressionism and the Problem of Postmodernity* (Cambridge: Cambridge University Press, 1999).

2. The most consequential, meaning meanwhile also most questioned, theoretical model of the historical avant-garde has been and, in spite of its lacunae, still is Peter Bürger, *Theory of the Avant-Garde*, trans. Michael Shaw, with a foreword by Jochen Schulte-Sasse (Minneapolis: University of Minnesota Press, 1984); originally published as *Theorie der Avantgarde* (Frankfurt: Suhrkamp, 1974). Bürger has credited the international movements with having made visible—at the instance of countering fin de siècle aestheticism—art's isolation from the life-worlds. The avant-garde is said to have delivered an all-out attack on aestheticism in terms of a fundamental "self-critique" of art that distinguishes it from the merely adversary stance of modernist formal innovations. The heuristic value of this model has significantly informed also Anglo-American criticism, tired of a nomenclature that subsumes as "avant-garde" everything from "aestheticism, decadence, and symbolism" to futurism as practiced by Renato Poggioli, *The Theory of the Avant-Garde* (Cambridge: Harvard University Press, Belknap Press, 1968), 227. Yet, inasmuch as the idea of a radical sublation of art into social life is necessarily also pointing to the ultimate failure of the avant-garde's grand project, such theory has to be historicized in turn. In critiquing and historicizing theory beyond Bürger, one should therefore further explore the avant-garde in a phase of becoming conscious of its own predicament, exploiting or, on the other hand, giving up on its critical and aesthetical potential *within* the institution of art. The Janus-faced quality and historical path of expressionism prescribes such a focus, which this study assumes.

3. See Helmut Heißenbüttel, "Die Demonstration des i und das Trivialgedicht. Der Dichter Kurt Schwitters," *Text und Kritik* 35/36 (1972): 5f.

4. See Edmund Husserl, *Die Krisis der europäischen Wissenschaften und die transzendentale Phänomenologie* (Hamburg: Felix Meiner, 1977), 13–15.

5. See Martin Jay, "The Discourse of Totality before Western Marxism," *Marx-*

ism and Totality: The Adventures of a Concept from Lukács to Habermas (Berkeley and Los Angeles: University of California Press, 1984), 21–80.

6. See Donald D. Egbert, *Social Radicalism and the Arts* (New York: Knopf, 1970), also Matei Calinescu, *Faces of Modernity: Avant-Garde, Decadence, Kitsch* (Bloomington: Indiana University Press, 1977), 100–4. ————. *Five Faces of Modernity: Modernism, Avant-garde, Decadence, Kitsch, Postmodernism* (Durham, N.C.: Duke University Press, 1987), 100–4.

7. Cf. Joachim Fest, *Der Zerstörte Traum. Vom Ende des utopischen Zeitalters* (Berlin: Siedler, 1991), 40, 49.

8. Paul Michael Lützeler, "The Avant-Garde in Crisis: Hermann Broch's Negative Aesthetics in Exile," in *Hermann Broch: Literature, Philosophy, Politics,* ed. Stephen Dowden (Columbia, S.C.: Camden House, 1988), 30. For a full discussion of the concept of a "negative aesthetics," see chapters 3 and 8 passim.

9. See Andreas Huyssen, "The Search for Tradition: Avant-Garde and Postmodernism in the 1970s," in *Postmodernism: A Reader* (New York, N.Y.: Columbia University Press, 1993), 226. For an incisive discussion of a postmodern negotiation of the experience of the avant-garde and modernism, see also Andreas Huyssen, *After the Great Divide: Modernism, Mass Culture, Postmodernism* (Bloomington: Indiana University Press, 1986), 168ff.

10. I here argue on the basis of Reinhart Koselleck, *Critique and Crisis: Enlightenment and the Pathogenesis of Modern Society* (Cambridge: MIT Press, 1988); originally published as *Kritik and Krise. Eine Studie zur Pathogenese der bürgerlichen Welt* (Freiburg and Munich: K. Alber, 1959).

11. I here argue on the basis of Paul de Man, "Criticism and Crisis," *Blindness and Insight: Essays in the Rhetoric of Contemporary Criticism* (Minneapolis: University of Minnesota Press, 1983), 12f.

12. Murphy, *Theorizing the Avant-Garde,* 259. Unfortunately, I could reflect on this groundbreaking study that supplies an innovative theoretical understanding of expressionism only at the very final stage of editing my own, thus merely in passing. Gottfried Benn is the only major author common to Richard Murphy's and my book.

13. Huyssen, *After the Great Divide,* 142f.

14. Thomas S. Kuhn, *The Structure of Scientific Revolutions* (Chicago and London: University of Chicago Press, 1962). See in particular chapters 7, "Crisis and the Emergence of Scientific Theories," and 8, "The Response to Crisis."

15. Ibid., 67, 79.

16. Paul Ricoeur, "Ist 'die Krise' ein spezifisch modernes Phänomen?," *Über die Krise*/Castelgandolfo-Gespräche 1985, ed. Krzysztof Michalski (Stuttgart: Klett-Cotta, 1986), 60f.

1. Gottfried Benn, "Gehirne," in *Gesammelte Werke*, 8 vols. ed. Dieter Wellershoff (Wiesbaden: Limes, 1968), 5:1191.

2. Peter Bürger, *Theory of the Avant-Garde*, trans. Michael Shaw, with a foreword by Jochen Schulte-Sasse (Minneapolis: University of Minnesota Press, 1984); originally published as *Theorie der Avantgarde* (Frankfurt: Suhrkamp, 1974). Bürger is paradigmatically concerned only with Dada and surrealism: "In their most extreme manifestations, their primary target is art as an institution such as it has developed in bourgeois society. With certain limitations that would have to be determined through *concrete analyses,* this is also true of Italian Futurism and German Expressionism" (109 n. 4; my emphasis). The most comprehensive exegesis and discussion of Bürger's model remains Jochen Schulte-Sasse's introductory essay to the English edition, "Foreword: Theory of Modernism versus Theory of the Avant-garde," vii–lvii, which situates it into the context from Poggioli to the poststructuralist debate, and concludes—via Benjamin and Kluge/Negt—significantly with a critique of Bürger's "reluctance to deal with future possibilities of aesthetic practice after the avant-garde."

3. Andreas Huyssen and David Bathrick, eds., *Modernity and the Text: Revisions of German Modernism* (New York: Columbia University Press, 1989). One of the merits of this collection of essays is that it characterizes as an essential feature of expressionism a certain "undecidebility in terms of established categories and traditional readings." Hence stems also a consensus to shift Peter Bürger's purist art/life model from its Hegelian totalizing schematics toward the "reading of individual texts in their specific historical inscriptions." Thus, the editors attempt "not only to accept expressionism as one exemplar of German modernism, but to claim its alleged anomaly for an expanded understanding of modernism's truly variegated nature" (10). See also Stephen Bronner and Douglas Kellner, eds., *Passion and Rebellion* (New York: Bergin, 1988).

4. See Peter Selz, *German Expressionist Painting* (Berkeley and Los Angeles: University of California Press, 1957), 9.

5. René Schickele, quoted in Thomas Anz and Michael Stark, eds., *Expressionismus: Manifeste und Dokumente zur deutschen Literatur 1910–1920* (Stuttgart: Metzler, 1982), 38.

6. Franz Marc, quoted ibid., 28.

7. For Reinhard Goering's obsession with Stefan George, see Robert Chapin Davis, *Final Mutiny: Reinhard Goering, His Life and Art,* Stanford German Studies, vol. 21 (New York: Lang, 1987), 85ff. Also Wolfgang Paulsen, *Deutsche Literatur des Expressionismus* (Bern and New York: Lang, 1983), 83f; Manfred Durzak, *Zwischen Symbolismus und Expressionismus: Stefan George* (Stuttgart: Kohlhammer, 1974), 119–53.

8. See Durzak, *Zwischen Symbolismus,* 107–12.

9. Anz and Stark, *Expressionismus,* 356.

10. Ibid., 44.

11. Ibid., 33.

12. See Raymond Furness, "The Religious Element in Expressionist Theatre," in *Expressionism Reassessed,* ed. Shulamith Behr, David Fanning, and Douglas Jarman (Manchester and New York: Manchester University Press, 1993), 163–73.

13. I here agree with Charles Haxthausen, "A Critical Illusion: 'Expressionism' in the Writings of Wilhelm Hausenstein," in *The Ideological Crisis of Expressionism: The Literary and Artistic War Colony in Belgium 1914–1918,* ed. Rainer Rumold and O. K. Werckmeister (Columbia, S.C.: Camden House, 1990), 172, that "the original concept of expressionism is more in harmony with Peter Bürger's theory of the avant-garde" than with Renato Poggioli's, as the latter stresses an "avant-garde" continuity of linguistic experimentalism from romanticism onward.

14. Douglas Kellner, "Expressionism and Rebellion," in *Passion and Rebellion,* ed. Stephen Bronner and Douglas Kellner (New York: Bergin, 1988), 5, referring to the flood of theoretical statements, manifestos, and reflections, observes that expressionism "was one of the most self-conscious movements in the history of art and literature." See also Geoffrey Perkins, *Contemporary Theory of Expressionism* (Bern and Frankfurt: Lang, 1974), 11.

15. Kurt Hiller, *Die Aktion,* no. 5 (1911): col. 138–39.

16. Anz and Stark, *Expressionismus,* 108.

17. Kurt Pinthus, "Zuvor (Berlin, Herbst 1919)," in *Menschheitsdaemmerung. Ein Dokument des Expressionismus,* 2d ed. (Hamburg: Rowohlt, 1955), 29. All translations from the German in this study are mine, unless indicated otherwise. For a translation differing from mine, see Kurt Pinthus, ed., *Menschheitsdämmerung/ Dawn of Humanity: A Document of Expressionism,* trans. and introduced by Joanna M. Ratych, Ralph Ley, Robert C. Conard, (Columbia, S.C.: Camden House, 1994), 35.

18. Quoted in Anz and Stark, *Expressionismus,* 108.

19. Friedrich Markus Huebner, "Der Expressionismus in Deutschland," in *Europas neue Kunst und Dichtung* (Berlin: Rowohlt, 1920), 80–95. See also Anz and Stark, *Expressionismus,* 3ff.

20. Quoted in Paul Raabe, "Der Expressionismus als historisches Phaenomen," in *Begriffsbestimmung des Literarischen Expressionismus,* ed. Hans Gerd Rötzer (Darmstadt: Wissenschaftliche Buchgesellschaft, 1976), 244.

21. Albert Soergel, *Dichtung und Dichter der Zeit. Neue Folge. Im Banne des Expressionismus* (Leipzig: R. Voigtlander, 1925), 370:

> Wir sind gegen die Musik—für die Erweckung zur Gemeinschaft.
> Wir sind gegen das Gedicht—für die Aufrufung zur Liebe.
> Wir sind gegen den Roman—für die Anleitung zum Leben.

Wir sind gegen das Drama—für die Anleitung zum Handeln.
Wir sind gegen das Bild—für das Vorbild.

22. The sudden emergence of "Doppelbegabungen," of artists creative in more than one artistic discipline, was symptomatic for an avant-garde esprit to transgress the boundaries of modern specialization. See Kent Hooper, *Ernst Barlach's Literary and Visual Art: The Issue of Multiple Talent* (Ann Arbor: UMI Research Press, 1987). For the other arts, including architecture, see Shulamith Behr, David Fanning, and Douglas Jarman, eds., *Expressionism Reassessed* (Manchester and New York: Manchester University Press, 1993).

23. See Haxthausen,"Critical Illusion," 187. Quotation from Wilhelm Worringer, *Künstlerische Zeitfragen* (Munich: R. Piper, 1921). Also see Anz and Stark, *Expressionismus,* 99.

24. Walter Sokel assessed the expressionist "writer in extremis" as the case of a heightened subjectivity that pivots in outright narcissism; see "The Other Face of Expressionism," *Monatshefte* 47 (1955): 1–10; while, for example, Roy Allen, *Literary Life in German Expressionism and the Berlin Circles* (Goeppingen: A. Kümmerle, 1974), 18–24, overly forces his argument of a unity of the expressionist movement in its antiestablishment revolt.

25. Shulamith Behr, introduction to *Expressionism Reassessed,* ed. Behr, David Fanning, and Douglas Jarman (Manchester and New York: Manchester University Press, 1993), 7.

26. For a comprehensive discussion of the concept "epoch," see the collection of greatly diversified interdisciplinary essays on the issue: Reinhart Herzog and Reinhart Koselleck, eds. *Epochenschwelle und Epochenbewusstsein* (Munich: W. Fink, 1987); and Hans-Ulrich Gumbrecht and Ursula Link-Heer, eds., *Epochenschwellen und Epochenstrukturen im Diskurs der Literatur—und Sprachhistorie* (Frankfurt: Suhrkamp, 1985). See also Jost Hermand, *Stile, Ismen, Etiketten. Zur Periodisierung der modernen Kunst* (Wiesbaden: Akademische Verlagsgesellschaft Athenaion, 1978), 7–16.

27. Silvio Vietta and Hans-Georg Kemper, *Expressionismus* (Munich: W. Fink, 1975), 21ff., constructively modify a long-standing two-track approach to expressionism (high modernism versus activism) dating back to Wolfgang Paulsen's study *Expressionismus und Aktivismus* from the mid-1930s. The authors understand "messianischer Expressionismus" as a naive activist attempt at "kollektive Menschheitserneuerung" (renewal of mankind), dialectically complementary to modernist expressionist developments of cognitive experimentation and exploration; both trends represent an "expressionist epoch's" will to revision and renewal. Anz and Stark, *Expressionismus,* xvff., use the construct of an expressionist epoch "only in a very limited sense, of course." They understand the expressionist "subculture which questioned and subverted the validity of established traditions and culture" as part of wider international developments, from French symbolism onward, as

an "intellektuell-avantgardistische Literatur." The authors in that sense opt for an expressionist "Avantgarde." Yet they do not address the fact, as does Matei Calinescu, *Five Faces of Modernity: Modernism, Avant-Garde, Decadence, Kitsch, Postmodernism* (Durham, N.C.: Duke University Press, 1987), 140f. that the historical avant-garde position implies a twofold strategy: It is set against the tradition of nineteenth-century bourgeois high culture (classicism, romanticism, realism, etc.) *and* it attempts to break away from the modernist adversary culture since Baudelaire (which tradition Anz and Stark mean by "intellektuell-avantgardistische Literatur"). Finally, it is conceivable to privilege the expressionist utopianism of the "new man," of "community" and "brotherhood" as constituting an "identity" of the "expressionist epoch." See Bernd Hüppauf, ed., *Expressionismus und Kulturkrise* (Heidelberg: C. Winter, 1983), esp. his introduction to the volume and his "Zwischen revolutionärer Epoche und sozialem Prozess. Bemerkungen über den Ort des Expressionismus in der Literaturgeschichte," 55–83, specifically 73f. Then, however, we exclude expressionism's self-reflective modernist components with which the previous critics are predominantly concerned. By contrast to German scholarly positions upholding, in degrees, the concept of an "expressionist epoch," the American scholars Bronner and Kellner, *Passion and Rebellion,* "seek to offer a new beginning for understanding Expressionism as a socio-cultural . . . avant-garde movement" (xi), emphasizing its "contradictory tendencies" (28). They simply point to an expressionist legacy, estrangement and montage techniques, developed by Brecht, which activate the public's critical reception toward intersubjective consciousness. For Paulsen, *Deutsche Literatur des Expressionismus,* an epochal term had meanwhile become "totally useless" (42).

28. Strindberg's theater, particularly the *Dream Play,* an experiment in subjective perspectivism in a wave of stagings, had just barely replaced the wave of naturalist plays. Baudelaire had left his mark on Stefan George's highly form-conscious poetry already before the turn of the century, but his themes and imagery continue to influence expressionists like Georg Heym or Georg Trakl in the early 1910s. And the explosive poetry of Rimbaud (in a translation by K. L. Ammer of 1907) is read just a few years earlier than Marinetti's iconoclastic "Futurist Manifesto" (in the German translation of *Der Sturm* [*The Storm*], 1912).

29. For the most comprehensive discussion of the transformations of the concept of "expressionism," see: Marit Werenskiold, *The Concept of Expressionism: Origins and Metamorphoses,* trans. Ronald Walford (Oslo: Universitetsforlaget, 1984), specifically 12ff, 33ff. See also Donald E. Gordon, "On the Origin of the Word Expressionism," *Journal of the Wartburg and Courtauld Institutes* 29 (1966): 377, and *Expressionism: Art and Idea* (New Haven and London: Yale University Press, 1987), 106f.; and Paul Poertner, "Was heisst 'Expressionismus'?" in *Begriffsbestimmung des literarischen Expressionismus,* ed. Hans Gerd Rötzer (Darmstadt: Wissenschaftliche Buchgesellschaft, 1976), 212.

30. See Paul Fechter, *Der Expressionismus* (Munich: R. Piper, 1914), 24; Wilhelm Worringer, "Künstlerische Zeitfragen," *Kunst und Künstler* 14 (February 1916): 262; Fritz Martini, "Was war Expressionismus," in *Begriffsbestimmung des Literarischen Expressionismus*, ed. Hans Gerd Rötzer (Darmstadt: Wissenschaftliche Buchgesellschaft, 1976), 138. In view of its international tendencies—which created extreme tensions with the conservative understanding of a specifically German superior national culture, pushed by a host of intellectuals from Carl Vinnen (in *Protest deutscher Künstler*, 1911) to Thomas Mann—there is clearly little reason to categorize expressionism as an epoch of a self-referential modernist sensibility.

31. Hans Mayer, "Rückblick auf den Expressionismus," in *Begriffsbestimmung des literarischen Expressionismus*, ed. Hans Gerd Rötzer (Darmstadt: Wissenschaftliche Buchgesellschaft, 1976), 279; see also John Willett, *Expressionism* (London: McGraw-Hill, 1970).

32. Anz and Stark, *Expressionismus*, 22.

33. Bürger, *Theory of the Avant-Garde*, 18.

34. Quoted in Anz and Stark, *Expressionismus*, 34.

35. Ibid.

36. See Burkhart Steinwachs, "Was leisten (literarische) Epochenbegriffe? Forderungen und Folgerungen," in *Epochenschwellen und Epochenstrukturen im Diskurs der Literatur—und Sprachhistorie*, ed. Hans-Ulrich Gumbrecht und Ursula Link-Heer (Frankfurt: Suhrkamp, 1985), 312–322; specifically 321f. Steinwachs suggests to relativize, if not abolish, the concept of an epoch through an independently differentiating notion of *Einstellungen* (dispositions): " 'Einstellungen' sind nicht per se an den Rahmen von Gattungs—und/oder Epochenerwartungen gebunden, koinzidieren aber häufig mit ihnen (z.B. 'romantisch' bzw. 'idyllisch')" (" 'Dispositions' are not per se linked to the frame of reference of genres or epochs but often coincide with them, e.g., 'romantic,' or 'idyllic,' respectively"). Steinwachs sees "dispositions" at work in the construction (1) of worldviews such as "realistic" or "romantic," (2) of self-understanding such as "ironic" or "satirical," and (3) of one's view of the times, as in "modern" or "avant-garde." As smaller units of interpretation, they are apt to deal with ambiguities, contradictions, and discontinuities erased by the normative epochal constructs.

37. Anz and Stark establish their categories for the documents and manifestos reprinted in *Expressionismus* mostly from within the realm of inner-German discourses, while I here focus on those that relate to the discourses of the international avant-garde.

38. Helmut Heißenbüttel, "Thesen zum Sprachgebrauch des deutschen Expressionismus," in *Expressionismus—sozialer Wandel und künstlerische Erfahrung* ed. Horst Meixner and Silvio Vietta (Munich: Wilhelm Fink, 1982), 42.

39. See "Aufstand der Landschaft gegen Berlin. Wilhelm Stapel und seine Zeitschrift 'Deutsches Volkstum,' Hamburg 1919–1938," and "Asphaltliteraten und

Dichter des total platten Landes. Der Streit in der Sektion für Dichtkunst der Preussischen Akademie der Künste" in *Berlin Provinz. Literarische Kontroversen um 1930*, ed. Jochen Meyer, *Marbacher Magazin* 35 (1985): 7–46, 47–86.

40. Walter Benjamin, "On Some Motifs in Baudelaire," in *Illuminations*, ed. Hannah Arendt, trans. by Harry Zohn, (New York: Schocken Books, 1969), 163ff.

41. See the discussion of Heym's allegoric poetry in scholarly criticism in Silvio Vietta and Hans-Georg Kemper, *Expressionismus*, 2d ed. (Munich: Wilhelm Fink, 1983), 49ff.

42. Walter Benjamin, *Gesammelte Schriften*, 7 vols., ed. Rolf Tiedemann and Hermann Schweppenhäuser (Frankfurt am Main: Suhrkamp, 1991) 3:182.

43. Pinthus, *Menschheitsdämmerung/Dawn of Humanity*, 65. The translation does not reproduce the rhyme of the original, for example, "Auf einem Häuserblocke sitzt er breit. / Die Winde lagern schwarz um seine Stirn. / Er schaut voll Wut, wo fern in Einsamkeit / Die letzten Häuser in das Land verirrn."

44. Reinhardt Tgahrt, ed., *Dichter lesen*, vol 3, *Vom Expressionismus in die Weimarer Republik* (Marbach am Neckar: Deutsche Schillergesellschaft, 1995), 43.

45. H. Pinthus, *Menschheitsdämmerung/Dawn of Humanity*, 67.

46. Quoted in Peter Demetz, *Worte in Freiheit. Der italienische Futurismus und die deutsche literarische Avantgarde 1912–1934* (Munich and Zurich: Piper, 1990), 332f: ". . . da plötzlich sprengt ein / Knall den aufgeschwollenen Stein. / Balkon-Gebisse blitzen knirschend drein. / Und Küchen klirren. Teppichklopfer prasseln. / Ein Mensch stürzt in den Kreis . . ."

47. Quoted in Anz and Stark, *Expressionismus*, 35.

48. Wilhelm Stapel, "The Intellectual and His People," in *The Weimar Republic Sourcebook*, ed. Anton Kaes, Martin Jay, and Edward Dimendberg (Los Angeles: University of California Press, 1994), 424; originally published as "Der Geistige und sein Volk," *Deutsches Volkstum* 12, no. 1 (1930): 5–8.

49. Anton Kaes, ed., *Kino-Debatte. Texte zum Verhältnis von Literatur und Film 1909–1929* (Tübingen: Max Niemeyer, 1978), 1ff.

50. Ibid., 2.

51. Franz Pfemfert, *Die Aktion*, 19 June 1910, 560–63; Kaes, *Kino-Debatte*, 62.

52. Kaes, *Kino-Debatte*, 72.

53. Walter Hasenclever, "Der Kintopp als Erzieher," *Die Revolution* ed. Hans Leybold, (Munich: Bachmair) 4 (1 December 1913): 3–4; Kaes, *Kino-Debatte*, 47f.

54. Kaes, *Kino-Debatte*, 6; Georg Simmel, "Die Großstadt und das Geistesleben," in *Die Großstadt. Jahrbuch der Gehe-Stiftung*, vol. 9 (Dresden, 1903), 188.

55. Translated by the author from Silvio Vietta, ed., *Lyrik des Expressionismus* (Tübingen: Niemeyer, 1976) 58:

Man zückt Revolver. Eifersucht wird rege, / Herr Piefke duelliert sich ohne Kopf. / Dann zeigt man uns mit Kiepe und Kropf / Die Älplerin auf mächtig steilem Wege. / . . . Und in den dunklen Raum-mir ins Gesicht- / Flirrt das hinein, entsetzlich! nach der Reihe! / Die Bogenlampe zischt zum Schluß nach Licht- / Wir schieben geil und gähnend uns ins Freie.

56. Quoted in Kaes, *Kino-Debatte*, 137.

57. Bertolt Brecht, *Gesammelte Werke*, 20 vols., *Schriften zur Literatur und Kunst* (Frankfurt am Main: Suhrkamp, 1967), 15:487.

58. Kaes, *Kino-Debatte*, 41, 45.

59. Ibid., 152.

60. Ibid., 18. See also Gerhard Wagner, *Walter Benjamin. Die Medien der Moderne* (Berlin: Vistas, 1992), 94.

61. See Demetz, *Worte in Freiheit*, 99–114.

62. F. T. Marinetti, *Let's Murder the Moonshine: Selected Writings*, ed. R. W. Flint; preface by Marjorie Perloff (Los Angeles: Sun and Moon Press, 1991), 70f.

63. Demetz, *Worte in Freiheit*, 68.

64. F. T. Marinetti, *Zang Tumb Tumb* (Milan: Edizioni Futuriste Di "Poesia," 1924), 181.

65. See Demetz, *Worte in Freiheit*, 88.

66. Pinthus, *Menschheitsdämmerung/Dawn of Humanity*, 108.

67. Quoted in Anz and Stark, *Expressionismus*, 53.

68. Quoted in Demetz, *Worte in Freiheit*, 222.

69. Franc Marc, quoted in Anz and Stark, *Expressionismus*, 28.

70. See Klaus H. Kiefer, *Diskurswandel im Werk Carl Einsteins. Ein Beitrag zur Theorie und Geschichte der Avantgarde* (Tübingen: Max Niemeyer, 1994), 170.

71. Quoted ibid., 181.

72. Ibid., 155.

73. Quoted in Anz and Stark, *Expressionismus*, 21.

74. Carl Einstein, *Negerplastik*, in *Werke*, 5 vols., ed. Rolf-Peter Baacke and Jens Kwasny, (Berlin: Medusa, 1980), 1:257.

75. Anz and Stark, *Expressionismus*, 46.

76. See Russell Berman, "German Primitivism/Primitive Germany: The Case of Emil Nolde," in *Cultural Studies of Modern Germany* (Madison: University of Wisconsin Press, 1993), 112–22.

77. Besides Carl Einstein's re-creations of "Afrikanische Lieder" and legends, only Carl Sternheim, more closely associated with him, introduced the motif of African "primitivism" in one of his novellas, "Ulrike," as a cynically flavored, primitivist critique of modern sexual mores. Significantly, it was Dada in Zurich that with Huelsenbeck at the front was to "drum literature" with fresh antiexpressionist, futurist-derived elemental energy "into the ground."

78. For a first (brief) discussion of Carl Einstein's input into *Documents* in American scholarship, see James Clifford, "On Ethnographic Surrealism," in *The Predicament of Culture: Twentieth-Century Ethnography, Literature, and Art* (Cambridge: Harvard University Press, 1988), 130; and Rainer Rumold, "Archeologies of

Modernity in *transition* and *Documents* 1929/30," in *Comparative Literature Studies* 37, no. 1 (2000): 45–67.

79. Huyssen and Bathrick, *Modernity and the Text*, 11.

80. Johannes Becher, "Vorbereitung," in *German Expressionist Poetry*, trans. Roy Allen (Boston: Twayne Publishers, 1979), 59.

81. Haxthausen, "Critical Illusion," 179; Joan Weinstein, "Wilhelm Hausenstein, the Leftist Promotion of Expressionism, and the First World War," in *The Ideological Crisis of Expressionism: The Literary and Artistic German War Colony in Belgium 1914–1918,* ed. Rainer Rumold and O. K. Werckmeister (Columbia, S.C.: Camden House, 1990), 195.

82. Carl Einstein, "Revolution durchbricht Geschichte und Überlieferung," *Werke,* ed. Herman Haarmann and Klaus Siebenlaar (Berlin: Fannei & Walz, 1992), vol. 4, 146–52. Also published in Berlin as "Absolute Kunst und absolute Politik," *alternative* 75 (1970): 253–57. Originally written in 1921.

83. Quoted in Anz and Stark, *Expressionismus,* 328.

84. Demetz, *Worte in Freiheit,* 103f.

85. Quoted in Pinthus, *Menschheitsdämmerung/Dawn of Humanity,* 308.

86. Demetz, *Worte in Freiheit,* 99.

87. See Gertrude Alexander,"Literaturbesprechung," in *Literatur im Klassenkampf. Zur Proletarisch—Revolutionären Literaturtheorie 1919–1923,* ed. Walter Faehnders and Martin Rector (Munich: Carl Hanser, 1971), 90f.

88. See Richard Sheppard, "Artists, Intellectuals and the USPD 1917–1922," in *Literaturwissenschaftliches Jahrbuch,* N.F. vol. 32 (Berlin: Duncker and Humblot, 1991), 175–216.

89. According to an analysis of the Social Democratic Party's council for *Arbeiter-Bildung* (workers' education), "Goethe and Schiller were the first and second most popular author among male workers and the first and third most popular authors among female workers." See Richard Sheppard, "The SPD, its Cultural Policy and the German *Avant-garde* 1917–1922," in *Internationales Archiv für Sozialgeschichte der deutschen Literatur* 20, no. 1 (1995) 62. If this were really more than an example of manipulated demoscopics, then there was, of course, no chance for a substantially different kind of cultural politics, avant-garde or proletarian, for any German political party. Hence also the success of NSPAD cultural politics, which cleverly perverted classical traditions later on. See Bernhard Zeller, ed. *Klassiker in finsteren Zeiten 1933–1945,* 2 vols., Marbacher Kataloge 38 (Marbach: Deutsche Schillergesellschaft e.V., 1983).

90. See Hanne Bergius, *Das Lachen Dadas: Die Berliner Dadaisten und ihre Aktionen* (Giessen: Anabas, 1989), 130–43.

91. See Chryssoula Kambas, *Die Werkstatt als Utopie. Lu Maertens literarische Arbeit und Formaesthetik seit 1900* (Tübingen: Niemeyer, 1988).

92. See Eva Hesse, *Die Achse Avant-Garde-Faschismus. Reflexionen über Filippo Tommaso Marinetti und Ezra Pound* (Zurich: Die Arche, 1991), 174f.

93. Quoted ibid., 191.

94. See Inca Rumold, *"Der Malik:* Else Lasker-Schüler's Anti-War Novel," *Women in German* 1 (1999): 143–61.

95. Gottfried Keller, *Gesammelte Briefe,* ed. Carl Helbing, 3 vols. (Bern: Benteli, 1950–54), 1:57.

96. See Marion Adams, "Der Expressionismus und die Krise der deutschen Frauenbewegung," in *Expressionismus und Kulturkrise,* ed. Bernd Hüppauf (Heidelberg: C. Winter, 1983), 105–30.

97. Else Lasker-Schüler, *Werke und Briefe,* vol. 1:1, *Gedichte,* ed. Karl Jürgen Skrodzki and Norbert Oellers (Frankfurt am Main: Suhrkamp, Jüdischer Verlag, 1996) 152f., 134f.

98. Pinthus, *Menschheitsdämmerung/Dawn of Humanity,* 223f.

99. Ibid., 350.

100. Rubiner and Zech were among the most radical, proletariat-oriented, activist expressionists. Heynicke and Zech were also exceptions as they did not have the higher education of most expressionists, who stemmed from wealthy professional families and who studied law or medicine. In contrast to, for example, the Russian cubo-futurists or neoprimitivists who came from rural Russia, most expressionists were born, raised, and by and large stayed in the city. Only Zech grew up on a farm and, out of committed idealism, gave up on his education in order to live as a worker, a miner. Rubiner was a clerk with little but self-education. Yet, Hasenclever or Werfel, equally leaning toward traditional expressions, were from the upper educated bourgeoisie and had a university education.

101. Heißenbüttel, "Thesen zum Sprachgebrauch," 42.

102. Walter Benjamin, "On Some Motifs in Baudelaire," *Illuminations,* ed. Hannah Arendt; trans. by Harry Zohn (New York: Schocken Books, 1969), 192.

103. See Markus Hallensleben's groundbreaking study, *Else Lasker-Schüler: Avantgardismus und Kuntstinszenierung* (Tübingen: Francke, 2000).

104. For a dedicated feminist reading of Else Lasker-Schüler, see Judith Kuckart, *Im Spiegel der Bäche finde ich mein Bild nicht mehr: Gratwanderung einer anderen Ästhetik der Dichterin Else Lasker-Schüler* (Frankfurt am Main: Fischer, 1985). See also Mary-Elisabeth O'Brien, "Ich war verkleidet als Poet . . . Ich bin Poetin!! The Masquerade of Gender in the Else Lasker-Schüler's Work," *German Quarterly* 65, no. 1 (1992): 1–17.

105. Pinthus, *Menschheitsdämmerung/Dawn of Humanity,* 170.

106. See David Bathrick, "Speaking the Other's Silence: Franz Jung's *Der Fall Gross,*" in *Modernity and the Text,* ed Andreas Huyssen and David Bathrick (New York: Columbia University Press, 1989), 23.

107. Quoted in Anz and Stark, *Expressionismus,* 150.

108. See Bathrick, "Speaking the Other's Silence," 19–35.

109. Raoul Hausmann, "Zur Weltrevolution," *Die Erde* 1 (1919): 12, 368–71.

110. Quoted in Anz and Stark, *Expressionismus,* 53.

111. Sander Gilman, *Smart Jews: The Construction of the Image of Jewish Superior Intelligence* (Lincoln: University of Nebraska Press, 1996) takes on the issue of the cultural construction of differences in "intelligence" and "creativity" on a large scale.

112. Quoted in Adams, "Der Expressionismus und die Krise," 108.

113. Pinthus, *Menschheitsdaemmerung/Dawn of Humanity,* 70.

114. Quoted in Vietta and Kemper, *Expressionismus,* 33. As Vietta omits a closer reading of "Dusk," his discussion of the "simultaneity of the disparate" remains more within the context of the problem of "the representation of urban perception" and is less informative for its mediation through the poet's "literary" predisposition.

115. Quoted in Anz and Stark, *Expressionismus,* 72f.

116. Quoted ibid., 70, 69, 71.

117. See Ernst Bloch, *Erbschaft dieser Zeit* (Frankfurt am Main: Suhrkamp, 1962) 104–22.

118. Quoted in Anz and Stark, *Expressionismus,* 110.

119. Demetz, *Worte in Freiheit,* 76.

120. Quoted in Anz and Stark, *Expressionismus,* 34.

121. Rainer Rumold, *Gottfried Benn und der Expressionismus. Provokation des Lesers; absolute Dichtung* (Königstein/Ts.: Scriptor/Athenaeum, 1982), 54f.

122. See Anz and Stark, *Expressionismus,* 80f.

123. Quoted ibid., 81, 282f.

124. Quoted ibid., 36.

125. See also Fredric Jameson, *The Political Unconscious: Narrative as a Socially Symbolic Act* (Ithaca, N. Y.: Cornell University Press, 1981), 225.

126. Bernd Hüppauf's observation that dropping the concept of an "expressionist epoch" would leave an "unstructured empty site," (Hüppauf, *Expressionismus und Kulturkrise,* 59) may explain why critics continue to insist on the unifying concept; however, it even more so explains the need for a reassessment. Expressionism may invoke the futurist "new," yet it may also revive the style of Goethe or Schiller. Thus Paul Raabe ("Der Expressionismus als historisches Phaenomen," 262) rightfully considered expressionism a "phenomenon of many voices," "a last current of the waning nineteenth century and simultaneously . . . a first manifestation of the vitality of a new literature in the twentieth century."

127. Raymond Williams, *The Politics of Modernism: Against the New Conformists,* ed. and intro. Tony Pinkney (London and New York: Verso, 1989), 46.

128. Ibid.

129. Jameson, *Political Unconscious,* 230.

130. The unconscious dimension of competing strategies of aestheticization can be stated in the more laconic terms of Alfred Döblin, who noted in 1918 that "economic parallels are likely." Alfred Döblin, "Von der Freiheit eines Dichter-

menschen," in *Theorie des Expressionismus,* ed. Otto Best (Stuttgart: Reclam, 1976), 28.

131. Paul de Man, "Criticism and Crisis," *Blindness and Insight. Essays in the Rhetoric of Contemporary Criticism* (Minneapolis: University of Minnesota Press, 1983), 12ff.

132. Paul Ricoeur,"Ist 'die Krise' ein spezifisch modernes Phänomen?" in *Über die Krise,* Castelgandolfo-Gespräche 1985, ed. Krzysztof Michalski (Stuttgart: Klett-Cotta, 1986), 38f.

133. Reinhart Koselleck, "Einige Fragen and die Begriffsgeschichte von 'Krise,'" in *Über die Krise,* 64–77.

134. For details, see beginning of chapter 8.

135. Koselleck, "Einige Fragen," 69.

136. See Ricoeur, "Ist 'die Krise' ein spezifisch modernes Phänomen?" 58.

137. De Man, "Criticism and Crisis," 14.

138. Ricoeur, "Ist 'die Krise' ein spezifisch modernes Phänomen?" 60f.

Chapter 2

1. Peter Sloterdijk, *Kritik der zynischen Vernunft* (Frankfurt: Suhrkamp, 1983) reviews dadaism in its two aspects of "kynical" reason which in recourse to vital, bodily experience resists all ideological confinement, and as "cynical," simultaneously, partaking in the destructiveness of modernity as a betrayal of the humanist enlightenment. For a discussion of the reaction of the avant-garde to World War I, see Theda Shapiro, *Painters and Politics: The European Avant-Garde and Society 1900–1925* (New York: Elsevier, 1976); Rudolf E. Kuenzli, "The Semiotics of Dada Poetry," in *Dada Spectrum: The Dialectics of Revolt,* ed. Stephen Foster and Rudolf E. Kuenzli (Madison: Coda Press, 1979), 52–70; Rudolf E. Kuenzli "Dada gegen den Ersten Weltkrieg: Die Dadaisten in Zürich," in *Sinn aus Unsinn. Dada International,* ed. Wolfgang Paulsen and H. G. Hermann (Bern and Munich: Francke, 1982), 87–100.

2. Richard Huelsenbeck, ed. *Dada; eine literarische Dokumentation* (Hamburg: Rowohlt, 1964), 13f.

3. Robert Motherwell, ed., *The Dada Painters and Poets* (Boston: G. K. Hall, 1981), 44.

4. Stephen C. Foster and Rudolf E. Kuenzli, eds., *Dada Spectrum: The Dialectics of Revolt* (Madison: Coda Press, 1979), 26.

5. Quoted in Burckhardt Lindner, "Aufhebung der Kunst in Lebenspraxis? Über die Aktualität der Auseinandersetzung mit den historischen Avantgardebewegungen," in *Theorie der Avantgarde. Antworten auf Peter Bürgers Bestimmung von Kunst und bürgerlicher Gesellschaft,* ed. Martin Luedke (Frankfurt: Suhrkamp, 1976), 78.

6. Thomas Anz and Michael Stark, eds., *Expressionismus: Manifeste und Dokumente zur deutschen Literatur 1910–1920* (Stuttgart: Metzler, 1982), 34.

7. Arnold Hauser, *Soziologie der Kunst* (Munich: Beck, 1974), 729.

8. Motherwell, *Dada Painters and Poets,* 29.

9. Walter Benjamin, "The Work of Art in the Age of Mechanical Reproduction," *Illuminations,* 237.

10. While Kuenzli, "Semiotics of Dada Poetry," assesses Zurich Dada as a phenomenon whose aesthetic strategies were deeply politically motivated, Reinhart Meyer and associates view it exclusively as an aesthetic event: *Dada in Zürich und Berlin 1916–1920,* (Kronberg/Ts.: Scriptor, 1973). Miklavz Prosence, *Die Dadaisten in Zürich* (Bonn: Bouvier, 1967), 107ff., goes to the extreme to see in Zürich Dada a movement of "radical leftist orientation."

11. See Peter A. J. Froehlich, "Reaktionen des Publikums auf Vorführungen nach abstrakten Vorlagen," in *Sinn aus Unsinn. Dada International,* ed. Wolfgang Paulsen and Helmut Hermann (Bern and Munich: Francke, 1982), 19.

12. Ibid., 19ff.

13. Herbert Read, *The Art of Jean Arp* (New York: H. N. Abrams, 1968), 156.

14. Hans Arp, "Dadaland" in *Dada in Zürich: Bildchronik und Erinnerungen der Gründer,* ed. Peter Schifferli (Zurich: Arche, 1957), 108.

15. See Read, *Art of Jean Arp,* 41; 40.

16. Richard Huelsenbeck, *Dada siegt! Eine Bilanz des Dadaismus* (Berlin: Malik, 1920), 27.

17. Motherwell, *Dada Painters and Poets,* 28.

18. See Hugo Ball, *Die Flucht aus der Zeit* (Munich: Duncker and Humblot, 1927; reprint, Lucerne: J. Stocker, 1946), 76, 81f. (page citations are to the reprint edition).

19. Hans Richter, *Dada: Kunst und Anti-Kunst. Der Beitrag Dadas zur Kunst des 20. Jahrhunderts* (Cologne: DuMont Schauberg, 1964), 169.

20. Ball, *Flucht aus der Zeit,* 84.

21. Ibid., 72.

22. Ibid., 143.

23. Ibid., 76.

24. Ibid., 74.

25. Ibid., 152.

26. Ibid., 95.

27. Richter, *Dada, Kunst und Anti-Kunst,* 169.

28. Ball, *Flucht aus der Zeit,* 144, 161.

29. Tristan Tzara, "Dada 1957," in *Dada in Zürich. Bildchronik und Erinnerungen der Gründer,* ed. Peter Schifferli (Zurich: Arche, 1957), 76: "Dada a essayé, non pas autant de détruire l'art et la littérature, que l'idée qu'on s'en était faite."

30. Ibid., 57: "On lance le Mouvement Dada. Création mystérieuse! Revolver magique!"

31. Ibid., 83; "Le mépris de Dada pour le 'modernisme' se basait surtout sur l'idée de relativité, toute codification dogmatique ne pouvant mener qu'à un nouvel académisme... Dada, qui se voulait mouvant et transformable, préférait disparaître plutôt que de donner lieu à la création de nouveaux poncifs."

32. Ibid., 57: "Le public s'accommode et rarefie les explosions d'îmbécilité élective, chacun retire ses penchants et plante son espoir dans l'esprit nouveau en formation 'Dada'."

33. Ibid., 62: "Victoire définitive de Dada."

34. Bernd Hüppauf, "Zwischen revolutionärer Epoche und sozialem Prozess. Bemerkungen über den Ort des Expressionismus in der Literaturgeschichte" in Hüppauf, ed. *Expressionismus und Kulturkrise* (Heidelberg: C. Winter, 1983), 55–83. The author discusses the creative aspects of alternative groupings such as the expressionists in times of cultural crisis; a cultural dialogue toward expanded communication makes possible at least the perception of alternatives. These insights can be made productive for the special mode of Dada's forms of communication as provocation.

35. Schifferli, *Dada in Zürich,* 81f.

36. Richard Huelsenbeck, ed., *Dada. Eine literarische Dokumentation,* (Reinbek beï Hamburg: Rowohlt, 1964), 29.

37. Raoul Hausmann, *Am Anfang war Dada,* ed. Karl Riha and Günther Kämpf, with an afterword by Karl Riha (Steinbach und Giessen: Anabas-Verlag Kämpf, 1972) 20f.

38. Carl Einstein, *Die Fabrikation der Fabrikationen,* ed. Sibylle Penkert (Reinbek beï Hamburg: Rowohlt, 1973).

39. Timothy O. Benson, *Raoul Hausmann and Berlin Dada* (Ann Arbor: UMI Research Press, 1987), 105.

40. See Rainer Rumold, *Sprachliches Experiment und literarische Tradition. Zu den Texten Helmut Heißenbüttels,* Stanford German Studies, vol. 9 (Bern and Frankfurt: Lang, 1975), 77f.

41. Huelsenbeck, *Dada. Eine literarische Dokumentation,* 14, 15ff., where the movement is reassessed as a "Kunstrichtung." See also Richard Huelsenbeck, "Dada und Existentialismus," in *DADA. Monographie einer Bewegung,* ed. Willy Verkauf (Teufen AR: A. Niggli, 1956), 45ff., where he attempts to resituate Dada within the twentieth-century existentialism; and Richard Huelsenbeck, *Mit Witz, Licht und Grütze. Auf den Spuren des Dadaismus* (Wiesbaden: Limes, 1957), 97, where Dada is reviewed less radically as opposed to the "Akademismus" of the aesthetic tradition. For further discussion, see Rainer Rumold, "Dada: A Critical History of the Literature. Germany and Central Europe," in *Dada and the Crisis in the Arts,* vol. 1, ed. Stephen Foster (New York: G. K. Hall; London: Prentice Hall, 1996), 197–221.

42. See Michael Stark, *Für und wider den Expressionismus* (Stuttgart: Metzler, 1982), 82.

43. John Heartfield, "Prospekt zur kleinen Grosz-Mappe," *Die Neue Jugend* 2, no. 2 (Berlin: Malik, June 1917).

44. Hanne Bergius, *Das Lachen Dadas. Die Berliner Dadaisten und ihre Aktionen* (Giessen: Anabas, 1989), 362. Bergius gives a full account of the Dada-Messe and its reception, pp 360ff.

45. Raoul Hausmann, *Am Anfang war Dada,* ed. Karl Riha and Günter Kämpf, with an afterword by Karl Riha (Steinbach and Giessen: Anabas-Verlag Kämpf, 1972), 20f.

46. See Bergius, *Lachen Dadas,* 365.

47. Motherwell, *Dada Painters and Poets,* 41.

48. Ibid.

49. Ibid.

50. Richard Huelsenbeck, *En avant Dada: Eine Geschichte des Dadaismus* (Hanover: P. Steegemann, 1920), 20, 43.

51. Hausmann, *Am Anfang war Dada,* 7.

52. Ibid., 12.

53. Ibid., 23, 24.

54. Ibid., 7.

55. Ibid.

56. Ibid., 12.

57. Ibid., 28.

58. Ibid., 13, 14.

59. Ibid., 28f.

60. Ibid., 15, 16.

Chapter 3

1. The foregoing phrases quoted in this paragraph appear in Jost Hermand and Frank Trommler, *Die Kultur der Weimarer Republik* (Munich: Nymphenburger, 1978), 115, 128ff.

2. Ibid., 129.

3. Ibid., 136.

4. Bertolt Brecht, *Gesammelte Werke,* 20 vols., *Schriften zur Literatur und Kunst I* (Frankfurt am Main: Suhrkamp, 1967), 18:129.

5. Gottfried Benn, *Briefwechsel mit Paul Hindemith,* ed. Ann Clark Fehn (Wiesbaden and Munich: Limes, 1978), 16, 29.

6. Gottfried Benn, "Gebührt Carleton ein Denkmal?" in *Gesammelte Werke,* 8 vols., (Wiesbaden: Limes, 1968), 3:763ff.

7. Benn, *Briefwechsel mit Paul Hindemith,* 47.

8. Stephanie Barron, ed., *"Degenerate Art" The Fate of the Avant-Garde in Nazi*

Germany (Los Angeles: Los Angeles County Museum of Art, New York: H. N. Abrams, 1991), 11, 366.

9. See Guy Stern, *Literatur im Exil. Gesammelte Aufsätze 1959–1989* (Ismaning: Max Hueber, 1989), 16.

10. Silvio Vietta, *Die literarische Moderne. Eine problemgeschichtliche Darstellung der deutschsprachigen Literatur von Hölderlin bis Thomas Bernhard* (Stuttgart: Metzler, 1992).

11. Paul Michael Lützeler, "The Avant-Garde in Crisis: Hermann Broch's Negative Aesthetics in Exile," in *Hermann Broch: Literature, Philosophy, Politics. The Yale Broch Symposium 1986,* ed. Stephen D. Dowden (Columbia: Camden House, 1988).

12. Stern, *Literatur im Exil,* 53f.

13. Serge Guilbaut, *How New York Stole the Idea of Modern Art* (Chicago and London: University of Chicago Press, 1983), 168–72.

14. Quoted in O. K. Werckmeister, *Paul Klee in Exile: 1933–1940* (Japan: Fuji Television Gallery, 1985), 36.

15. Klaus Weissenberger, "Yvan Goll," in *Deutschsprachige Exilliteratur seit 1933,* ed. John M. Spalek and Joseph Strelka (Bern: Francke, 1989), vol. 2. *New York,* part 1, 239.

16. Dieter Schiller, et al., eds., *Exil in Frankreich* (Frankfurt am Main: Röderberg, 1981), 331.

17. Manfred Durzak, ed., *Die deutsche Exilliteratur 1933–1945* (Stuttgart: Philipp Reclam, 1973), 11.

18. Ernst Schürer, "German Drama in Exile: A Survey," in *Exile: The Writer's Experience,* ed. John M. Spalek and Robert F. Bell (Chapel Hill: University of North Carolina Press, 1982), 52.

19. Wolfgang Emmerich, "Welt, gesehen mit dem rebellischen Auge des Dichters. Die Exillyrik Erich Arendt's," in *Deutschsprachige Exilliteratur. Studien zu ihrer Bestimmung im Kontext der Epoche 1930 bis 1960,* ed. Wulf Koepke and Michael Winkler (Bonn: Bouvier, 1984), 145f.

20. Adrienne Ash, "Lyric Poetry in Exile," in *Exile: The Writer's Experience,* 18.

21. Theodor Ziolkowski, "Form als Protest. Das Sonett in der Literatur des Exils und der Inneren Emigration," in *Exil und Innere Emigration,* ed. Reinhold Grimm and Jost Hermand (Frankfurt a.M.: Athenaeum, 1972), 153, 172.

22. Quoted ibid., 165, 160, 154.

23. Ibid., 158.

24. Emmerich, "Welt," 146.

25. Ibid., 151.

26. Ibid., 154.

27. Ibid., 155.

28. Ibid., 153.

29. John M. Spalek and Penelope D. Willard, "Ernst Toller," in *Deutschsprachige*

Exilliteratur seit 1933, ed. John M. Spalek and Joseph Strelka (Bern: Francke, 1989) 2. *New York,* part 2, 1723–65.

30. Stern, *Literatur im Exil,* 42.

31. Ibid., 54.

32. Ibid., 42.

33. Ibid., 79.

34. Ulrich R. Fröhlich, "Fritz von Unruh," in *Deutschsprachige Exilliteratur seit 1933,* ed. John M. Spalek and Joseph Strelka (Bern: Francke, 1989) 2. *New York,* part 2, 914–32.

35. Ernst Schürer,"Verinnerlichung, Protest und Resignation. Georg Kaisers Exil," in *Die deutsche Exilliteratur 1933–1945,* ed. Manfred Durzak (Stuttgart: Philipp Reclam, 1973), 263–81.

36. Cf. Werner Vortriede, "Vorläufige Gedanken zu einer Typologie der Exilliteratur," in *Akzente* 15, no. 6 (1968): 570f.

37. Markus Hallensleben, *Else-Lasker-Schüler. Avant-gardismus und Kunstinszenierung* (Tübingen and Basel: Francke, 2000), 269ff.

38. Sigrid Bauschinger, *Else Lasker-Schüler. Ihr Werk und ihre Zeit* (Heidelberg: Lothar Stiehm, 1980), 273.

39. Else Lasker-Schüler, *Werke und Briefe,* vol. 1.1, *Gedichte,* ed. Karl Jürgen Skrodzki and Norbert Oellers (Frankfurt am Main: Suhrkamp, Jüdischer Verlag, 1996), 284f.

40. Bauschinger, *Else Lasker-Schüler,* 275.

41. Ash, "Lyric Poetry in Exile," 2.

42. Thomas Mann, *Doctor Faustus,* trans. H. T. Lowe Porter (New York: Vintage, 1948), 321f.

43. Ziolkowski, "Form als Protest," 153.

44. Lützeler, "Avant-Garde in Crisis," 23.

45. Lützeler, "Avant-Garde in Crisis," 23f.

46. Ibid., 25f.

47. Ibid., 26.

48. Peter Bürger, *Theory of the Avant-garde,* 17, 22.

49. James Rolleston, "Short Fiction in Exile: Exposure and Reclamation of a Tradition," in *Exile: The Writer's Experience,* ed. John M. Spalek and Robert F. Bell (Chapel Hill: University of North Carolina Press, 1982), 37.

50. Stern, *Literatur im Exil,* 71.

51. Klaus H. Kiefer, " 'BEB II'—Ein Phantombild," in: *Carl Einstein. Text + Kritik,* ed. Heinz Ludwig Arnold (Munich: text + kritik, 1987), 95:62.

52. Ibid., 61.

53. Ibid., 60f.

54. See Klaus H. Kiefer, *Avantgarde—Weltkrieg—Exil. Materialien zu Carl Einstein und Salomo Friedländer/Mynona* (Frankfurt am Main, Bern, and New York: Peter Lang, 1986), 26.

55. Ibid.

56. Stern, *Literatur am Exil,* 13.

57. Werner Fuld, *Walter Benjamin. Eine Biographie* (Reinbek bei Hamburg: Rowohlt, 1990), 243.

58. Ibid., 245.

59. M. Kay Flavell, *George Grosz: A Biography* (New Haven, Conn., and London: Yale University Press, 1988), 153.

60. Wulf Koepke and Michael Winkler, eds., *Deutschsprachige Exilliteratur. Studien zu ihrer Bestimmung im Kontext der Epoche 1930 bis 1960,* (Bonn: Bouvier, 1984), 5.

61. Lützeler, "Avant-Garde in Crisis," 30.

62. See Hans Mayer, "Sprechen und Verstummen der Dichter," in *Zur deutschen Literatur der Zeit* (Reinbek bei Hamburg: Rowohlt, 1967), 86f.

Chapter 4

1. The rediscovery of Carl Einstein began with Helmut Heißenbüttel's "Ein Halbvergessener: Carl Einstein," *Deutsche Zeitung,* 15–16 December 1962; reprinted in *Über Literatur* (Olten: Walter, 1966). Heißenbüttel, at the time the most prominent author and theoretician of experimental writing, compared Einstein's cultural criticism and skepticism with that of Gottfried Benn and contrasted his philosophy of history with Walter Benjamin's much more developed critical thought. Sibylle Penkert, *Carl Einstein. Beiträge zu einer Monographie* (Göttingen: Vandenhoeck and Ruprecht, 1969); and *Carl Einstein. Existenz und Ästhetik* (Wiesbaden: F. Steiner, 1970), pioneered in the rediscovery of the author in terms of his biography and aesthetic theory. Ernst Nef's limited edition of Einstein's *Gesammelte Werke* (Wiesbaden: Limes, 1962) has become a historical token in view of the large-scale undertaking of the edition of Carl Einstein, *Werke,* vols. 1–5, ed. by various scholars (Vienna and Berlin: Medusa, 1980, 1981, 1985); (Berlin: Fannei & Walz, 1992, 1996). Most informative for the multiple aspects of Einstein's work are the critical essays in *Carl Einstein. Text und Kritik* (Munich: text + kritik, 1987) vol. 95, and Klaus Kiefer, ed. *Carl Einstein-Kolloquium 1986* (Frankfurt am Main: Peter Lang, 1988). Klaus Kiefer, *Diskurswandel im Werk Carl Einsteins. Ein Beitrag zur Theorie und Geschichte der europäischen Avantgarde* (Tübingen: Niemeyer, 1994) is a definitive achievement that virtually covers all aspects of Einstein's work, which the author has interpreted in numerous previous articles. The study's bibliography by itself is an important source for Einstein criticism. Carl Einstein's far-reaching theoretical significance is most succinctly discussed by Heidemarie Oehm, *Die Kunsttheorie Carl Einsteins* (Munich: Fink, 1976), and Jochen Schulte-Sasse, "Carl Einstein; or, The Postmodern Transformation of Modernism," in *Modernity and the Text: Revisions of German Modernism,* ed. Andreas Huyssen and David Bathrick

(New York: Columbia University Press, 1989), 36–59. For a detailed biographical account of Einstein's exile years, see Heidemarie Oehm, "Carl Einstein: Leben und Werk im Exil," in *Exil* 3 (1982): 41–59.

2. Helmut Heißenbüttel, "Ein Halbvergessener: Carl Einstein," in *Über Literatur. Aufsätze* (Munich: DTV, 1970), 36–41; and "Carl-Einstein-Portrait," in *Zur Tradition der Moderne. Aufsätze und Anmerkungen 1964–1971* (Neuwied and Berlin: Luchterhand, 1972), 262–90.

3. For detailed historical information, see Marianne Kroeger, "Carl Einstein und die 'Grupo Internacional'' der Kolonne Durruti — Ein Beitrag zur Auseinandersetzung Carl Einsteins mit der Realität des Spanischen Bürgerkriegs," in *Carl Einstein-Kolloquium 1986* (Frankfurt am Main: Peter Lang, 1988), 261–71; and "Carl Einstein im Spanischen Bürgerkrieg: Gratwanderungen zwischen Engagement und Desillusionierung. Die Jahre 1937 und 1938 anhand von Briefen und Interviews in 'La Vanguardia' vom 24. Mai, 1938," *Archiv für die Geschichte des Widerstands und der Arbeit* 12 (1992): 79–96.

4. Schulte-Sasse, "Carl Einstein," 39.

5. Ibid., 43.

6. Kiefer consistently argues against Oehm's *Kunsttheorie Carl Einsteins*. Oehm's assumption of Einstein's turn to materialism in the 1930s; see Kiefer, *Diskurswandel,* 524, 544ff. Instead, the leading Einstein scholar describes the author's "transformation of discourses" as a series of attempts to generate for art "a quality of difference" that impacts the social realm (535). The first such attempt is the expressionist's deconstructionist aestheticization of a religious transcendence. It is followed by a discourse that deconstructs the polarity of the modern versus the archaic experience by fusing (in *Negerplastik* [*Negro Sculpture;* 1915]) a turn to the "primitive" with the cubist renewal in the act of "seeing." Einstein's subsequent embrace of the surrealistic discourse culminates in his treatise *Georges Braque,* of the early 1930s, which roots the chaotic energies of the unconscious in the sexual. In all cases, Einstein vies to liberate the aesthetic experience from its confinement in the institution of art.

7. Carl Einstein, *Werke,* 5 vols. (Vienna and Berlin: Medusa, 1985), vol. 3, ed. Marion Schmid and Liliane Meffre, 178 (hereafter cited in text as *W* with volume and page number).

8. Rainer Rumold, "Carl Einstein and Buenaventura Durruti: The Poesy and Grammar of Anarchism," in *German and International Perspectives on the Spanish Civil War: The Aesthetics of Partisanship,* ed. Luis Costa et al. (Columbia, S.C.: Camden House, 1992), 64–77; Kiefer, *Diskurswandel,* 523–29.

9. Schulte-Sasse, "Carl Einstein," 58.

10. Carl Einstein as Bataille's coeditor of *Documents. Archéologie, Beaux-Arts, Ethnographie, Variétés,* Paris 1929–1930. Walter Benjamin's contacts to Bataille are to be traced via the Collège de Sociologie; see Georges Bataille, *Visions of Excess: Selected Writings 1927–1939,* ed. and trans. Allan Stoeckl (Minneapolis: University of

Minnesota Press, 1985), xxi. There is no reference to each other in either Benjamin's or Einstein's essays, diaries, or notes.

11. A comparison of Einstein's theory of the avant-garde with Benjamin's is still to be written; neither Heidemarie Oehm, Klaus Kiefer, nor Jochen Schulte-Sasse go beyond more than allusions. My own references to Benjamin made in this chapter indicate that such study would establish more differences than similarities.

12. See Christoph Braun, "Carl Einstein's *Schlimme Botschaft* und ihre Leser. Zum Literaturalltag der Weimarer Republik," in *Carl-Einstein-Kolloquium 1986* (Frankfurt am Main: Peter Lang, 1988), 175–84.

13. Penkert, *Beiträge,* 120.

14. Eugene Jolas, *Man from Babel,* ed., intro., and annotated by Andreas Kramer and Rainer Rumold (New Haven, Conn., and London: Yale University Press, 1998), 123.

15. See *Exil in Frankreich,* ed. Dieter Schiller (et al.), *Kunst und Literatur im antifaschistischen Exil 1933–1945,* vol. 7 (Frankfurt am Main: Röderberg, 1981), 310.

16. See Rainer Rumold, *Gottfried Benn und der Expressionismus. Provokation des Lesers; absolute Dichtung* (Königstein/Ts.: Scriptor, 1982), 62f.

17. See Andreas Kramer and Rainer Rumold, introduction to Jolas, *Man from Babel,* xxvii.

18. See, for example, Gottfried Benn, "Answer to the Literary Emigrants," in *Primal Vision,* ed. E. B. Ashton (New York: New Directions, 1971), 48.

19. Gottfried Benn, "Expressionismus," in *Gesammelte Werke,* 8 vols., ed. Dieter Wellershoff (Wiesbaden: Limes, 1968), 3:810.

20. Penkert, *Existenz und Ästhetik,* 55.

21. Less concerned with the second thoughts Benjamin has about surrealism, Paul Westheim's review "Aufgabe der Kunst heute" (*Pariser Tageblatt,* Paris 1934) focuses on and reinforces precisely Einstein's view of Braque as a surrealist avant-gardist whose work goes beyond mere formalist significance. Einstein's assessment of the painter is also confirmed by Herbert Read, who cites his interpretation of Braque for defining the political paradigm among the various tendencies of the surrealist movement ("What Is Revolutionary Art?," 1935). Paul Westheim, "Aufgabe der Kunst heute" in Einstein, *Werke* 3:583f. Herbert Read, "What Is Revolutionary Art?" in *Modern Art and Modernism: A Critical Anthology,* ed. Francis Frascina and Charles Harrison (New York: Harper and Row, 1982), 126.

22. Carl Einstein, *Die Fabrikation der Fiktionen,* ed. Sibylle Penkert (Reinbek bei Hamburg: Rowohlt, 1973), 316 (hereafter cited in text as *FF* with page number).

23. Carl Einstein, "Entwurf einer Landschaft," trans. Eugene Jolas, *transition: An International Quarterly for Creative Experiment* 19–20 (June 1930): 213.

24. Quoted in Penkert, *Beiträge,* 119.

25. Quoted in Kiefer, *Diskurswandel,* 521.

26. Quoted in Penkert, *Beiträge,* 125.

27. See *Exil in Frankreich,* 311; *Exil in den Niederlanden und Spanien* ed. Klaus

Hermsdorf, et al. (Leipzig: Röderberg, 1981), 207f. See also Oehm, "Leben und Werk," 57.

28. Quoted in Penkert, *Beiträge*, 123.

29. Ibid., 124.

30. Kiefer, *Diskurswandel*, 524.

31. See Ibid., 534. See also Klaus Kiefer, "Carl Einstein and the Revolutionary Soldiers' Councils in Brussels," in *The Ideological Crisis of Expressionism: The Literary and Artistic German War Colony in Belgium 1914–1918*, ed. Rainer Rumold and O. K. Werckmeister (Columbia, S.C.: Camden House, 1990), 97–12.

32. Schulte-Sasse, "Carl Einstein," 43.

33. Cf. Kiefer, *Diskurswandel*, 371.

Chapter 5

1. Walter Benjamin, *Briefe I*, ed. Gershom Scholem and Theodor W. Adorno (Frankfurt am Main: Suhrkamp, 1978), 121.

2. Chryssoula Kambas, *Walter Benjamin im Exil. Zum Verhältnis von Literaturpolitik und Ästhetik* (Tübingen: Niemeyer, 1983), 45–63, 71–80, is the only study to date which devotes sufficient space to Benjamin as, in his own words, "a strategist in the literary struggle" against the literary politics of what he very broadly regards as the legacy of expressionism. She is quite aware that for Benjamin this legacy ranges from the activism of Kurt Hiller to Alfred Döblin's pacifist humanist and New Objectivity's "geistige" alternative to the politics of the Communist Party. And Kambas does address Benjamin's differences with the art theorist Riegl, influential for the development of an expressionist self-understanding. She, however, often questions Benjamin's harsh criticism of expressionist activism on *political* grounds, without decisively drawing a connection between his long-term epistemological stance against expressionist subjectivity and his political position.

3. See Ulrich Weisstein, "Literaturkritik in deutschen Exilzeitschriften: Der Fall *Das Wort*," in *Exil und Innere Emigration II*, ed. Peter Uwe Hohendahl and Egon Schwarz (Frankfurt am Main: Athenaeum, 1973), 19–46.

4. Gottfried Benn, "Expressionismus," in *Gesammelte Werke*, 8 vols., ed. Dieter Wellershoff (Wiesbaden: Limes, 1968), 3, 804f.

5. The contributions to *Das Wort* are reprinted in Hans-Jürgen Schmitt, ed., *Die Expressionismusdebatte. Materialien zu einer marxistischen Realismuskonzeption*, (Frankfurt am Main: Suhrkamp, 1973).

6. Walter Benjamin, *Gesammelte Schriften*, 7 vols., ed. Rolf Tiedemann and Hermann Schweppenhäuser (Frankfurt am Main: Suhrkamp, 1991), 1:1023 (hereafter cited in text and notes as *GS* with volume and page number).

7. Alfred Döblin, *Wissen und Verändern! Offene Briefe an einen jungen Menschen* (Berlin: S. Fischer, 1931), 126.

8. Richard Sheppard, "Georg Lukács, Wilhelm Worringer and German Expressionism," *Journal of European Studies* 25 (1995): 241–82.

9. Benjamin, "Strenge Kunstwissenschaft," *GS* 3:372.

10. Benjamin, *Ursprung des deutschen Trauerspiels, GS* 1:234–37.

11. Klaus Garber, *Rezeption und Rettung. Drei Studien zu Walter Benjamin* (Tübingen: Niemeyer, 1987), 86.

12. Walter Benjamin, letter to Scholem, *Briefe 1*, 368. See also *GS* 1:880.

13. See Gershom Scholem, *Walter Benjamin: The Story of a Friendship*, trans. Harry Zohn (Philadelphia: Jewish Publication Society of America, 1981), 16; Momme Brodersen, *Spinne im eigenen Netz. Walter Benjamin. Leben und Werk* (Buehl-Moos: Elster, 1990), 89. Gustav Wyneken contributed the essay "Schöpferische Erziehung" to Hiller's *Das Ziel* (Munich: Mueller, 1916).

14. For Benjamin's relation to Fritz Heinle against the background of expressionism, see Werner Kraft, "Friedrich C. Heinle," *Akzente. Zeitschrift für Literatur* 31, no. 1 (1984): 9–21.

15. Brodersen, *Spinne im eigenen Netz*, 65, 68.

16. See Benjamin's positive reaction to a performance of "Frank Wedekind: Frühlings Erwachen," *GS* 4:551f.

17. Scholem, *Story of Friendship*, 65, writes: "Benjamin never developed a positive relationship to literary Expressionism as a movement, though the movement did originate in the prewar years in a circle to which Benjamin was personally quite close. . . . To be sure, he regarded Georg Heym as a great poet and recited for me verses from his collection *Der ewige Tag* (The eternal day) from memory—a very unusual practice for him." See also Kraft, "Friedrich C. Heinle," 9–21.

18. See Richard Sheppard, ed. *Die Schriften des Neuen Clubs. 1908–1914,* vol. 2 (Hildesheim: Gerstenberg, 1983), 529f.

19. See Brodersen, *Spinne im eigenen Netz,* 66, 74.; Sheppard, *Schriften des Neuen Clubs,* 585.

20. See O. K. Werckmeister, *Versuche über Paul Klee* (Frankfurt am Main: Syndikat, 1981), 98–123.

21. Scholem, *Story of Friendship,* 65.

22. Walter Benjamin, *Briefe 2,* ed. Gershom Scholem and Theodor W. Adorno (Frankfurt am Main: Suhrkamp, 1978), 706.

23. Benjamin, *Briefe 1,* 214, 260.

24. John McCole, *Walter Benjamin and the Antinomies of Tradition* (Ithaca, N.Y., and London: Cornell University Press, 1993), 206–52, in my opinion, inflates Benjamin's criticism of surrealism—marginally inherent in the surrealism essay itself and more explicitly stated in Benjamin's notes for the essay—from hindsight.

25. E.g., Richard Wolin, *Walter Benjamin: An Aesthetics of Redemption* (New York: Columbia University Press, 1982), 126–37; Margaret Cohen, *Profane Illumination: Walter Benjamin and the Paris of Surrealist Revolution* (Berkeley, Lon-

don, and Los Angeles: University of California Press, 1993). Other studies focus more on the philosophical German context, e.g., Josef Fürnkäs, *Surrealismus als Erkenntnis. Walter Benjamin— Weimarer Einbahnstraße und Pariser Passagen* (Stuttgart: Metzler, 1988) focuses on the Weimar connection only in regard to Bloch and Kracauer. Susan Buck-Morss, *The Origin of Negative Dialectics* (New York: Free Press, 1977), 122–35, places Benjamin's surrealism essay in terms of Adorno's rejection of the immediacy of surrealist poetics in favor of Schönberg as a "dialectical composer" into the context of their Königstein program. McCole, *Benjamin and the Antinomies of Tradition,* 206–52, significantly discusses Benjamin's relation to surrealism mainly via Klages and refers to the critic's antiexpressionist stance. While he thus concerns himself with the cultural environment in Germany, his arguments are more focused on issues of intellectual influence and opposition than on the textual strategies of Benjamin's criticism.

26. Benjamin had read the 1922 edition of Klages's *Vom kosmogonischen Eros; GS* 7:451.

27. Ernst Bloch, "Gesänge der Entlegenheit," *Gesamtausgabe,* vol. 4 (Frankfurt am Main: Suhrkamp, 1962) 200f. For Klages's significance for expressionism, see Walter Sokel, *The Writer in Extremis* (New York: McGraw-Hill, 1964), 95.

28. See McCole, *Benjamin and the Antimonies of Tradition,* 176, 178ff. For Benjamin on Klages, see *GS* 3:44; 2:229.

29. Ludwig Klages, *Vom Kosmogonischen Eros,* 2d ed. (Jena: Eugen Diederichs, 1926), 110.

30. Walter Benjamin, *Reflections,* trans. Edmund Jephcott; ed. and intro. Peter Demetz (New York: Schocken, 1986), 191f.

31. Ibid., 192.

32. Ibid., 178.

33. In the surrealism essay, Benjamin contrasts Paul Scheerbart's utopianism with Guillaume Apollinaire's misconception of an anticipation of the marvels of modern technology by the imagination of avant-garde poets (*GS* 2:303). Elsewhere Scheerbart's utopia is defined as "bodily" (*GS* 6:148).

34. *GS* 2:147, 150, 157. See Winfried Menninghaus, *Walter Benjamins Theorie der Sprachmagie* (Frankfurt am Main: Suhrkamp, 1980), 15, for a discussion of the language essay's erasing of the distinction between "language as such" and "poetic" language.

35. *Reflections,* 184.

36. Klages, *Vom Kosmogonischen Eros,* 128; 134.

37. His previous criticism of Fritz von Unruh had been phrased in a portrait of the expressionist playwright, once prowar but now pacifist turncoat, as an "overeating profiteer"; "Friedensware" (1926), *GS* 3:23–28.

38. See Kambas, *Benjamin im Exil,* 160ff.

39. See Kambas, *Benjamin im Exil,* 46.

40. Benjamin, *Briefe 2,* 609.

41. For an excellent account of the relationship of Brecht's theater to expressionist drama, see Ernst Schürer, *Georg Kaiser und Bertolt Brecht* (Frankfurt: Athenaeum, 1971).

42. See Alfred Döblin, *Schriften zur Politik und Gesellschaft*, ed. Walter Muschg and Heinz Graber (Freiburg: Walter Verlag, 1972), 275.

43. *Alfred Döblin 1878–1978*, ed. Bernhard Zeller (Marbach: Deutsche Schillergesellschaft, 1978), 302f.

44. Ibid., 304.

45. Ibid., 294.

46. For the concept of "relative autonomy," see Peter Bürger, *Theory of the Avant-Garde*, trans. Michael Shaw, with a foreword by Jochen Schulte-Sasse (Minneapolis: University of Minnesota Press, 1984), 82. For a full discussion, see Burckhardt Lindner, "Aufhebung der Kunst in Lebenspraxis?" in *Theorie der Avant-garde. Antworten auf Peter Bürgers Bestimmung von Kunst und Gesellschaft*, ed. Martin Lüdke (Frankfurt am Main: Suhrkamp, 1976), 99f.

47. Benjamin, *Reflections*, 222–32.

48. David Pike, *Lukács and Brecht* (Chapel Hill and London: University of North Carolina Press, 1985), 217; Kambas, *Benjamin im Exil*, 172f; Hans Albert Walter, *Deutsche Exilliteratur*, vol. 7, *Exilpresse I* (Darmstadt: Luchterhaud, 1973), 310, 335.

49. Walter Benjamin, "Pariser Brief I," *GS* 3:482–95.

50. See reprint of the Gestapo's document, dated "2. 23. 1939," in Ingrid and Konrad Scheurmann, eds., *Für Walter Benjamin: Dokumente, Essays und ein Entwurf* (Frankfurt am Main: Suhrkamp, 1992), 108.

51. See Pike, *Lukács and Brecht*, 198f.; Kambas, *Benjamin im Exil*, 163ff.

52. Georg Lukács,"Realism in the Balance" (1938), in *Aesthetics and Politics*, with an afterword by Fredric Jameson (London and New York: Verso, 1988), 29. In contrast to Benjamin, Lukács identifies expressionism as part of the international avant-garde that includes surrealism. In his contribution to *Das Wort*, he identifies "specific literary trends leading from Naturalism and Impressionism via Expressionism to Surrealism" as "so-called avant-garde literature."

53. Quoted from Fritz J. Raddatz, ed., *Marxismus und Literatur*, vol. 2 (Hamburg: Rowohlt, 1969), 35.

54. Pike, *Lukács and Brecht*, 214.

55. See Reinhard Müller, ed. *Die Säuberung. Moskau 1936: Stenogramm einer geschlossenen Parteiversammlung* (Reinbek bei Hamburg: Rowohlt, 1991), 16.

56. *GS* 1:1006, 1032. Kambas, *Benjamin im Exil*, 167 n. 29, disagrees with the editor's stress of the theses' competitive relation to Brecht. She also does not give much weight to Adorno's assertion that Benjamin had in mind "mit der Reproduktionsarbeit Brecht an Radikalismus übertrumpfen zu wollen" (to want to surpass Brecht's radicalism), repeated in Theodor W. Adorno, "Interimsbescheid," *Über Walter Benjamin* (Frankfurt am Main: Suhrkamp, 1968), 95. My own discussion is

less interested in a verification of Adorno's statement. Rather, I aim to show, by way of tracing and interpreting Benjamin's long-standing attack on expressionism on the basis of a surrealist inspired "anti-art" disposition, that his stance against autonomous "artistic creativity" surpassed Brecht's interest in "literature."

57. Benjamin, *Reflections*, 186.

58. *GS* 1:1023. See also Benjamin, *Briefe 2*, 716, 721, 729.

59. See Benjamin, "Die Politische Gruppierung der russischen Schriftsteller," *GS* 2:747.

60. *GS* 3:493. For a discussion of Benjamin's disagreement with the "Literatur-politik" of the KP, see Kambas, *Benjamin im Exil*, 156.

61. See Müller, *Säuberung*. This publication renders a revealing account of an inquisitional investigation of German writers in Soviet exile that took place already before the Moscow public tribunals in 1936. The meetings (September 4–9, 1936) are masterminded by Georg Lukács and evolve into a terrorizing trial of the participants themselves, among them Johannes Becher, Friedrich Wolf, Willi Bredel, Alfred Kurella, Ernst Ottwalt, et al. While Ernst Bloch would declare his solidarity with the public tribunals foreshadowed here, for Brecht they were, of course, a major case for his opposition to Stalinist politics, as later voiced to Benjamin in 1938.

62. Benjamin, *Reflections*, 184.

63. Ibid., 234.

64. Walter Benjamin, *Illuminations*, trans. Harry Zohn, ed. and intro. Hannah Arendt (New York: Schocken, 1969), 249f.

65. Ibid., 238.

66. Ibid., 236f.

67. Benjamin, *Illuminations*, 233.

68. Klages, *Vom Kosmogonischen Eros*, 134.

69. Benjamin, *Illuminations*, 231.

70. See Thomas Mann, "Ein Bruder," in *Essays*, vol. 2, ed. Hermann Kurzke (Frankfurt am Main: Fischer Taschenbuch, 1977), 225f.

71. Benjamin, *Illuminations*, 235, 241f.

72. Russell Berman, "The Aestheticization of Politics: Walter Benjamin on Fascism and the Avant-garde," *Stanford Review* 8, no. 1–2 (1990): 48ff., also interprets the artwork essay as relating to the "German cultural tradition." He makes his case by drawing on, for example, Thomas Mann's novella "Mario and the Magician" (1930). Berman views the novella as a critique of the powerful role that the fascination with the aesthetic can play not only in the context of Italian fascism but also for the German intellectual observer, the narrator, who implicitly comments on developments in Germany.

73. Berman, "Aestheticization of Politics," also argues that the essay is focused on the symbolic work of art as a critique of the "structure of communicative relationships within the political interaction" (49). He fails to see, however, that "the

attack on the autonomous work of art of bourgeois culture" is not simply "an extension of the avant-gardist campaign of the dadaists (and, for that matter, the futurists as well)." Rather, it involves, as I have shown here, a further critique of the historical avant-garde as a still "literary" performance. In that sense, the communication of "Geist" and "body" within political interaction is, for Benjamin, only restored in film. And on that level the essay *emphatically* attacks futurism (as well as expressionism) as even more linked to traditional modernist aesthetics than surrealism. Berman's reference to Alfred Kurella's *Mussolini without a Mask* (1931) as a suggestion of a mere "metaphoric relationship between fascist politics and an aesthetic discourse" (46) from the point of view of an enlightenment rhetoric enhances our understanding of the nature of the literary struggle which Benjamin intended to enter with his artwork essay in *Das Wort*. Kurella, of course, was one of the most representative debaters in Lukács's camp.

74. *GS* 5:590. In the fragment "Negativer Expressionismus," Benjamin addresses a "sublation of the inner impulses and the bodily center" as a chief characteristic of expressionism; *GS* 6:132.

75. See Bertolt Brecht, "Popularity and Realism," in *Aesthetics and Politics,* with an afterword by Fredric Jameson (London and New York: Verso, 1980), 79–85; "Volkstümlichkeit und Realismus," in Schmitt, *Die Expressionismusdebatte,* 329–36.

76. *GS* 7:377. In the wider context of the modernism debate, Theodor Adorno, too, objected to Benjamin's sweeping assessment of filmmaking per se as "a revolutionary criticism of the concept of art." Instead, Adorno pointed to the practice of Hollywood film given to "infantile mimetism" rather than dialectical montage techniques, thus producing mass illusions for the all too receptive masses (see *Aesthetics and Politics,* with an afterword by Fredric Jameson, 123f.). Hollywood's Mickey Mouse therefore would have to be considered as a commodity, a reification of collective dreaming. Adorno's distaste for popular culture is well known. Less familiar is the fact that he wrote his very first essay in 1920 as a critique of expressionism's "absolute scream" against the "rusty wire fence between life and art"; see Theodor Adorno, *Gesammelte Schriften,* vol. 11, ed. Rolf Tiedemann (Frankfurt am Main: Suhrkamp, 1974), 609. His other early essays on expressionism and its context are " 'Platz' zu Fritz von Unruhs Spiel" and "Frank Wedekind und sein Sittengemälde 'Musik'," ibid., 613–26. From there he proceeded to valorize the breaking up of the aura of the autonomous work of art through the dialectic of technique and the very materiality of the artistic medium (his prime example is Arnold Schönberg's twelve-tone method of composition). Averse to "unstylized expression" as a form of "hostility to art," in his essay on "Arnold Schönberg (1874–1951)" Adorno is still concerned with a critique of the expressionist movement: "Unstylized, naked expression and hostility to art are one" (*Gesammelte Schriften,* vol. 10 [Frankfurt am Main: Suhrkamp, 1977], 167). He continued to reject any form of "Heimzitierung der Kunst ins Leben" (summoning art home into life), the project of the historical

avant-garde and of Brecht's ideological theater; see Theodor W. Adorno, *Ästhetische Theorie*, ed. Gretel Adorno and Rolf Tiedemann (Frankfurt am Main: Suhrkamp, 1970), 347, 355.

77. Ernst Bloch, "Der Expressionismus jetzt erblickt" (1937), in *Gesamtausgabe*, vol. 4 (Frankfurt am Main: Suhrkamp, 1962), 257: "Die Übereinstimmung einiger Moskauer Intellektueller schematischen Schlags mit Hitler ist folglich nicht angenehm" (The concurrence of some dogmatic intellectual types in Moscow with Hitler is not pleasant). See a variant of this statement made a year later in his contribution to *Das Wort*, "Discussing Expressionism," *Aesthetics and Politics*, 17: "To concur with Hitler in his denunciation of Expressionism must have been a shock to Ziegler, for such a coincidence of views would be lethal to any man."

78. Bertolt Brecht,"Über den Realismus," in Schmitt, *Expressionismusdebatte*, 323.

79. Ibid., 314, 312, 313.

80. Bertolt Brecht, "On the Formalistic Character of the Theory of Realism," in *Aesthetics and Politics*, 74; Schmitt, *Expressionismusdebatte*, 315.

81. Bertolt Brecht, *Gesammelte Werke*, vol. 15 (Frankfurt am Main: Suhrkamp, 1967), 43f.

82. Brecht, quoted in Bernhard Zeller, ed., *Alfred Döblin 1878–1978*, Sonderausstellung des Schiller-Nationalmuseums (Marbach: Deutsche Schillergcsellschaft, 1978), 282.

83. Ernst Bloch, "Diskussionen über Expressionismus," in Schmitt, *Expressionismusdebatte*, 184; *Aesthetics and Politics*, 20.

84. Ernst Bloch, "Marxismus und Dichtung" (1935), in *Gesamtausgabe*, vol. 9 (Frankfurt am Main: Suhrkamp, 1962), 142.

85. For the most comprehensive and illuminating discussion of the function of the "dialectical image" in Benjamin's criticism and thought, see Michael Jennings, *Dialectical Images: Walter Benjamin's Theory of Literary Criticism* (Ithaca, N.Y.: Cornell University Press, 1987).

86. Bloch, "Expressionismus jetzt erblickt," 260. In apparent suppression of the dream as a nightmare, Bloch thus overprivileges the "daydream" as a *literary* activity. Between the conscious and unconscious, art's teleological narrative would reconnect with the collective heritage of fairy tales, legends, and myths (as Freud had written); see Sigmund Freud, "Creative Writers and Day-Dreaming," in *The Freud Reader*, ed. Peter Gay (New York and London: Norton, 1989), 440. Bloch's crucial deviation from a Marxist theory of agency and Freud's own emphasis of the fundamental limitations of the self through the unconscious thus is based on his belief in the power of *literary* narrative.

87. Bloch, "Gesänge der Entlegenheit," 200f.

88. *GS* 1:608. Ernst Bloch repeated his vigorous attacks on Benn in his lecture at the Congress for the Defense of Culture (Paris, 1935) and the subsequent essays

devoted to expressionism. See Ernst Bloch, "Marxismus und Dichtung," in *Litera-rische Aufsätze* (Frankfurt am Main: Suhrkamp, 1965), 137; "Expressionismus jetzt erblickt," 256f., 260; "Diskussionen über den Expressionismus," 264.

89. For the case of Georg Lukács, see Sheppard, "Lukács and Expressionism," 241–82. In reference to "Es geht um den Realismus," Sheppard writes in n. 84 that "it is a strange fact that this is the first time . . . that Lukács ever mentions Benn in his published writings . . . instead of using Benn's life and work as a living proof of his ideas about Expressionism and its political implications, he refuses to get involved" in the discussion about Benn as a typical expressionist. Instead Lukács's invective is leveled against Hiller and the "Geistige," as documented by Sheppard in great detail.

90. Benjamin, "Pariser Brief I," *GS* 3:485. If we can take any stock in Benjamin's personal list of his extensive readings, where expressionist works are conspicuously lacking, he was interested closer only in Gottfried Benn's essay collection *Nach dem Nihilismus* (1932); *GS* 7:466. Benn's introductory essay stressed the "bio-negative" aspects of art being elevated over life, a thesis Benjamin must have found confirming his view of expressionism. I discuss Benn's view of art as "bio-negative" in chapter 7.

91. See Christina Ujma, "Lumpensammler. Bloch's Benjaminsche Sicht des Sur-realismus. Walter Benjamin zum 100. Geburtstag." in *Bloch-Almanach,* vol. 12, ed. Karlheinz Weigand (Ludwigshafen: Ernst-Bloch-Archiv der Stadtbibliothek Ludwigshafen, 1992), 79; Kambas, *Benjamin im Exil,* 153. Arno Münster, *Utopie, Messianismus und Apokalypse im Frühwerk von Ernst Bloch* (Frankfurt am Main: Suhrkamp, 1982), e.g., 223, altogether overlooks the tensions and differences be-tween Bloch and Benjamin, which can be traced from Benjamin's epistolary re-action (*Briefe 1,* 232f.) to Bloch's *Geist der Utopie.*

92. Ernst Bloch, "Revueform in der Philosophie," *Vossische Zeitung,* 1 August 1928. See Ujma, "Lumpensammler," 79.

93. After all, for Bloch, surrealism was merely a late, impure form of expres-sionism. Like Paul Fechter in his 1914 monograph on expressionism, he had placed expressionism, beginning with *Geist der Utopie* (1918), in the spiritual center of the historical avant-garde movements. As he stated in a retrospective of 1937, he had written the messianic treatise during the years 1915–1917 as his "testimony to the original expressionist impulse." See Bloch, "Expressionismus jetzt erblickt," 261f. For Benjamin this expressionist testimony had already been a problem at the time of its publication *(Briefe 1,* 232f.).

94. *Briefe 2,* 648. Bloch's *Spuren (Traces;* 1930) and the essays on "Denkende Surrealismen" in his *Erbschaft dieser Zeit* (1935), however, had been indebted to Benjamin's surrealist vision. See Ujma, "Lumpensammler," 92f. In the latter work, Bloch still praised Benjamin's practice (in *One-Way Street*) of quoting and ruptur-ing through montage the commodified object that dominates modern experience.

The technique of montage, in the center of his own aesthetic theory, is, of course, the key for understanding Benjamin's "surrealist" method. In his use of montage, Benjamin employed, as Bloch wrote, "dialectical experiment figures" that were to initiate a "public process" of recuperating suppressed collective dreams. See Bloch, *Gesamtausgabe*, 4:371. For a first selection of representative essays by Bloch in English translation, see Ernst Bloch, *Ernst Bloch. The Utopian Function of Art and Literature: Selected Essays,* trans. Jack Zipes and Frank Mecklenburg (Cambridge: MIT Press, 1988).

Chapter 6

1. See M. Kay Flavell, *George Grosz: A Biography* (New Haven, Conn., and London: Yale University Press, 1988), 6ff.

2. George Grosz, *Briefe 1913–1959,* ed. Herbert Knust (Reinbek bei Hamburg: Rowohlt, 1979), 178. (All translations are mine, unless indicated otherwise).

3. Grosz, *Briefe,* 274.

4. For biographical details concerning Grosz, see Flavell, *George Grosz: A Biography;* Uwe Schneede, *George Grosz: His Life and Work* (London: Gordon Fraser, 1979); and Lothar Fischer, *George Grosz* (Reinbek: Rowohlt, 1976).

5. For biographical details concerning Bertolt Brecht, see James K. Lyon, *Bertolt Brecht in America* (Princeton, N.J.: Princeton University Press, 1980).

6. See Rainer Rumold, "Ein kleines Ja und ein großes Nein. George Grosz im Spiegel seiner Begegnung mit Gottfried Benn und Bertolt Brecht," in *Probleme der Moderne,* ed. Benjamin Bennet, Anton Kaes, and William J. Lillyman (Tübingen: Niemeyer, 1983), 389–403.

7. Kurt Tucholsky, *Gesammelte Werke,* vol. 2, ed. Mary Gerold-Tucholsky and Fritz J. Raddatz (Reinbek: Rowohlt, 1961), 1065.

8. Bertolt Brecht, "Anmerkungen zu Stücken und Aufführungen 1918 bis 1956," in *Gesammelte Werke,* vol. 17 (Frankfurt am Main: Suhrkamp, 1967), 944.

9. Ibid., 961.

10. Ibid., 965.

11. die Avantgarde—Notizen; Notizbuch, geh., 1937; BBA 827/41. Thanks are due to Barbara Brecht and the Bertolt-Brecht-Archiv for permission to quote Brecht's entry:

> die Avantgarde
> der dadaismus
> der expressionismus
> die neue sachlichkeit
> das zeitstück
> die gefrorene musik, die konzertante musik, die gebrauchsmusik,

das massenlied, das lehrstück, die revue, der rote
faden, der in szene gesetzte aphorismus, die gespielte losung
wir kritisierten die zeit und die zeit kritisierte uns

12. Bertolt Brecht, "Kunsthistoriker sind Leute . . . ," *Uhu,* 7 (Dec. 1930): 84f.

13. Grosz, *Briefe,* 200.

14. Ibid., 202.

15. Ibid., 216f.

16. Postscriptum omitted in Knust's edition of George Grosz's letters; BBA 482/73.

17. Bertolt Brecht, *Briefe 1913–1956,* ed. Günther Glaeser (Berlin and Weimar: Aufbau-Verlag), 520f.

18. Grosz, *Briefe,* 389.

19. Grosz, *Briefe,* 390.

20. Fischer, *George Grosz,* 118.

21. Grosz, *Briefe,* 439; cf. also 441, 445.

22. In a letter, dated "9. Dezember 1930," Grosz had told Benn that "ich liebe Deine Prosa sehr und viele Deiner Gedanken sind mir ausserordentlich nahe. 'Fazit der Perspektiven' — Seite 138 bis Schluss: Grossartig!!" (I love your prose very much, and many of your ideas are extremely close to me. "Result of Perspectives" — page 138 to the end. Superb!!) Grosz repeats his admiration for Benn two decades later in a letter, dated "Dezember 11. 1952," as he writes (in English), "I like your you and your work very much." See Benn Archiv, Deutsches Literaturarchiv, Marbach am Neckar.

23. Grosz, *Briefe,* 448.

24. George Grosz, *Ein kleines Ja und ein großes Nein. Sein Leben von ihm selbst erzählt* (Hamburg: Rowohlt, 1955), 122.

25. See Bertolt Brecht, "Das Portrait des Beschauers" (circa 1920), in *Werke,* 30 vols., ed. Werner Hecht, Jan Knopf, Werner Mittenzwei, and Klaus-Detlev Müller (Berlin: Aufbau-Verlag; Frankfurt: Suhrkamp, 1989), vol. 17, 414f., 417.

26. Ibid., 417.

27. Bertolt Brecht, "Verfremdungseffekt in den erzählenden Bildern des älteren Breughel," in *Gesammelte Werke,* vol. 18 (Frankfurt am Main: Suhrkamp, 1967), 268.

28. Bertolt Brecht, *Über Lyrik* (Frankfurt: Suhrkamp, 1964), 74.

29. Grosz, *Briefe,* 205; 209; 265; 460.

30. Ibid., 390.

31. Brecht, "Das Portrait des Beschauers," 414f., 417.

32. Grosz, *Briefe,* 390.

33. Cited and translated by Jochen Schulte-Sasse, foreword to Peter Bürger, *Theory of the Avant-Garde,* trans. Michael Shaw (Minneapolis: University of Minnesota Press, 1984), xxxvi.

34. Brecht, *Gesammelte Werke,* 20 vols. (Frankfurt am Main: Suhrkamp, 1967), vol. 17, 961.

Chapter 7

1. Gottfried Benn, *Gesammelte Werke,* 8 vols., ed. Dieter Wellershoff (Wiesbaden: Limes, 1968), 8:1960.

2. See Reinhold Grimm, "Innere Emigration als Lebensform," in *Exil und innere Emigration [I],* ed. Reinhold Grimm and Jost Hermand (Frankfurt: Athenaeum, 1972), 70f.

3. Quoted ibid., 49.

4. Reinhold Grimm, "Gottfried Benn's *Urerlebnis,*" in *The Ideological Crisis of Expressionism: The Literary and Artistic German War Colony in Belgium 1914–1918,* ed. Rainer Rumold and O. K. Werckmeister (Columbia, S.C.: Camden House, 1990), 142.

5. See Peter Uwe Hohendahl, ed. *Wirkung wider Willen* Dokumente zur Wirkungsgeschichte Benns (Frankfurt: Athenaeum, 1971), 52f., 58f. Except for a renaissance of Benn's (as well as Ernst Jünger's) work (in translations) in conservative French circles, not much has changed since Hohendahl's appraisal, clearly not for English-speaking audiences.

6. Eugene Jolas, "Gottfried Benn," *transition* 5 (August 1927): 147.

7. See Andreas Kramer and Rainer Rumold, introduction to Eugene Jolas, *Man from Babel* (New Haven, Conn.: Yale University Press, 1989), xxvii.

8. Eugene Jolas, *Man from Babel* (New Haven, Conn.: Yale University Press, 1989), 126, 232.

9. See, for example, Michael Hamburger, *Reason and Energy* (London: Routledge & Paul, 1957), 273–312; *From Prophecy to Exorcism* (London: Longmans, 1956), 67–70; and *The Truth of Poetry* (New York: Weidenfeld & Nicholson, 1969); B. Ashton, ed., *Primal Vision: Selected Writings of Gottfried Benn,* (New York: New Directions, 1971), vii–xxvi; J. M. Ritchie, *Gottfried Benn: The Unreconstructed Expressionist* (London: Wolff, 1972); Reinhard Alter, *Gottfried Benn: The Artist and Politics (1910–1934)* (Bern: Peter Lang, 1976).

10. Jürgen Habermas, "Modernity versus Postmodernity," *new german critique* 22 (1981): 14. Habermas here talks of the whole development of modernist culture from Baudelaire up to the later Benn; the notion of the "privacy" of the aesthetic experience alludes specifically to the latter.

11. See, for example, Inge Jens, *Dichter zwischen rechts und links. Die Geschichte der Sektion der Dichtkunst der Preussischen Akademie der Künste dargestellt nach den Dokumenten* (Munich: Piper, 1971), or Jürgen Schröder, *Gottfried Benn. Poesie und Sozialisation* (Stuttgart: Kohlhammer, 1978). For an analysis of the Benn affair as viewed in criticism from 1933 onward, see Hohendahl, *Wirkung wider Willen,* 39–50, and its respective documentation.

12. See Rainer Rumold, *Gottfried Benn und der Expressionismus: Absolute Dichtung; Provokation des Lesers* (Königstein/Ts.: Scriptor, 1982), 49f.

13. Gottfried Benn, "Nietzsche nach fünfzig Jahren," *Gesammelte Werke,* 4:1046.

14. Bruno Hillebrand, *Artistik und Auftrag. Zur Kunsttheorie von Benn und Nietzsche* (Munich: Nymphenburger, 1966), 32, 165; Rumold, *Benn und Expressionismus,* 108–38.

15. See Grimm, "Gottfried Benn's *Urerlebnis;*" and Jürgen Schröder, "The Birth of Art from the Anti-Spirit of the War: Gottfried Benn's *Etappe,*" in *The Ideological Crisis of Expressionism: The Literary and Artistic German War Colony in Belgium 1914–1918,* ed. Rainer Rumold and O. K. Werckmeister (Columbia, S.C.: Camden House, 1990), 133–49; 151–67.

16. Quoted in Thomas Anz and Michael Stark, eds., *Expressionismus: Manifeste und Dokumente zur deutschen Literatur 1910–1920* (Stuttgart: Metzler, 1982), 35.

17. Thomas Mann, "Nietzsches Philosophie im Lichte unserer Erfahrung," in *Schriften und Reden zur Literatur, Kunst und Philosophie,* vol. 3 (Frankfurt: Suhrkamp, 1968), 27.

18. Gottfried Benn, "Weinhaus Wolf," in *Gesammelte Werke,* 8 vols., ed. Dieter Wellershoff (Wiesbaden: Limes, 1968), vol. 5, 1319; Gottfried Benn, "Wolf's Tavern," in *Primal Vision,* ed. E. B. Ashton (New York: New Directions, 1971), 79.

19. Bernard Pautrat, *Versions du soleil. Figures et systeme de Nietzsche* (Paris: Editions du Seuil, 1971), 266.

20. See Rudolph Kuenzli, "Nietzsche's Zerography: *Thus Spoke Zarathustra,*" *Boundary 2* [special issue on Nietzsche] (spring-fall 1981): 95–113.

21. Friedrich Nietzsche, "Über Wahrheit und Lüge im aussermoralischen Sinn," in *Werke,* 3 vols., ed. Karl Schlechta (Munich: Hanser, 1966), 3:378, 375f, 383.

22. Ibid., 379.

23. Habermas, "Modernity versus Postmodernity," 10.

24. Unfortunately for a wider critical understanding of Benn in international literary studies, only a few of these important essays are available in English translation. See Gottfried Benn, "Answer to the Literary Emigrants," "Art and the Third Reich," in E. B. Ashton, ed. *Primal Vision* (New York: New Directions, 1971); reprinted in Gottfried Benn, *Gottfried Benn: Prose, Essays, Poems,* ed. Volkmar Sander (New York: Continuum, 1987).

25. For the dating of the text, see Benn, *Gesammelte Werke,* 8:2207. The oldest typescript is dated May 17, 1938; an authorized copy, signed by Benn himself, bears the date 1937.

26. Benn, "Wolf's Tavern," 79.

27. See Günter Martens, "Im Aufbruch das Ziel. Nietzsches Wirkung im Expressionismus," in *Nietzsche. Werk und Wirkungen,* ed. Hans Steffen (Göttingen: Vandenhoeck und Ruprecht, 1974).

28. Benn, "Nietzsche nach fünfzig Jahren," 1053.

29. Paul de Man, "Literary History and Literary Modernity," in *In Search of*

Literary Theory, ed. Morton W. Bloomfield (Ithaca, N.Y., and London: Cornell University Press, 1972), 251.

30. Gottfried Benn, *Briefe an F. W. Oelze 1932–1945*, 4 vols., ed. Harald Steinhagen and Jürgen Schröder (Frankfurt am Main: Fischer, 1979), vol. 1, 191f.

31. Benn, "Wolf's Tavern," 65.

32. See Klaus Gerth, "Absolute Dichtung," in *Gottfried Benn*, ed. Bruno Hillebrand (Darmstadt: Wissenschaftliche Buchgesellschaft, 1979), 247.

33. See Schröder, *Benn. Poesie und Sozialisation*, 94f.

34. Benn, "Wolf's Tavern," 64, 75, 72.

35. Ibid., 65.

36. Ibid., 72.

37. Jürgen Habermas, "The Entwinement of Myth and Enlightenment: Re-Reading *Dialectic of Enlightenment*," *new german critique* 26 (1982): 25; expanded version in *The Philosophical Discourse of Modernity*, tr. F. Lawrence (Cambridge: MIT Press, 1987), 122f.

38. Max Horkheimer and Theodor W. Adorno, *Dialectic of Enlightenment* (New York: Continuum, 1991), 37.

39. Benn, "Wolf's Tavern," 74, 78.

40. Ibid., 79 [my emphasis and changes in the translation].

41. Grimm, "Gottfried Benn's *Urerlebnis*," 142f.

42. Gottfried Benn, "Nach dem Nihilismus," in *Gesammelte Werke*, 3:721.

43. Benn, "Wolf's Tavern," 80.

44. Benn, *Gesammelte Werke*, 4:1075.

45. Cf. Paul de Man, "Literary History and Literary Modernity," in *In Search of Literary Theory*, ed. Morton W. Bloomfield (Ithaca, N.Y., and London: Cornell University Press, 1972), 256.

46. Habermas, "Modernity versus Postmodernity," 14.

47. See Habermas, *Discourse of Modernity*, 86ff.

48. See, for instance, Gottfried Benn, "Can Poets Change the World? Radio Dialogue," in *Benn: Prose, Essays, Poems*, 102ff.

49. Benn, *Briefe an Oelze*, 189f.

50. Ibid., 180; 166; 182f.

51. Benn, "Answer to Emigrants," 51.

52. Benn, *Briefe an Oelze*, 175.

53. Ibid., 171.

54. See Benn, "Answer to Emigrants."

55. Benn, *Briefe an Oelze*, 180.

56. Jean-François Lyotard, *The Postmodern Condition: A Report on Knowledge* (Minneapolis: University of Minnesota Press, 1984), 79f.

57. Benn, *Gesammelte Werke*, 8:1874.

58. Ibid., 8:1960.

59. Grimm, "Gottfried Benn's *Urerlebnis,*" 142f.

60. Benn, Gesammelte Werke, 4:1075.

Chapter 8

1. Joan Weinstein, *The End of Expressionism: Art and the November Revolution in Germany, 1918–19* (Chicago and London: University of Chicago Press, 1990), 11.

2. Paul de Man, "Criticism and Crisis," in *Blindness and Insight: Essays in the Rhetoric of Contemporary Criticism* (Minneapolis: University of Minnesota Press, 1983), 14.

3. Andreas Huyssen, "Mapping the Postmodern," *New German Critique* 33 (1984): 22.

4. See Andreas Huyssen, *After the Great Divide: Modernism, Mass Culture, Post-modernism* (Bloomington: Indiana University Press, 1986), 142ff.

5. John Barth, "The Literature of Replenishment: Postmodern Fiction." *Atlantic Monthly,* 245, no. 1 (January 1980): 65–71.

6. Gerald Graff, "The Myth of the Postmodern Breakthrough," *Literature Against Itself* (Chicago: University of Chicago Press, 1979), 31–62.

7. Paul Ricoeur,"Ist 'die Krise' ein spezifisch modernes Phänomen?," in *Über die Krise,* ed. Krzysztof Michalski (Stuttgart: Klett-Cotta, 1986), 60.

8. For a survey of postmodern politics, see Hans Bertens, *The Idea of the Post-modern: A History* (London and New York: Routledge, 1995), 185–208.

9. Quoted in Thomas Anz and Michael Stark, eds., *Expressionismus: Manifeste und Dokumente zur deutschen Literatur 1910–1920* (Stuttgart: Metzler, 1982), 93.

10. Ibid., 99.

11. Ibid., 108f.

12. Ibid., 98ff.

13. Quoted in Paul Raabe, "Der Expressionismus als historisches Phaenomen," in *Begriffsbestimmung des Literarischen Expressionismus,* ed. Hans Gerd Rötzer (Darmstadt: Wissenschaftliche Buchgesellschaft, 1976), 317. For a discussion of the terror of utopian thought and movements, see Joachim Fest, *Der zerstörte Traum. Vom Ende des utopischen Zeitalters* (Berlin: Siedler, 1991), 62ff.

14. See James A. Robinson, "Crisis," in *International Encyclopedia of the Social Sciences* (New York: Macmillan, 1968), 510f.; Reinhart Koselleck, *Kritik und Krise. Ein Beitrag zur Pathogenese der bürgerlichen Welt* (Freiburg: K. Alber, 1959); Reinhart Koselleck, *Futures Past: On the Semantics of Historical Time* (Cambridge: MIT Press, 1985).

15. See Ernst Bloch, *Erbschaft dieser Zeit* (Frankfurt am Main: Suhrkamp, 1962) 104–22.

16. Walter Benjamin, *Reflections,* 184.

17. See Reinhart Koselleck, "Einige Fragen und die Begriffsgeschichte von

'Krise,' *Über die Krise,* Castelgandolfo-Gespräche 1985, ed. Krzysztof Michalski (Stuttgart: Klett-Cotta, 1986), 68f.

18. See Walter Sokel, ed., *Anthology of German Expressionist Drama: A Prelude to the Absurd* (Ithaca, N.Y., and London: Cornell University Press, 1984), 265–78.

19. The USPD understood the potential of film for influencing and shaping mass opinion. The Communist Party would be the first to actually use it for that purpose. See Richard Sheppard, "Artists, Intellectuals and the USPD 1917–1922," in *Literaturwissenschaftliches Jahrbuch,* vol. 32 (1991), 211f; and "The SPD, Its Cultural Policy, and the German *Avant-garde* 1917–1922," in *Internationales Archiv für Sozialgeschichte der deutschen Literatur* 20, no. 1 (1995): 49f.

20. Jochen Schulte-Sasse, "Carl Einstein; or, The Postmodern Transformation of Modernism," in *Modernity and the Text: Revisions of German Modernism,* ed. Andreas Huyssen and David Bathrick (New York: Columbia Press, 1989), 42.

21. de Man, "Criticism and Crisis," 14.

22. Fredric Jameson, "Postmodernism and Consumer Society" in *The Anti-Aesthetic: Essays on Postmodern Culture,* ed. Hal Foster (Port Townsend, Wash.: Bay Press, 1983), 114. See also his essay "The Cultural Logic of Late Capitalism," in *Postmodernism or The Cultural Logic of Late Capitalism* (Durham, N.C.: Duke University Press, 1992), 17f.

23. Jameson, "Postmodernism and Consumer Society," 125.

24. See Andreas Huyssen, "The Search for Tradition," in *Postmodernism A Reader,* ed. Thomas Docherty (New York: Columbia University Press, 1993), 226.

25. See Anz and Stark, *Expressionismus,* 99.

26. I agree with Lyotard, who ascribes to expressionism a "melancholy" disposition, and understand his view that both modernist and postmodern productions are involved with the question of the "unrepresentable in presentation itself." But I cannot work with his distinction of the former, modernism, as still based on a "consensus of taste" and "the solace of good forms" and certain "preestablished rules," while the latter is articulating its own necessities free from any restrictions through the production itself as an "*event*" (Jean-François Lyotard, *The Postmodern Condition: A Report on Knowledge* [Minneapolis: University of Minnesota Press, 1984], 81). Such an "event"-based model would make expressionists like Kandinsky (*The Yellow Sound*), Kokoschka (*Murder: Hope of Women*), and, of course, Dada "postmodern." Yet, as I have shown in my first chapter, the expressionist artists and writers are still part and parcel of an agon of art over art that, while it relativizes "styles" as "dispositions," is enacted in deference to aesthetic autonomy and its continued grand expectations from art.

27. Paul Michael Lützeler, "The Avant-Garde in Crisis," in *Hermann Broch: Literature, Philosophy, Politics,* ed. Stephen Dowden (Columbia, S.C.: Camden House, 1988), 25.

28. Schulte-Sasse, "Carl Einstein," 42. Talking about institutionalization processes of the arts, Schulte-Sasse states, "My thesis is that the degree to which art-

ists gained such an insight determines the difference between modernism and the avant-garde/postmodernism."

29. See Rainer Rumold, *Gottfried Benn und der Expressionismus. Absolute Dichtung; Provokation des Lesers* (Königstein/Ts: Scriptor, 1982) 65–70, 148–51, 160f.

30. See Rosalind E. Krauss, "The Originality of the Avant-Garde: A Postmodernist Repetition," in *Zeitgeist in Babel: The Postmodernist Controversy,* ed. Ingeborg Hoesterey (Bloomington and Indianapolis: Indiana University Press, 1991), 70f.

31. Carl Einstein, *Werke,* 5 vols., ed. Marion Schmid and Liliane Meffre (Vienna and Berlin: Medusa, 1985), 3:59.

32. Gottfried Benn, *Gesammelte Werke,* 8 vols., ed. Dieter Wellershoff (Wiesbaden: Limes, 1968), 5:1217.

33. Hugo von Hofmannsthal, "Der Brief des Lord Chandos," in *Gesammelte Werke,* 6 vols. (Berlin: Fischer, 1924), 2:175ff.

34. Schulte-Sasse, "Carl Einstein," 56.

35. For a reprint of the poem and its interpretation by Helmut Heißenbüttel, see Helmut Heißenbüttel, "Carl-Einstein-Portrait," in *Zur Tradition der Moderne. Aufsätze und Anmerkungen 1964–1971* (Neuwied and Berlin: Luchterhand, 1972), 262–90.

36. Ibid., 287.

37. Ibid., 284.

38. See Rainer Rumold, *Sprachliches Experiment und literarische Tradition. Zu den Texten Helmut Heißenbüttel,* Stanford University Department of German Studies series, vol. 9 (Bern and Frankfurt: Lang, 1975), 104–10.

39. Hans Magnus Enzensberger, "Die Aporien der Avantgarde," in *Einzelheiten II Poesie und Politik* (Frankfurt am Main: Suhrkamp, 1963), 75.

40. Helmut Heißenbüttel, *Zur Tradition der Moderne. Aufsätze und Anmerkungen 1964–1971* (Neuwied and Berlin: Luchterhand, 1972), 159.

41. Helmut Heißenbüttel, *Das Textbuch* (Freiburg i. Breisgau: Walter-Olten, 1967), 140.

42. Ibid.

43. Paul Celan, "Entwurf einer Landschaft," in *Sprachgitter* (Frankfurt am Main: Fischer, 1959), 44.

44. Theodor Adorno, "Kulturkritik und Gesellschaft," in *Prismen* (Munich: DTV, 1963), 26.

45. Paul Celan, "Entwurf einer Landschaft," 44.

46. See Wilfried Ihrig, "Landschaftsentwürfe. Paul Celan und Carl Einstein," in *Archiv für das Studium der neueren Sprachen und Literaturen* 221 (Berlin: Erich Schmidt, 1984): 298–305. Ihrig's detailed comparison of the two poems by way of tracing motifs like "Atem," "Wort," "Eis," "Gestein," and "Tod" (breath, word, ice, rock, and death) well establishes his thesis "that Einstein's poem touches on central problems of Celan's poetics" and that Celan's poem constitutes a differing answer to Einstein's" (305).

47. G. W. F. Hegel, *Vorlesungen über die Ästhetik*, 20 vols., ed. Eva Moldenhauer and Karl Markus Michel (Frankfurt: Suhrkamp, 1986), 2:231ff.

48. Hans Egon Holthusen, "Utopie und Katastrophe. Der Lyriker Hans Magnus Enzensberger 1957–1978," in *Sartre in Stammheim. Zwei Themen aus den Jahren der grossen Turbulenz* (Stuttgart: Klett-Cotta, 1982), 14f.

49. See, for example, Theo Buck, "Enzensberger und Brecht," *Text und Kritik* 49 (1976): 5–16; or Arthur Zimmermann, *Hans Magnus Enzensberger, Die Gedichte und ihre literaturkritische Rezeption* (Bonn: Bouvier, 1977).

50. Walter Boehlich, "Autodafé," *Kursbuch* 15 (Frankfurt am Main: Suhrkamp, 1968).

51. Hans Magnus Enzensberger, *Gedichte 1955–1970* (Frankfurt am Main: Suhrkamp, 1971).

52. Holthusen, "Utopie und Katastrophe," 66f.

53. Ibid., 71, 75.

54. Ibid., 90, 92, 75, 96.

55. Reinhold Grimm, "Poetic Anarchism? The Case of Hans Magnus Enzensberger," in *Texturen. Essays und anderes zu Hans Magnus Enzensberger* (New York: Peter Lang, 1984), 112ff.

56. Ibid., 127.

57. Hans Magnus Enzensberger, "Commonplaces on the Newest Literature," in *Critical Essays,* ed. Reinhold Grimm and Bruce Armstrong (New York: Continuum, 1982), 43. Originally published as "Gemeinplätze, die Neueste Literatur betreffend" in *Kursbuch* 15 (1968): 195.

58. Hans Magnus Enzensberger, "Scherenschleifer und Poeten," in *Mein Gedicht ist mein Messer,* ed. Hans Bender (Munich: List, 1969) 147.

59. Hans Magnus Enzensberger, "Poesie und Politik," in *Einzelheiten II* (Frankfurt am Main: Suhrkamp, 1964) 136.

60. Ibid., 133; 136.

61. Hans Magnus Enzensberger, *Blindenschrift* (Frankfurt am Main: Suhrkamp, 1964), 67.

62. Enzensberger, "Poesie und Politik," 133.

63. Enzensberger, "Aporien der Avantgarde," 79.

64. Enzensberger, "Scherenschleifer und Poeten," 147.

65. See Hans Magnus Enzensberger, "Eurozentrismus wider Willen. Ein politisches Vexierbild" and "Der höchste Stand der Unterentwicklung. Eine Hypothese über den Real Existierenden Sozialismus," in *Politische Brosamen* (Frankfurt am Main: Suhrkamp, 1982).

66. Peter Weiss, *Aesthetik des Widerstands. Roman,* vol. 3 (Frankfurt am Main: Suhrkamp, 1981), 265.

67. For a critical account of contemporaneous doomsday literature, see Reinhold Grimm, " 'Eiszeit und Untergang' Zu einem Motivkomplex in der deutschen Gegenwartsliteratur," in *Texturen. Essays und anderes zu Hans Magnus Enzensberger*

(New York, Bern, and Frankfurt: Lang, 1984). For a critical account of Sloterdijk's postmodern negotiation of the apocalyptic, see Andreas Huyssen, "The Return of Diogenes as Postmodern Intellectual," foreword to Peter Sloterdijk, *The Critique of Cynical Reason* (Minneapolis: University of Minnesota Press, 1987), ix–xxv.

68. Hans Magnus Enzensberger, *Der Untergang der Titanic. Eine Komödie* (Frankfurt am Main: Suhrkamp, 1978), 97.

69. Ibid., 100.

70. Ibid., 101.

71. Walter Benjamin, *Gesammelte Schriften,* 7 vols., ed. Rolf Tiedermann and Hermann Schweppenhäuser (Frankfurt am Main: Suhrkamp, 1991), 1, 2:700, 703; 5:593.

72. Hans Magnus Enzensberger, "Zwei Randbemerkungen zum Weltuntergang," in *Politische Brosamen,* (Frankfurt am Main: Suhrkamp, 1982), 236, 234, 225. Cf. also Leszek Kolakowski, "Die Moderne auf der Anklagebank," in *Über die Krise,* ed. Krzysztof Michalski (Stuttgart: Klett-Cotta, 1986), 79ff. For Kolakowski, too, the topos of the apocalypse belongs to a core of a universal stock of myths that embody the recurrent conflict between the old and the new, between "progress" and tradition, serving as a means to symbolically cope and come to terms with rapid changes. The topos functions as a counterbalance against Western culture's predilection for the "new," as expressed in an always ill-defined positive valorization of the "progressive" and an always pejorative usage of the label "reactionary."

73. Rainer Naegele, "Freud, Habermas and the Dialectic of Enlightenment: On Real and Ideal Discourses," *new german critique* 22 (winter 1981): 43.

74. Hans Magnus Enzensberger, "Aporien der Avantgarde" (1962) in *Einzelheiten II,* 79.

Index

Absurdism, 139, 145, 148, 171, 175; "aesthetics of," 188

Adorno, Theodor, 78, 89, 134, 149, 172; versus Brecht, xvii; as critic, 86, 92, 127, 184, 222n25, 225n76; and the writing of poetry, 184; *Dialectic of Enlightenment,* 164

Advertising, 47, 49–50, 54; boundaries between art and, 136

Aestheticism: avant-garde attack on, 199n2; expressionists react against, 5–7; fin de siècle, 199n2; "negative aesthetics," xiv, 67, 77–90, 171, 178; and politics, xvi, 23–25, 168; Western tradition questioned, xi

African art (masks and tattoos) and culture, 20–23

Agitprop, 50, 64, 172

Agon: of art over art, 7–9, 154, 177; of discourses, (concept of) xi, xii, 34–35, 36, 39, (history of) 59

Aichinger, Ilse: *Buttons,* 171

Aktion, Die (journal), 14, 18, 32, 116

Allegory, 12

America: American Left, 69, 138, 139, 143, 145; art in, 172, (as art center of the world) 148, (surrealist) 77; exiles in, xii, 69, 70, 71, 75, 78, 83–84, 137–39, 141; expressionist theater in, 68, 143; hegemony of, 171; pessimism about, 145; poets and writers of, 70; popular culture of, xviii, xx, 172, (Mickey Mouse) 84, 132; postmodern literature of, 173

Ammer, K. L., 8

Anarchism, 27, 47, 48; Berlin Dada and, 50, 51, 52; of exiles, 48; Groszian, 141; individualist men-

tality, 139; and language, 45; mentality shared by artist and writer, 102, 139; poetic, 188; in Spanish Civil War, xv, 74, 80, 92, 94, 105–8

Anfang, Der (journal), 116, 117

Angelus Novus (Klee painting), 118

Angelus Novus (planned journal), 113

"Anti-art" concept, xiii, xiv, 40, 88; anti-art art, 41–49, 88, (politicizing) 49–55, (surrealist) 111, 116

Antifascists. *See* Fascism

Anti-Semitism. *See* Jews

Apocalypse. *See* "Doomsday" mentality

Apollinaire, Guillaume, 222n33

Aporia, 173, 184, 187, 191

Aragon, Louis, 50, 97, 120

"Archaic" image, 114, 119, 134

Architecture: Bauhaus, x; utopian visions of during World War I, 7

Arendt, Erich, 66, 73, 74, 75, 77, 88; "The Hands," 74

Arp, Hans (Jean), 25, 31, 47, 96; in exile, 39, 66, 75, 95; poems of, 41–45; way of working described, 48. WORKS: *Cloud Pump,* 42; "Strassburgian Configuration," 183; "Toward the Exit," 42

Art: "absolute," 96; abstract, 148, 172; African, 20–23; in America, 148, 172; art market attacked, 62; "degenerate," 172; "fatal hour of," 87; folk, 134; French, in Germany, 21; gender and, 25–29, 33; -life relation, 165; pop, xx–xxi, 172; crisis of, 136; revolution in, *see Kunstrevolution;* as weapon, 54. *See also* "Anti-art" concept; Visual arts; Western culture

239

65, 96–97, 110–11, 134–35, 154, 156, 161, 166, 167–68, (criticized, attacked for support) 138, 155, 163; (falls from) xv, 153–54, 157, 160–69 passim; and Nietzsche, 153, 157–69; poetry defined by, 101, 165; poetry of, 173; postfascism of, 159–60, 163, 166; postwar, 156; and "primitive" collective experience," xv; radio debate with Becher, 62, 63, 163, 187; Right represented by, 64; and "world of expression," xiii. WORKS: "Answer to the Literary Emigrants," 138, 160; "Art and the Third Reich," 160; "The Birthday," 155, 168; "Brains," 3–4, 168; "Breeding I," 160; "Breeding II," 160; "Confessing Expressionism," 65, 110, 160; "Home Front," 140; "The Island," 155; *Morgue* poems, 132, 140; "Nietzsche after Fifty Years," 157, 161, 163–64; "No Solace," 28; "Oratory: The Unending," 63; "Primal Vision," 65, 155–56; "Probleme der Lyrik," 169; "Roman des Phänotyp," 169; Rönne novellas, 3–4, 64, 70, 154, 165, 168, 180; *Static Poems,* 155; "The Structure of the Personality," 156; "The Three Old Men," 145; "Weizenstück," 63; "Wolf's Tavern," xv, xvii, 153, 155, 157–69; works translated, 95

Berlin Dada, 45, 50, 64, 91, 178; and anti-art art, 49–55; as countermovement, ix, xiv, 179; Einstein and Grosz and, 33, 49, 50, 53–54, 145; female member of, 25; politicized, 54, 61, 89

Beuys, Joseph, xx

Blass, Ernst, 6

Blätter für die Kunst (journal), 119

"Blindness" of language. *See* Language

Bloch, Ernst, 32, 105, 111, 112, 119, 126, 132; avant-garde assessed by, 175; Benjamin versus, 135; Benn versus, 134–35, 163; defends expressionism, xvi, 134; and montage technique, 129; and Moscow tribunals, 224n61. WORKS: "Discussing Expressionism," 134; *Legacy of Our Times,* 64, 135; *Spirit of Utopia,* 8; *Traces,* 64

Blue Rider (almanac), 20

Blutige Ernst, Der (journal), 53

Boccaccio, Giovanni: *Decameron,* 82

Boldt, Paul, 5

Borchert, Wolfgang: *Homeless,* 171

Bourgeoisie: dadaist attack on, 62; Einstein's criticism of, 101, 102, 105, 106; film seen as end of culture of, 127; ideal of beauty of, 149

Braque, Georges, xv, 21, 96, 98; Einstein's treatise on, 93, 96, 97–98, 99, 101, 102–7 passim; exhibit on, 93

Brecht, Barbara, 228n11

Brecht, Bertolt, 54, 87, 94, 101, 135; aesthetic theories of, xvii; Benn versus, ix, xvi, xviii, 154, 172, 187, 189; as critic of avant-garde, 111, 137; as editor of *Das Wort,* 127–28; epic theater of, *see* Theater; in exile, 72, 88, 139; and expressionism, 133–34; and film, 16, 129, 132, 139; "formalism" of, 126–27; Grosz and, xii, xvi, xxii, 137, 139–49; influence of, 156, 182, 190, 191; poetry of, 122, 140, 173, (as anarchist poet, 188); silenced, 66; Soviet sympathies of, 139; and "television," 143, 144. WORKS: "The Anachronistic Procession or Freedom and Democracy," 144; *Baal,* 133; "Ballad of the Dead Soldier," 140–41; commentaries on his own plays, 140; "Conversation with George Grosz," 141; "Defamil-

official culture of Third Reich, xvii;
vision of change of, 6

signs for Landscape," 182–83, 186; "Teaching/Learning Poem about History," xviii

Hemingway, Ernest, 71

Hémisphères (journal), 70

Hennings, Emmy, 25

Hermand, Jost, 61; (coauthor) *Die Kultur der Weimarer Republik*, 61

Herzfelde, Wieland, 50, 141, 143, 144, 145

Hesse, Hermann, 13, 32; *Steppenwolf*, 64

Heym, Georg, 6, 15, 18, 24, 29, 64, 117, 197; influence on, 204n28; sonnet form used by, 5; "visual" poetics of, 32; "The God of the City," 10–13

Heynicke, Kurt, 32; "Psalm," 27

Hillebrand, Bruno, 157

Hiller, Kurt, 9, 13, 31, 116, 158, 220n2; ethical rationalism of, 32; as expressionist, 5, 6, 33, 125; opposition to, 117, 227n89; populist goal of, 113; *The Leap into the Light*, 123

Hindemith, Paul, 62–63

Hitler, Adolf, 75, 135, 142, 156, 167, 168; caricatured, 138; comes to power, 70, 95, 99, 124, 138, 139; Moscow equated with, 69, 132; pact with Stalin, 87, 138; rejects modern art, 65; and Schwabing tradition, 130. *See also* National Socialism (Nazis)

Hoech, Hannah, 25

Hofmannsthal, Hugo von, 9, 18. WORKS: "Chandos Letter," xii–xiii, 16, 67, 87, 180, 195; "Substitute for Dreams," 16–17

Hohenzollern monarchy, 147

Hölderlin, Friedrich, 11

Hollywood. *See* Film

Holthusen, Hans Egon, 187–88, 189

Horkheimer, Max, 86, 164

Huch, Ricarda, 154

Huelsenbeck, Richard, xiv, 53, 59; and Dada, 9, 40, 43–44, 45, 47, 61, 207n77; and Dadaist Manifesto, 50, 51; in exile, 39, 75; versus Tzara, 48, 50. WORKS: *En Avant Dada. Eine Geschichte des Dadaismus*, 51; *Fantastic Prayers*, 46

Husserl, Edmund: concept of crisis, xi

Huyssen, Andreas, 177

Idealism, German, 8, 33, 123, 171, 172; idealist language, 52

Ideologies: critiques of, 191–92, 195–96; Left, 62, 64, 195–96, (American) 69, 138, 139, 143, 145; New Left, 172, 182, (revolt of) xx; Right, 64, 195. *See also* Fascism; Marx, Karl, and Marxism; National Socialism (Nazis); Popular Front

"Image/body realm," xiii, xvi, 4, 104; artistic versus surrealist image, 45; intrusion of, into writing, 9, 122, 127. *See also* "Archaic" image

"Imaginary museum" concept, 34, 36

Imperialism, 105

Impressionism, 223n52

In Bloody Earnest (journal), 53

Institute for Social Research (New York), 86

Intellectuals/intelligentsia: criticized, 13, 64, 122; "free-floating," 24, 39; French, 118; leftist, 64

International avant-garde, 68, 160; Moscow consensus against, 126. *See also* Exile period

International Writers' Congress (Paris, 1935), 87

Internationale Literatur (Moscow journal), 124

Italian avant-garde, 60

Italian futurism, ix, xviii, 4, 5, 6, 99, 130, 180, 201n2; and aesthetization of politics, xvi, 23, 24; criticized, 97, 131; impact of, 18, 65; war as viewed by, 18–19, 25; women scorned by, 25

Jameson, Fredric, 33, 88, 177
Janco, Marcel, 39
Jews, 65, 186; prejudice against, 29, 95, 110–11, 160, 167
Johst, Hanns, 61, 110, 155. WORKS: *Schlageter*, 54; *The Solitary One*, 133
Jolas, Eugene, x, 70, 96, 100, 180, 181. WORKS: "Gottfried Benn," 155; *Man from Babel*, 95, 156
Joyce, James, 71, 79, 126, 155. WORKS: *Finnegans Wake*, 80, 95; *Ulysses*, 80
Jung, Carl G., 132, 134, 135
Jung, Franz, 26–27, 28, 29; Berlin journal of, 51
Jünger, Ernst, 64, 119, 131, 230n5. WORKS: *The Adventurous Heart*, 64; *War and Warrior*, 123

Kafka, Franz, and Kafkaesque thought, xvii, 64, 146, 166, 171, 191, 197; first English translations of, 70, 95
Kahnweiler, Daniel-Henry, 21
Kaiser, Georg, 133–34; in exile, 66, 75; film and plays of, 14, 158, 175. WORKS: "Alkibiades Saved," 133; *Gas II*, 61; *From Morning to Midnight*, 15
Kandinsky, Wassily, 43, 118, 234n26; *Judgment Day*, 3–4, 35
Kant, Immanuel, 13
Kapp Putsch (1920), 61
Kästner, Erich, 122, 124
Kiefer, Klaus, 84, 219n11
Kinobuch, Das (anthology), 14
"Kinostil" as literary term, 16
Kisch, Egon, 62, 163
"Kitsch," 174

Klages, Ludwig, xvi, 120, 134, 135, 222n25; and images, 114, 121, 129; lectures, 130. WORKS: *The Mind as Adversary of the Soul*, 119; "On the Nature of Ecstasy," 119; *Vom Kosmogonischen Eros*, 119
Klee, Paul, 69, 117–18, 135, 138, 148
Koepke, Wulf, 88
Kokoschka, Oskar, 61, 234n26
Kracauer, Siegfried, 124
Kraus, Karl, 20, 75, 179
Kubin, Alfred: *The Other Side*, 196–97
Kuhn, Thomas, xxi
Kunstrevolution (art revolution), xiv, 31, 34, 40, 91
Kurella, Alfred, 224n61, 225n73
Kursbuch (journal), 188, 191

Lacis, Asja, 116
Lang, Fritz: *Metropolis*, 62
Langgässer, Elisabeth, 154
Language: anarchist play of, 45; "blindness of," xiii, xvii, xviii, 100, 198; Dadaist, 47–48, 52, (international) 60; denial of, 179, 180; of expressionism, inflated, 115; futurism and, 131; idealist, 52; limits of, 182; "linguistic turn," xi; literary, visual arts and, 16–17, 100; metaphorical nature of, 32, 47, 121, 158, 161, 185–86, 195, (surrealism and) 120; of poetry, *see* Poetry; versus style, 9; universal, poetry as, 173
Lasker-Schüler, Else, x, 14, 25–27, 75, 88; Benjamin's reaction to, 118; in exile, 60, 66; poetry of, 28, 29, 184. WORKS: "For the Barbarian," 26, 28; *IandI*, 75, 77; *The Malik: An Emperor's Story*, 25–26, 28; *My Blue Piano*, 76; "Sabaoth," 26–27, 28; "The Song of the Play Prince," 26, 28

Nolde, Emil, 22
Nouvelle Revue (journal), 86
Novel, the. See Literature

Oberdada, 50, 53
Oehm, Heidemarie, 219n11
Oelze, F. W., 162, 167, 168
O'Neill, Eugene: The Hairy Ape, 68
Open Road (journal), 51
Opera, 62, 63
Opitz, Martin, 114
Orwell, George: Homage to Catalonia,
   108
Otten, Karl, 75
Ottwalt, Ernst, 224n61

Pacifism, 18, 25, 220n2
Painting. See Visual arts
Panizza, Oscar, 146
Paris: exiles in, 71, 74, 78, 83–86 pas-
   sim, 94, 136, 179; German-French
   avant-garde in, 21, 32, 68, 86, 118;
   International Writers' Congress in,
   87
Parisian Institute for the Study of
   Fascism, 124
Patchen, Kenneth, 70
Patera, 197
Pechstein, Max, 22
Pessimism, cultural, 145, 164, 170,
   172, 180, 187–88; dystopian reversal
   of, 197; language, 171, 180. See also
   "Doomsday" mentality (apocalypse)
Pfemfert, Franz, 14, 18, 116
Picasso, Pablo, 16, 21, 43, 138; Guer-
   nica, 71
Pieck, Wilhelm, 127
Pinthus, Kurt, 14, 173; The Dawn of
   Humanity (anthology), 6, 32, 70
Piscator, Erwin, 62, 64, 141
Plays: Dadaist, 53–54, 61; expression-
   ist, 61, 171, (in U.S.) 68, 143; learn-

ing, 154; Nazi, 54; postwar, 175–76;
   radio, 62–63, 171. See also Theater
Pleite, Die (journal), 54, 138
Poetry: "absolute," xi, 65; anarchist,
   188; Baroque, 12; Benn's definition
   of, 101, 165; of Brecht and Grosz,
   compared, 140; dadaist, 49; expressionist, 6, 9–13, 23–25, 75; gender
   and, 26–29; German Academy of,
   155; German poets, "Fichte spirit"
   of, 96; idealist, 122; language of,
   28, 73, 115, ("bio-negative" view)
   168, 191; "language poetry," experimental, 9; modernist, 173; as
   monologue, 101, 165; poet as "flâ-
   neur," 11, 12; poets in exile, 75–77;
   postwar German, 189–91, 195; "pre-
   expressionist," 117; radio debate
   about, 62, 63; simultaneist, 50;
   sonnets, 5, 73–74, 77; "static," 183;
   "stepchild of exile research," 72–
   73; of the subjective, 111; surrealist
   elements in, 64, ("poetic politics")
   52, 53, 107, 116, 118; as universal
   language, 173; of war, 18, 19–20
Poggioli, Renato, 5, 201n2
Politics: aesthetization of, xvi, 23–25,
   168; expressionism isolated from,
   24; literature intersects with, 88;
   political exile, see Exile period;
   politically staged events, 54, 61;
   radical, see Radicalism
Pollock, Jackson, 68
Pop art, xviii, xx–xxi, 172. See also Art
Popular Front, 71, 105–6, 126;
   Benjamin and, 87, 111, 128
Populism, 113
Postmodernism, xii, 100, 176–77, 196;
   distinction between modernism
   and, 34; as "endgame of avant-
   garde," xv; exile and, 89; "linguistic
   turn" of, xi; of literature, 67, 173;

Toller, Ernst, 66, 74, 75, 133; postwar plays of, 175; and "theater of the idea," 124. WORKS: *Man and the Masses*, 61; *No More Peace*, 77

Trakl, Georg, 5, 204n28

Transatlantik (journal), 188

transition (journal), x, 70, 95, 96, 100, 180

Treitschke, Heinrich von, 29

Trommler, Frank: (coauthor) *Die Kultur der Weimarer Republik*, 61

Tucholsky, Kurt, 122, 140

Tzara, Tristan, xiv, 39, 44; attacks on, 43, 50; as mastermind of Dada, 45–46. WORKS: "Chronique Zurichoise 1915–1919," 46; "Dada 1957," 45; "The Heart of Gas," 46

Ulysses theme, 75

United States. *See* America

Urban experience, 10–14, 209n100; film and, 14–18

USPD (Independent Socialist Party of Germany), 24, 234n19

Utopianism, ix, 192; apocalyptic vision of, 35; architecture and, 7; dystopian reversal of, xiv–xv, 36, 103, 171, 173, 175, 190, 193, 197; Einstein's view of, 84–85; expressionist, 36, 77, 175; futility of, 148; historical, return to, 198; naïve, xix, 195; "negative," 196; Nietzsche's, 157, 159, 164; postutopianism, xix, 36; rationalism and, 163, 166; rejected, 153; of Saint-Simon and Fourier, xi; and totalitarianism, 154

Van den Bruck, Moeller, 18

Van Gogh, Vincent, 8

Van Hoddis, Jakob, 6, 29, 197. WORKS: "End of the World"/"Doomsday," 15, 35, 195; "Kinematograph," 15

Vietnam, 192

Vietta, Silvio: *Die Literarische Moderne*, 66

Vinnen, Carl: "Protest of the German Artists," 21

Visual arts, 71; absurdist, 139; dadaist, 49 (*see also* "Anti-art" concept); expressionist, 8, 68–69, 118, 170, 178, (abstract) 68–69, 148; futurist, 18, 52; impact of African primitivism on, 22–23; and literary language, 16–17, 99–100; pop art, xx–xxi, 172; prewar, 175; Rubens painting and art debate, 61–62; surrealist, 68–69; on theme of Last Judgment, 3, 35–36; typography, 60. *See also* Cubism; Film; Grosz, George; Surrealism

Völkische Beobachter (periodical), 163

"Voltaire Society," 44. *See also* Cabaret (or Café) Voltaire

Von Unruh, Fritz, 66, 75, 222n37

Vortriede, Werner, 76

Vossische Zeitung (periodical), 135

Walden, Herwarth, 19, 126, 131

Walser, Robert, 64

War: Italian and fascist glorification of, 18–19, 25, 125, 129, 131; poetry of, 18, 19–20; resigned reaction to, 26; technology and, 5, 123, 131. *See also* Spanish Civil War; World War I; World War II

Warhol, Andy, 177

Wedekind, Frank, 116

Wegener, Paul: *Der Golem*, 16

Weill, Kurt, 62; *Mahagonny*, 63

Weimar culture, x, 8, 60–65, 89, 126; and Left versus Right, 64; and literary culture, 154

Weimar Republic, xix, 54, 61, 64, 65, 124, 138; blasphemy trials of, 94, 141; fall of, 124

Weininger, Otto, 25, 29; *Sex and Character,* 28

Weinstein, Joan, 170

Weiss, Peter, x, 172. WORKS: *Aesthetics of Resistance,* 192; *Discourse on Vietnam,* 192; *Song of the Lusitanian Bogey,* 192

Werfel, Franz, ix, 14, 27, 130; poetry of, 29; *Troerinnen,* 114

Western culture: aesthetic totality questioned, xi; artist as "spiritual" authority, 118; art traditions, 41, (and "end of art" thesis) 65; and avant-garde productions, xviii; and conflict between old and new, 237n72; Dada entwined with, 51; Dada's revolt against, 39, 40, 46; hegemony questioned, 162–63; of history, 164; international avant-garde and, 68; modernism in, 89; Postwar Germany's reconnection with, 171; widening of scope toward, 75. *See also* America

Western democracies, 106

Wiene, Robert: *Das Kabinett des Dr. Caligari,* 16

"Wiener Gruppe," x

Wiesengrund, Theodor. *See* Adorno, Theodor

Williams, Raymond, 33

Williams, William Carlos, 70

Winkler, Michael, 88

Wittgenstein, Ludwig, 171, 182

Wolf, Friedrich, 62, 224n61

Wolfenstein, Alfred, 66, 77; *Frank* (novel), 75

Women: avant-garde artists among, 25–29; and feminism, 25, 173; prejudice against, 25, 29

"Work of art," as concept, xi

World War I, 5, 8, 22, 130, 165, 172; dadaism during, 54; effect of, 38, 46–47, 55, 60, 147, 157; exile during, xiv, 33, 48, 67, 154, 169; pro- and antiwar divisions brought about by, 25–26; spiritualized, 123; utopian ideas during, 7

World War II, xiv; U.S. enters, 69

Worringer, Wilhelm, 7, 8, 9, 21, 61, 115, 177; Lukács versus, 114; *Abstraction and Empathy,* 4

Wort, Das (Moscow periodical), 87, 125–26, 127, 128, 130, 135; debate on expressionism in, xv, 110, 132, 149, 160

Wortkunst (language art), 19, 20

Wyneken, Gustav, 110, 116

Youth movements (Germany), 10

Zarathustra figure. *See* Nietzsche, Friedrich (works)

Zech, Paul, 29, 75; "This Is the Hour," 27

Ziegler, Bernhard, 226n77

Ziel, Das (periodical), 116

Ziolkowski, Theodore, 73, 79

Zurich Dada, 38–40, 43–46, 49, 51, 53, 178, 179, 182, 207n77; as countermovement, ix, x, xiv; criticism of, 43–44; group mentality of, x, 18; multinational, 33, 39, 59–60; women in, 25

9414